Lay Counseling

D1040840

Lay Counseling

EQUIPPING CHRISTIANS FOR A HELPING MINISTRY

SIANG-YANG TAN

Foreword by Gary R. Collins

ZondervanPublishingHouse
Academic and Professional Books
Grand Rapids, Michigan

A Division of HarperCollinsPublishers

Requests for information should be addressed to:
Zondervan Publishing House
Academic and Professional Books
1415 Lake Drive S.E.
Grand Rapids, Michigan 49506

Library of Congress Cataloging-in-Publication Data
Tan, Siang-Yang, 1954–
    Lay counseling : equipping Christians for a helping ministry /
Siang-Yang Tan.
        p.   cm.
    Includes bibliographical references and index.
    ISBN 0-310-52931-X
    1. Peer counseling in the church. I. Title.
BV4409.T35   1991   90-48197
253.5—dc20   CIP

Edited by Lori Walburg

Printed in the United States of America

91 92 93 94 95 96 / AK / 10 9 8 7 6 5 4 3 2 1

Contents

Foreword   7

Acknowledgments   11

Introduction   13

1. *The Need for Lay Counseling Ministries*   17
2. *Biblical Basis for Lay Counseling*   23
3. *A Biblical Model for Effective Lay Counseling*   32
4. *The Literature of Lay Counseling*   61
5. *Building a Ministry of Lay Counseling*   82
6. *Selection of Lay Counselors*   96
7. *Training of Lay Counselors*   115
8. *Supervision of Lay Counselors*   135
9. *Evaluation of Lay Counselors*   159
10. *The Local Church and Lay Counseling*   188
11. *Potential Pitfalls in Lay Counseling*   212
12. *Conclusions About Lay Counseling*   227

Appendices

   A. *Postcounseling Questionnaire—Client Form*   232

   B. *Postcounseling Questionnaire—Counselor Form*   235

   C. *Some Local Churches with Lay Counseling Ministries*   237

   D. *Ethical Standards for Christian Counselors*   239

   E. *Christian Association for Psychological Studies, Proposed Code of Ethics*   241

   F. *Sample Forms:*
     (1) Progress Notes   246

(2) *Informed Consent Forms*   247
(3) *Release of Information Form*   251

Indexes   253

Biographical Sketch   256

Foreword

Several years ago I attended a seminar on lay counseling. The participants were all professionals, and the teacher was a man who had written several widely acclaimed books on this topic. For two or three days we heard his lectures, watched videos, practiced training exercises, and learned a great deal about lay counselor training. The whole conference was stimulating, informative, and a lot of fun.

Never once, however, did the leader mention the church. He talked about lay counseling in prisons, classrooms, and businesses and over the back fence in neighborhoods, but the church was ignored. When I raised this during a question-and-answer period, our instructor got a strange look on his face.

"I never thought of that!" he exclaimed. "Teaching people in the church how to help one another is a really creative and novel idea."

I chose not to mention that lay counseling has been around for centuries. Exodus 18 gives one of the clearest and earliest Old Testament examples of dedicated laypeople giving guidance to one another. Moreover, when he walked on earth, Jesus modeled care-giving and so did the disciples. The New Testament epistles not only mention problems, but instruct Christians to "bear one another's burdens" when the stresses of life get heavy. Do not "become weary in doing good," the apostle Paul wrote to the laypeople at Galatia. "As we have opportunity, let us do good to all people, especially to those who belong to the family of believers." Throughout the centuries of church history believers have continued to encourage, care for, and challenge each other. Technically this caring went beyond, but also included what we now know as lay counseling.

Within the past thirty years, however—beginning perhaps with the U.S. government's report on mental health in the early sixties—lay counseling (including Christian lay counseling) has expanded, blossomed, and become more prevalent. Training programs, seminars, written and audiovisual materials, telephone hotlines, national care-giving ministries, church peer-counseling centers, suicide prevention programs, and a host of other initiatives have demonstrated that lay counseling is growing in sophistication and influence.

Some professionals may raise legitimate questions about the validity of nonprofessional counselors, but church leaders continue to ask how they can train and use lay counselors effectively, politicians and educators have begun to wonder how lay helpers can be used to meet human need, and a few researchers have turned their scientific methods to evaluating lay counseling effectiveness. Of course, there have been examples of poorly prepared "counselors" who have caused more harm than good. Some people have wondered if lay counseling is as valuable as some of its proponents suggest. But lay counselor training is getting better, and increasing numbers of people are getting involved. Clearly this is a growing movement within the church and without.

Despite the activity, relatively few professional counselors have stepped into this swirl of change, growth, training, and utilization of nonprofessional people helpers. Several counselors have designed and proposed their own approaches to lay counseling, but few have systematically looked at the field with its growing professional literature. Few have tried to propose guidelines for training and practice that are practical, data-based, and consistent with biblical truth. The author of this book is one who has taken that challenge.

When I first met Dr. Siang-Yang Tan several years ago, he had already become an expert in lay counseling. Over the years his familiarization with what others have written on this subject, his own research, and his personal experiences in developing and directing lay counseling ministries have all established him as a leader—perhaps *the* leader—in this field. When he joined the faculty at the Fuller Graduate School of Psychology, Siang-Yang

was able to teach courses on lay counseling and develop
carefully designed research to evaluate the effectiveness of
Christian lay counseling. As the following pages show, this book
is written by a man who has a masterful grasp of his subject,
accompanied by a Christian commitment and practical orientation that shine through repeatedly.

This new book is a thoroughly documented, realistic, practical, relevant, psychologically sound, biblically based survey of
the field of Christian lay counseling. The author shows a clear
sensitivity to the needs of the local church and an awareness of
the importance of denominational and cross-cultural differences.
He is not hesitant to evaluate existing programs of lay counseling, but he is consistently fair, gracious, and without any
evidence of "putting down" the work of others. Drawing on the
contemporary psychological literature, on his experiences with
lay counseling in a local church, on his research involving lay
counselors, and on his interaction with others in the field—
including his doctoral students—Siang-Yang Tan has written a
book against which all others will be measured for years to
come.

This volume is "must reading" for anyone who is pondering,
establishing, directing, giving training in, or evaluating lay
counseling, especially as it relates to the Christian community.
The following pages are enlightening, informative, insightful,
and interesting. I recommend the book highly and enthusiasti-
cally.

GARY R. COLLINS, Ph.D.

Acknowledgments

The main focus of this book on lay counseling is on compassion and caring for people. I would like to express my deepest appreciation to two special people who have been examples of caring to me—my late father, Siew Thiam Tan, and my mother, Madam Chiow Yang Quek. I would also like to especially thank my wife, Angela, for her faithful support, love, prayers, encouragement, and helpful insights, particularly while this book was being written, and my two children, Carolyn and Andrew, for the joy and blessings they have brought to our lives, and for their patience and prayers while Daddy was writing his book.

Others who have been of help and encouragement in my work on lay counseling include the following: lay counselors and students who have worked with me over the years; former Singapore Youth For Christ leaders Rev. Donald Chia and Mr. Harry Quek; Rev. Donald Hamilton, when he was pastor of Peoples Church of Montreal; Dr. William McRae, when he was pastor-teacher and elder of North Park Community Chapel; Dr. Eddie Lo, pastor of First Evangelical Church in Glendale, California; Rev. George Hay, Dr. Robert Duez, and others at Ontario Bible College; and my colleagues and students at Fuller Theological Seminary. Special thanks are due to Dr. Gary Collins for so kindly writing the foreword, to Dr. Thomas Needham, Associate Dean of Marriage and Family Therapy in the Graduate School of Psychology at Fuller Theological Seminary, and Mr. Michael Smith of Zondervan for their feedback and significant editorial help, and to Mrs. Freda

Carver, my secretary, for her excellent and efficient secretarial assistance.

Finally, and above all, I want to thank God for his grace and love manifested in Jesus Christ, who has motivated my work described in this book, by the power and enabling of the Holy Spirit.

Siang-Yang Tan, Ph.D.
Pasadena, California

The author is grateful for permission to use extensive quotations from the following books and periodicals:

Geraldine L. Cerling, "Selection of Lay Counselors for a Church Counseling Center," *Journal of Psychology and Christianity* 2, no. 3 (1983). Chart of selection criteria used by permission.

Gary R. Collins, *How to Be a People Helper*, copyright © 1976. Used by permission of Regal Books, 2300 Knoll Drive, Ventura, CA 93003.

A. A. Lazarus, *The Practice of Multimodal Therapy*, copyright © 1981 by McGraw-Hill, Inc., 1221 Avenue of the Americas, New York, NY 10020. Used by permission of the publisher.

H. Newton Malony, Thomas L. Needham, and Samuel Southard, *Clergy Malpractice*, copyright © 1986 by The Westminster Press. Used by permission of Westminster/John Knox Press, 100 Witherspoon Street, Louisville, KY 40202-1396.

R. Paul Stevens, *Liberating the Laity*, copyright © 1985 by InterVarsity Christian Fellowship of the USA. Used by permission of InterVarsity Press, P.O. Box 1400, Downers Grove, IL 60515.

Joan Sturkie and Gordon Bear, *Christian Peer Counseling: Love in Action*, copyright © 1989 by Word Books, Dallas, Texas. Used by permission.

Introduction

"Your problem, Mr. Jones, is that you are a sinner. Give up your drinking and running around, and God will resolve all your conflicts."

Is that what we mean by "lay Christian counseling"? Indeed, the idea of some inept, nonprofessionally trained person blundering around in the minefields of personality may sound hazardous. One can easily visualize the problems inherent in such a situation.

Is lay Christian counseling helpful or dangerous? Is it a realistically beneficial activity or a woefully inadequate tinkering with people's urgent problems? Is it always necessary and essential that a professional counselor enter the picture in order to deal with any and all emotional maladjustments, neurotic reactions, or just plain mental misery?

Can we expect an average person without a master's or doctoral degree in counseling to be able to meet the needs of someone plunged into depression or wracked with indecision by some complex problems in his or her life? If lay counseling can really be helpful, then what are the principles and guidelines needed to begin a lay counseling ministry?

These were questions posed by my secretary when I mentioned I was writing a book on lay Christian counseling. It is the purpose of this book to investigate questions like these and to provide some helpful answers. More specifically, it covers the selection, training, supervision, and evaluation of lay Christian counselors, as well as how to set up and administer a lay counseling service or ministry in a responsible and effective way. It also presents the biblical basis for such a ministry and a biblical model for effective lay counseling.

Counseling has been defined by Dr. Gary Collins as "a caring relationship in which one person tries to help another deal more effectively with the stresses of life."[1] Collins has described lay counselors as individuals who lack the training, education, experience, or credentials to be professional counselors, but who nevertheless are involved in helping people cope with personal problems.[2] Lay counselors have also been called nonprofessionals with little or no training in people-helping skills, or paraprofessionals with some limited training in such skills.

Interest in lay counseling has grown considerably in recent years, both in the secular world as well as in Christian circles, including churches and parachurch organizations. The burgeoning literature on both secular as well as Christian lay counseling will be reviewed in a later chapter of this book. Dr. George Albee, a former president of the American Psychological Association, has pointed out that the demand for mental health professionals will always exceed the supply.[3] Recently Albee referred to a survey completed by the National Institute of Mental Health which indicated that about 20 percent of the American population (i.e., 43 million people) suffer at some point from a mental disorder, and he emphasized that the notion that there will ever be enough therapists to treat that many individuals "is sheer folly."[4] The shortage of professional mental health workers has, therefore, led to an increasing use of lay counselors to provide mental health services to the millions who need them, so much so that one author has referred to this trend as "the nonprofessional revolution in mental health."[5]

Lay counseling has not only become a significant part of the contemporary mental health scene,[6] but it has also begun to occupy an important place in Christian ministries, particularly in churches.[7] I have written this book to present an overview of lay counseling, covering both the secular and Christian literature, but focusing on a biblical, Christian approach to lay counseling which I have developed and used for more than a decade now. Most of my work in lay counseling ministries has been done in two local churches in Canada (Peoples Church of Montreal, 1976–80, and North Park Community Chapel in

London, Ontario, 1980–83), and at the Institute of Christian Counseling, which I set up at Ontario Bible College in Toronto in 1984 for the training of lay or paraprofessional Christian counselors. At present I conduct lay counselor training in local church and parachurch contexts and evaluate the effectiveness of such *training* as well as the effectiveness of the *counseling* done by lay counselors, in collaboration with doctoral students in the Graduate School of Psychology at Fuller Theological Seminary.

The present book contains enough information to be used as a practical manual for the establishment of a lay counseling ministry, especially within a local church. It can be best utilized, however, in conjunction with some other books and materials which are cited and recommended in several chapters. I trust and pray that this book will be of significant help and blessing to all of us who desire to be channels of Christ's love and truth, and hence to bring his grace and healing to the many people who are hurting in this broken world.

NOTES

[1] G. R. Collins, *Innovative Approaches to Counseling* (Waco, Tex.: Word, 1986), 73.

[2] Ibid., 74.

[3] G. W. Albee, "Conceptual Models and Manpower Requirements in Psychology," *American Psychologist* 23 (1968): 317–20.

[4] See "Prevention—Here to Stay," *APA Monitor* 17 (January 1986): 17.

[5] F. Sobey, *The Nonprofessional Revolution in Mental Health* (New York: Columbia University Press, 1970).

[6] See, e.g., S. Alley, J. Blanton, and R. Feldman, *Paraprofessionals in Mental Health: Theory and Practice* (New York: Human Sciences Press, 1978); M. Gershon and H. B. Biller, *The Other Helpers: Professionals and Nonprofessionals in Mental Health* (Lexington, Mass.: Lexington Books, 1977); S. S. Robin and M. O. Wagenfeld, eds., *Paraprofessionals in the Human Services* (New York: Human Sciences Press, 1981). Two significant books published earlier, over twenty years ago, are: B. G. Guerney, Jr., ed., *Psychotherapeutic Agents: New Roles for Non-Professionals, Parents, and Teachers* (New York: Holt, Rinehart & Winston, 1969); and F. Sobey, *The Nonprofessional Revolution in Mental Health.*

A significant part of lay counseling is peer counseling (i.e., peers in age, status, and knowledge helping each other), which has spread to elementary and secondary schools, colleges and universities, social agencies, businesses, and churches. In a recent book (see J. Sturkie and G. R. Bear, *Christian Peer Counseling: Love in Action* [Dallas: Word, 1989], 18), Sturkie and Bear pointed out that in 1988 the estimated number of peer counseling programs in elementary and secondary schools across the nation was over twenty thousand! A number of significant peer counseling associations have also been formed recently, including the California Peer Counseling Association, which started in 1984, with its fourth conference in San Francisco in 1988 having an attendance of over three thousand people; and the National Peer Helpers Association, which was founded in 1986, with its first national conference held in 1987 in St. Louis having representatives from thirty-three states.

[7]See, e.g., G. R. Collins, "Lay Counseling Within the Local Church," *Leadership* 1 (1980): 78–86; S. Y. Tan, "Lay Counseling: The Local Church," *CAPS Bulletin* 7, no. 1 (1981): 15–20.

1

The Need for
Lay Counseling Ministries

We all live in a fallen world that is tainted by the effects of sin. Despite the psychological sophistication of our modern society (which one author has called "The psychological society"),[1] we are all living in a broken world where things are not really getting better. Dr. Armand Nicholi, a well-known psychiatrist from Harvard Medical School, has actually predicted that with the rapid and widespread breakdown of caring and meaningful relationships, especially within the family, the incidence of mental illness will increase to the point where 95 percent of our hospital beds may be taken up by mental patients. He has further suggested that a lack of self-control will be a primary characteristic of future mental or emotional disorders.[2]

Dr. Scott Peck, another psychiatrist and author of the well-known book, *The Road Less Traveled,* has written: "Life is difficult. . . . Life is a series of problems."[3] This great truth is valid not only in the secular world, but also in Christian circles, including churches. There are many hurting people in our congregations and Christian institutions who are struggling with life. They need help, but they often find it almost impossible to open up and share their burdens. This may be because no one is available to listen and care, and/or their Christian beliefs (or misbeliefs) make them feel guilty, as if their struggles make them second-class citizens in the kingdom of God. Many of them are, therefore, afraid of being judged as bad or poor Christians.

Let us take a closer look at some examples of such situations.

While these examples are fictitious and details have been changed, they are based on composites of real-life cases.

A common problem among Christians is reflected in the case of Ron. Ron is a bright, energetic, and deeply committed Christian who has been serving in his local church as a lay leader for over a decade. He is a deacon and also serves as the advisor to the college fellowship in the church. He often sings in the choir and for special worship services. He also teaches an adult Sunday school class. He is highly respected as a mature, spiritual man of God, and he is well-liked by his peers as well as by the pastoral leaders in his church.

At thirty-five years of age, Ron has done well as a professional accountant, having just been made partner of the firm in which he has been working for many years. He is married to a spiritually mature wife who works part-time as a music teacher and is choir director at the church. They have three lovely young children. On the surface, Ron and his wife appear to be the perfect couple with an ideal family.

In recent months, however, Ron has been feeling very physically fatigued and emotionally drained. He does not enjoy life as much as he used to and has begun to lose his appetite. He has also been having some difficulty falling asleep. Deep within he feels spiritually dry and empty, but he has not been able to tell anyone until recently, when he spoke to his wife about the "burnout" symptoms he has been experiencing lately. He has realized that he has had too many demands placed on him over too long a period of time and now feels that he cannot meet them any longer.

Ron and his wife are both deeply concerned and worried about his health and "burnout" symptoms. However, they do not know where to turn for help. Ron tried recently to talk to a close friend and fellow deacon at church but was told he just needed a vacation and should not worry so much. Both Ron and his wife are now reluctant to talk to anybody else in church about how depressed Ron has really been feeling. Out of frustration and desperation, they eventually make an appointment with a professional therapist recommended by their family physician. However, they do so with mixed feelings and are afraid that someone in church may find out Ron is seeing a "shrink."

Another situation that often arises in a church context is in the area of marital conflict. Take, for example, Jack and Rachel, who have been married five years and have a two-year-old son, Peter. Both of them have been church members for many years and have served in various capacities, including teaching elementary Sunday school and working with the high school youth group.

Since their son, Peter, was born two years ago, they have had a very difficult time adjusting to their new status of parenthood, with all its demands as well as joys. They love Peter very much and were happy to have him, since they had planned to have a child. However, they had not anticipated how much having a child would change their lives. Peter had been a colicky baby who cried frequently and awoke several times during the night, so that Rachel felt very exhausted most of the time, especially in the first year of Peter's life. Jack was also affected and often felt tired, though not as exhausted as Rachel. As a result, their communication with each other, as well as their sexual relationship, suffered. They had significantly less time to spend with one another, since most of their time and energy were being spent on taking care of Peter and his needs.

While Peter is somewhat less demanding now that he is older and able to sleep through more nights, Jack and Rachel have not quite recovered from the stress they have experienced. They find themselves easily irritated and upset with each other, even over small things. They argue frequently and still feel fatigued most of the time. Jack is working full-time as an engineer in a very demanding job, with the ever-threatening possibility of a layoff, and this only makes things worse. Rachel works part-time as a tutor to help out financially. They still do not have much time to spend with each other and have gone out by themselves without Peter only a couple of times. Their sexual relationship has improved but not to their satisfaction.

Both Jack and Rachel are aware that their marriage is rocky and that they are experiencing some significant problems. They did not expect that the birth of a wanted child would involve so much stress and change. They still care deeply for each other and do not want their marital relationship to get any worse. However, they are not sure to whom they should talk about their marital and sexual problems, since they feel these are very personal in nature. They are also afraid that people in church might judge them to be poor Christians if they find out about their marital difficulties. Jack and Rachel feel they need to maintain a good example of victorious Christian living to their youth group. However, they have experienced too much marital conflict and emotional pain to go on pretending that everything is fine and dandy. Their own spiritual lives too have been affected adversely so that they no longer pray together on a regular basis. They often wonder angrily why God has allowed all these things to happen. They sometimes think back to the "good old days" before their son was born. They know they need help and counseling from someone but again are hesitant and unsure as to whom they should turn.

Let me provide one more example of a common situation that may occur in Christian circles. Paul is a twenty-eight-year-old youth worker on the staff of a parachurch youth organization specializing in outreach to troubled teenagers living in urban ghettos. He has been in full-time ministry with this organization for five years. A gifted and effective youth worker, he has won a number of honors from churches, as well as from the city, for the good work he has done.

Despite all the outward signs of a success, Paul struggles inwardly with a deep sense of insecurity and fear of failure. He has done well so far partly because he is driven to succeed and has worked very hard and long hours. Although he is a very good public speaker and communicator with adolescents, deep down inside Paul is still afraid of "blowing it." He has not told anyone about his insecurity and fears, since most people have complimented him on his obvious gifts and effectiveness in youth ministry.

Paul has often wished he could tell someone his deepest fears and struggles. He grew up under strict and demanding parents who set such perfectionistic standards of behavior that he often felt inadequate and inferior although he usually did very well in whatever endeavors he undertook.

Recently Paul decided to "spill his guts" to one of his most trusted friends, a colleague in the same parachurch organization. It was very difficult for him to open up, but eventually he succeeded in talking about his feelings. His friend tried to be understanding, but eventually he told Paul that he should not think so negatively. He suggested instead that Paul should pray for the Lord's deliverance from such oppressive thoughts, which he believed were satanic in source. Paul has prayed for deliverance with some relief, but he feels he still needs someone to talk to in more depth about his inner struggles. He is afraid, however, to open up again to someone else in case he is told once more to just pray for deliverance.

All three examples—Ron, Jack and Rachel, and Paul—demonstrate the great need for helping and caring ministries in the church. Christians are human beings with real needs and struggles. Yet often, as these three examples have illustrated, Christians with problems do not know where or to whom to turn, because the church is more often a museum for saints rather than a hospital for sinners. The church therefore tends to miss many significant opportunities to manifest itself as a caring community.

The recent scandals of televangelists are further real-life examples of how good Christian folks may be hurting in their lives without receiving the help they need. At times, problems like these are caused when help is not sought even if available, or not received even if given. However, it is my opinion that in many cases, help is not easily available or forthcoming because many of us are either not sensitive enough to such needs around us, or even if we are, we do not know how to minister to those in need (including ourselves!). Many of us do not even know that we *can* minister to others in need, since there is a tendency to believe that only mental health professionals can help or counsel effectively.

As already mentioned in the beginning of this chapter, we are living in a world where things are actually getting worse, and emotional or psychological problems will be increasingly evident. The church and Christian organizations are also being affected. We can no longer afford to pretend problems do not exist and go on playing our religious games and "churchianity." Yet there is hope. I have received many inquiries from pastors and church leaders about how to meet people's needs through a lay caring and counseling ministry, so there are leaders and people out there in our churches and Christian communities who really do care and are moved enough to want to do something about ministering to broken lives.

True Christianity centered in the Gospel of Jesus Christ calls us to love one another as deeply as Christ loves us and to reach out to each other, to bear one another's burdens, and to be instruments of God's grace and healing as we help one another.

There are several scriptural passages or texts that challenge us to live this way, and they form the biblical basis for lay caring ministries, including lay counseling. Those passages will be covered in the next chapter.

NOTES

[1]M. L. Gross, *The Psychological Society* (New York: Random House, 1978).

[2]A. M. Nicholi, Jr., "The Fractured Family: Following It Into the Future," *Christianity Today* (May 25, 1979): 10–15.

[3]M. Scott Peck, *The Road Less Traveled* (New York: Touchstone, 1978), 15.

2

Biblical Basis for
Lay Counseling

I have conducted numerous training courses and workshops in local churches on lay Christian counseling. In doing so, I have sensed that one of the key questions pastors and church leaders have in their minds, even if unspoken, is whether lay counseling is a legitimate ministry for Christians to be involved in; that is, whether a lay counseling ministry has adequate biblical support. Some of them wonder whether lay counseling may simply be a means of getting secular psychology into the church through the back door and under the guise of a "Christian ministry." In the more conservative circles of evangelicalism today, there is a deep concern about the "seduction of Christianity" by secular psychology.[1] This is a valid concern that must be addressed before a lay Christian counseling ministry or training program is attempted.

Every Christian ministry must begin with a theological and biblical basis. Adequate biblical support for a lay Christian counseling ministry is of particular importance because of the questions and concerns already raised. Christians should not be involved in lay counseling or people-helping just because the world is doing so or because there is a shortage of mental health professionals. Christians and churches should get involved in lay counseling primarily because the Lord, through his Word, the Bible, has called us to be engaged in such a ministry to people.

Two categories of scriptural references do provide biblical support for lay counseling as a ministry by Christians. The first category of references emphasizes the calling of all Christians, including the so-called "laity" (who are not ordained or professional pastors), to be involved in ministry or service in general. The second category of references more specifically directs all believers to be involved in ministries to one another which can be grouped together under the general umbrella of lay counseling (i.e., people-helping by nonprofessionals and paraprofessionals).

The Call to Ministry in General

The Bible clearly teaches that all Christians belong to the universal priesthood of believers (1 Peter 2:5, 9) and are called to minister to each other so that we can all achieve the ultimate goal of maturity in Christ (see Eph. 4). Lay pastoral care and ministry are topics that have justifiably received much attention in recent years, as a growing number of authors have written on themes such as liberating the laity, Christian caregiving, lay caregiving, helping laity help others, and training church members in pastoral care.[2] For example, Paul Stevens, teaching elder at Marineview Chapel in Vancouver, British Columbia, Canada, has emphasized that every church has far more work than any one person or pastor can do. In his book *Liberating the Laity*, he uses Ephesians 4:1–16, among other passages, to demonstrate that it is God's will for all the saints to be equipped for ministry or service.[3]

Stevens first points out that in the Bible "the laity (Gk. *laikoi*) is the whole people of God—both clergy and so-called laity. It is a term of honor since the whole people of God in Christ is chosen to be a 'royal priesthood, a holy nation, a people [*laikoi*] belonging to God' (1 Peter 2:9). Christianity arose as an essentially lay movement."[4] He then goes on in chapter 2 of his book to argue for the abolition of the laity. The common Christian deserves to be accorded more than second-class status, because Jesus himself honored his people by giving gifts of ministry to *all* Christians. The laity of the church, just as much as an ordained pastor, has been called to a respectable vocation of serving the Lord and his people. Stevens asserts that the whole *environment*, not just programs, of the church should be designed to equip all Christians or members for such a high calling.

Using Ephesians 4:1–16 as the main scriptural text, Stevens makes the following points as biblical foundations for the laity's call to ministry.

1. Unity of Calling

He notes that "vocation or calling . . . is what you do with who you are in Christ. Every believer has been called to be Jesus' disciple and to serve in the kingdom of God. This is the 'one hope' to which we are called (4:4). Fundamentally, then, there is no clergy-laity distinction. All are called by God."[5]

2. Unity of Ministry

Stevens points out that though there is one calling (Eph. 4:1), there are many expressions of grace (v. 7) and many gifts for ministry (v. 11). It is because of such diversity, which reflects how essential and needed each of the various ministries is, that the unity of the whole body can be achieved. Each member of the body is therefore indispensable, and unity in ministry results as each part does its work effectively (v. 16).

Stevens clarifies that

> the gifts of the Spirit for ministry are not mere functions or activities carried out by the members. The gifts are *people*, the men and women to whom you are connected in Christ . . . when Paul speaks of gifts for ministry in verse 11, giving apostles, prophets, evangelists and pastor-teachers as examples, the emphasis is not on these gifts but on these people. In receiving the grace of Christ we *become* ministers. We don't *have* a ministry; we *are* one.[6]

3. Unity in Common Life

Stevens emphasizes that it is impossible for believers to be in Christ alone or live independently of each other without losing their spiritual health. He points out the frequent and innovative ways the word *together* occurs in Paul's epistle to the Ephesians (e.g., see Eph. 2:5, 6, 19, 21, 22; 3:6; 4:16). The interdependence of every member in the body of Christ (see also 1 Cor. 12) reflects the unity in common life of all Christians. He concludes that in Ephesians 4:16, "Paul is saying that every member *in his or her contact with other members* supplies something the body needs. . . . In order to be an equipping environment, therefore, the local church must be structured for relationships."[7]

4. Unity in Purpose

Stevens notes that Ephesians 4:13 and 15 provide the goal of the equipping ministry and the climax of Ephesians 4:1–16—maturity in Christ. Therefore the body of Christ is unified in its common purpose of achieving maturity in Christ.

The theme of unity—in calling, in ministry, in common life, and in purpose—provides the biblical or theological setting for the heart of equipping, which must involve not just individual members but the whole environment of the local church such that the whole body together is given clerical status for service or ministry. Ordained pastors should make themselves dispensable by equipping others (all the saints) for ministry or service. However, the Ultimate Equipper is the Lord Jesus himself, the head of the church, who has given grace and spiritual gifts to his people.

Stevens concludes:

> In short, the equipping ministry of the Lord effectively abolishes what we call the laity by providing for every member to become engaged in ministry. The notion that one person could so embody the charismatic gifts of ministry for the church that he or she might be called *the* minister is not only a practical heresy. It is an affront to the intention of the Head Equipper. . . . The goal of equipping is not to make people dependent on the leaders but dependent on the Head. This is the highest possible calling. It requires the strongest possible leadership in the church to lead people in such a way that they do not become dependent on the human leaders.[8]

Scripture, therefore, calls all Christians to ministry and service. As Stevens puts it: "By the grace of God we have been chosen, appointed and anointed, a special people, a holy nation, priests to our God. We are all clergy—priestly ministers."[9]

The Call to Lay Counseling as a Specific Ministry

If lay ministry in general has biblical support, what about lay *counseling* as a ministry in particular? I believe there is also a strong biblical basis for lay counseling as a specific ministry. The Bible teaches explicitly that the Lord Jesus came not only to save sinners but also to call us to a radically different lifestyle characterized by agape love. He has given a new commandment to all Christians to love one another as he has loved us (John

13:34–35). One way to show Christlike love to one another and hence to fulfill the law of Christ is to bear or carry each other's burdens (Gal. 6:2). This directive was given by the apostle Paul to all Christians—and especially mature, spiritual Christians (v. 1)—to get involved in a burden-bearing or "restoring" ministry to fellow believers who are struggling with sin in their lives. This "restoring" ministry involves counseling in its broad sense of people-helping, but restoring also involves more. For example, James tells us to confess our sins to each other and to pray for one another so that we may be healed (James 5:26). Confession and prayer are critical components of *Christian* people-helping.

Other passages in the Bible (e.g., Rom. 15:14; Col. 3:16; 1 Thess. 5:14) direct all believers to be involved in admonishing, encouraging, or helping one another. These verses also emphasize that spiritual qualities or qualifications like goodness or caring, knowledge, and wisdom (rather than credentials or professional training) are crucial for effective Christian counseling. Such scriptural texts also support the legitimacy of a lay caring and counseling ministry for all believers. However, it should be noted that the Bible also teaches that some Christians may be specially gifted with appropriate spiritual gifts like exhortation, or *paraklesis* (Rom. 12:8), and are therefore called to spend much of their time and service in lay counseling.

Dr. C. Peter Wagner, noted authority on church growth, has written a helpful book entitled *Your Spiritual Gifts Can Help Your Church Grow*.[10] In it, he defines the spiritual gift of exhortation as "the special ability that God gives to certain members of the Body of Christ to minister words of comfort, consolation, encouragement and counsel to other members of the Body in such a way that they feel helped and healed."[11] Wagner goes on to state:

> All Christians, of course, have a role of caring for one another. Hebrews 3:13 says, "Exhort one another daily." The life-style of Christians in contact with one another should be to counsel and share and encourage at all times. But over and above this, some Christians have a special gift of counseling that should become recognized to the extent that people in the church who are hurting know where to go to find help. When this happens, the Body is in good health. It is a positive growth characteristic.[12]

The proper exercise of spiritual gifts is therefore essential to the healthy growth of a church as a caring community. Our present society especially needs such a community because of the impact of individualism and the breakdown of a sense of genuine community and meaningful interpersonal relationships.

More recently, Dr. Rodger K. Bufford, professor and chairman of the psychology department, and Dr. Robert Buckler, associate professor of psychiatry in the psychology department—formerly at Western Seminary in Portland, Oregon, and now at George Fox College—have proposed a strategy for ministering to mental health needs in the church.[13] They state that the church's mission has many facets, centering on loving submission to God and ministry to people around us (cf. Matt. 28:18–20; Mark 12:30–31; John 13:34), and note that meeting personal needs to minimize mental health problems definitely falls within the scope of this mission. Hence, ministries like lay counseling are important aspects of the church's role and mission in the world. Bufford and Buckler conclude:

> Trained counselors, forming a coordinated multilevel network of care, can extend pastoral counseling care to all members of the church, while relieving the pastoral staff of often unbearable burdens in this area. The use of different echelons of counselors within the local church also recognizes differing abilities and spiritual gifts in the church Body. Those with the gifts of exhortation, helps, and administration are fulfilled as they exercise their gifts, and those to whom they minister are edified through receiving their specialized ministry.[14]

Some authors have noted that there are several biblical words from Scripture that have meanings closely associated with the concept of lay counseling or people-helping. For example, Dr. Jay Adams, who developed nouthetic counseling, has pointed out that many of the "one another" passages in the New Testament (including those already cited) pertain in some way to lay counseling.[15] Adams has asserted that directive or nouthetic counseling (based on a New Testament Greek word nouthesia), which involves "change through confrontation out of concern" is the appropriate designation for biblical counseling.[16] However, Dr. John Carter, professor of psychology at Rosemead School of Psychology, has proposed that biblical counseling is more adequately based on parakaleo and parakle-

sis, than only on *noutheteo* or *nouthesia.* *Parakaleo* or one of its forms is translated twenty-nine times in the King James Version as "comfort," twenty-seven times as "exhort," fourteen times as "consolation," and forty-three times as "beseech," whereas *noutheteo* and its cognate appear only thirteen times in the New Testament. *Paraklesis* is also listed as a spiritual gift in Romans 12:8.[17] I agree with Carter that biblical counseling (including lay counseling) includes not only the nouthetic or directive approach (and the "restoring" ministry referred to earlier), but also includes comforting, encouraging, and supporting others at appropriate times.

Christian psychiatrist Dr. Frank Minirth has noted that there are at least five verbs in the New Testament that are relevant to the ministry of counseling: *parakaleo, noutheteo, paramutheomai, antechomai,* and *makrothumeo.*[18] All five of these Greek words appear in 1 Thessalonians 5:14 thus:

> And we urge [*parakaleo*] you, brothers, warn [*noutheteo*] those who are idle, encourage [*paramutheomai*] the timid, help [*antechomai*] the weak, be patient [*makrothumeo*] with everyone.

In their recent book on healing relationships and lay counseling,[19] Stephen Grunlan and Daniel Lambrides review the meanings of these Greek words based on Kittel's *Theological Dictionary of the New Testament.*[20] They conclude that 1 Thessalonians 5:14 is addressed to all believers, who are urged "to be involved in exhorting, encouraging, comforting, and helping—in short, counseling,"[21] and that this verse emphasizes the importance of a flexible and balanced approach to counseling, one that is sensitive to the needs and specific problems of the individual. A biblical model for effective lay counseling that is consistent with this view will be presented in chapter 3. Such a model will also take into consideration a number of Old Testament passages that are relevant to a biblical approach to effective counseling (e.g., Ex. 18:5–26; 1 Kings 12:9, 28; Ps. 55:13–14; Prov. 12:15; 13:10; 19:20; 20:18). They contain Hebrew words that are often translated as "counsel," with the main connotation of advice in the form of guidance or direction.[22]

There are, therefore, many scriptural passages that provide a biblical basis or rationale for lay ministry in general and lay counseling in particular. The Lord has called us to reach out to one another in love, bearing each other's burdens as we help and counsel one another. In so doing, we demonstrate the reality of a genuinely caring and compassionate community that reaches out with the love of Christ to draw more people to him.

NOTES

[1]See. D. Hunt and T. A. McMahon, *The Seduction of Christianity* (Eugene, Ore.: Harvest House, 1985); D. Hunt, *Beyond Seduction* (Eugene, Ore.: Harvest House, 1986). See also M. Bobgan and D. Bobgan, *Psychoheresy: The Psychological Seduction of Christianity* (Santa Barbara, Calif.: Eastgate, 1987). For examples of responses to Hunt and McMahon's views, see E. Paulk, *That the World May Know* (Atlanta, Ga.: K-Dimension Publishers, 1987), as well as R. Wise, "Speaking Out: Welcome to the Inquisition," *Christianity Today* (May 16, 1986), 10; T. C. Muck, "Open Season," *Christianity Today* (November 21, 1986): 16–17; W. C. Lantz, "Book Reviews—The Seduction of Christianity," *Journal of Psychology and Christianity* 5, no. 1 (1986): 55–58; and K. L. Williams, "Seduction of the Innocents (Featured Book Review)," *Journal of Psychology and Theology* 15 (1987): 168–70.

[2]See, e.g., D. Detwiler-Zapp and W. C. Dixon, *Lay Caregiving* (Philadelphia: Fortress, 1982); R. E. Grantham, *Lay Shepherding: A Guide for Visiting the Sick, the Aged, the Troubled, and the Bereaved* (Valley Forge, Pa.: Judson, 1980); K. C. Haugk, *Christian Caregiving— A Way of Life* (Minneapolis: Augsburg, 1984); S. J. Menking, *Helping Laity Help Others* (Philadelphia: Westminster, 1984); A. Schmitt and D. Schmitt, *When a Congregation Cares* (Scottdale, Pa.: Herald, 1984); S. Southard, *Comprehensive Pastoral Care* (Valley Forge, Pa.: Judson, 1975); S. Southard, *Training Church Members for Pastoral Care* (Valley Forge, Pa.: Judson, 1982); R. P. Stevens, *Liberating the Laity* (Downers Grove, Ill.: InterVarsity Press, 1985); H. W. Stone, *The Caring Church* (San Francisco: Harper & Row, 1983).

[3]Stevens, *Liberating the Laity*, 26–42.

[4]Ibid., 21.

[5]Ibid., 29.

[6]Ibid., 30.

[7]Ibid., 31–32.

[8]Ibid., 36–37.

[9]Ibid., 41.

[10]C. Peter Wagner, *Your Spiritual Gifts Can Help Your Church Grow* (Ventura, Calif.: Regal Books, 1979).

[11]Ibid., 154.

[12]Ibid., 154.

[13]R. K. Bufford and R. E. Buckler, "Counseling in the Church: A Proposed Strategy for Ministering to Mental Health Needs in the Church," *Journal of Psychology and Christianity* 6, no. 2 (1987): 21–29.

[14]Ibid., 28.

[15]See Jay Adams, *Ready to Restore: The Layman's Guide to Christian Counseling* (Grand Rapids: Baker, 1981), 4.

[16]Ibid., 9.

[17]John Carter, "Adams' Theory of Nouthetic Counseling," *Journal of Psychology and Theology* 3 (1975): 143–55.

[18]F. B. Minirth, *Christian Psychiatry* (Old Tappan, N.J.: Revell, 1977), 37.

[19]S. Grunlan and D. Lambrides, *Healing Relationships: A Christian's Manual for Lay Counseling* (Camp Hill, Pa.: Christian Publications, 1984).

[20]G. Kittel, ed., *Theological Dictionary of the New Testament*, 10 vols. (Grand Rapids: Eerdmans, 1967).

[21]Grunlan and Lambrides, *Healing Relationships*, 25.

[22]Ibid., 21–23; see also H. N. Wright, *Training Christians to Counsel: A Resource Curriculum Manual* (Eugene, Ore.: Harvest House, 1977), 22.

3

A Biblical Model for Effective Lay Counseling

The title of chapter 2 of Lawrence Crabb's book *Effective Biblical Counseling* is "Christianity and Psychology: Enemies or Allies?"[1] This crucial question strikes at the heart of the integration of psychology and theology or Christianity. The literature on this topic of integration has grown considerably in recent years. A number of important books,[2] as well as journal articles,[3] have been published. Before I present a biblical model for effective lay Christian counseling in this chapter, a few comments about integration are necessary, including the model of integration I am adopting.

Four Main Approaches to Integration

First, four main approaches to, or models of, integration have been described. For example, Crabb has suggested that psychology and Christianity may be viewed as: (a) separate but equal; (b) tossed salad (equal and mixable); (c) nothing buttery (psychology is irrelevant and unnecessary; only the Scriptures are needed to deal with human problems and needs); and (d) spoiling the Egyptians (using whatever concepts or methods from secular psychology that are consistent with Scripture, hence subjecting them to the authority of Scripture).[4] The "spoiling the Egyptians" approach is similar to the "Integrates" model of integration,[5] and this is the one I have chosen to use as a foundation for developing a biblical model for effective Christian counseling, including lay counseling. A recent trend in the literature proposes an alternative model called the perspectival model. In this model each discipline is approached from the perspective of the other, and therefore is formed and informed by the other, but psychology is not to be under the authority of theology.[6] One author has even suggested that the term integration and its conceptual model should be disposed of, in favor of such a perspectival model.[7] I am aware of the problems and limitations inherent in any human endeavor, including the interpretation of Scripture.[8] Nevertheless, I believe that a position for the authority of *Scripture* (not theology as a discipline per se) is still required for true, biblical integration of psychology and Christianity to occur. Several authors agree with me, including Everett Worthington, who recently wrote an incisive book review in which he briefly critiqued the perspectival model.[9]

A Biblical Model for Effective Lay Counseling

The model to be described is based mainly on three well-known approaches to Christian counseling briefly mentioned in chapter 2: Jay Adams' "Nouthetic Counseling," Gary Collins' "People-Helping," and Lawrence Crabb's "Biblical Counseling."[10] It also incorporates the views and methods advocated more recently by William Backus and his approach to Christian counseling called "Misbelief Therapy,"[11] and Everett Worthington and his practical guide to counseling, both of which are mainly cognitive-behavioral in perspective (i.e., problem feelings are usually due to problem behavior and, more fundamentally, problem thinking).[12] The model also uses concepts, principles, and techniques from secular approaches advocated by Robert Carkhuff,[13] Gerard Egan,[14] and cognitive-behavior therapists like Aaron Beck, Albert Ellis, and Donald Meichenbaum[15] that are in line with Scripture and rejects those that are inconsistent with, or directly contradictory to, Scripture. The model therefore can best be described as a biblically based, comprehensive, somewhat eclectic one, with a strong cognitive-behavioral component. It is *one* approach to effective lay counseling from a biblical perspective, and as such has its strengths and weaknesses. No claim is being made for it as *the* (or *only*) biblical model. It is *a* biblically based model that is similar to and consistent with H. Norman Wright's book on self-talk, imagery, and prayer in counseling.[16] The model will now be described in more detail under three major headings:

(1) Basic View of Humanity,
(2) Basic View of Counseling, and
(3) Basic Principles of Effective Counseling

Basic View of Humanity

Much has been written about the *basic psychological and spiritual needs* of human beings, and different lists can be made up, depending on which theoretical position one takes. The model assumes that such basic needs include the need for meaning and direction in life, and the need for hope or forgiveness, as Adams has pointed out.[17] Lawrence Crabb asserts that human beings basically need a sense of self-worth (*not* self-worship) which consists of a need for security or love, as well as a need for significance or purpose.[18] Ultimately, such needs can only be fully met in the context of a personal relationship with Jesus Christ.

More recently, Crabb has preferred to speak of such needs for security and significance with different words—he now calls them "deep longings in the human heart for relationship and impact,"[19] which only the Lord alone can quench. Such longings will also not be completely satisfied while we live in a fallen world, and hence full satisfaction of them in the Lord can only be experienced in heaven. However, these deep longings can begin to be substantially (not fully) satisfied as we give up our self-protective defenses and admit our need for the Lord and his love and grace. Ultimately we depend on Christ alone to help us to live life the way he designed it to be lived, and that includes living in the context of a caring community of believers in a local church. Crabb has changed his terminology primarily because some people have misinterpreted him to be teaching a human-centered focus on fulfillment (due to his previous emphasis on a person's "needs" for security and significance, as if such needs define the essential nature of a human being), rather than a God-centered focus on obedience. Like Crabb's model, my model proposes that people have some fundamental needs or longings God has put within them which only he can ultimately or fully meet, and they include longings for relationship or security and for impact or significance.

Second, the model views humanity's *basic problem* as having to do with *sin*. The breaking of God's moral laws as revealed in Scripture and the satanic belief that we can handle our own affairs and meet our basic needs or longings without God underlie most mental-emotional problems that are nonorganic in nature.[20] However, the model does *not* assume that *all* emotional suffering or anguish is due to sin (whether personal sin or the sin of others); at times, such anguish may be part of God's process of perfecting his children in the image of Christ. Jesus himself experienced deep distress in the Garden of Gethsemane. While he struggled with his Father's will to go to the cross and die for a sinful world (Matt. 26:36–39; Mark 14:32–36; Luke 22:40–44), he never sinned (Heb. 4:15).[21] We must therefore discern between sin-induced mental-emotional suffering, and anguish or deep distress which may be part of obedience to God's will and growing as a Christian.

More specifically, there are "mystical" aspects of the spiritual life which we may not fully comprehend, including what St. John of the Cross has described as the "dark night of the soul" (cf. Isa. 50:10). Richard Foster in his classic book, *Celebration of Discipline*, has described such an experience thus:

> The "dark night" . . . is not something bad or destructive. . . .
> The purpose of the darkness is not to punish or afflict us. It is to set us free. . . .
> What is involved in entering the dark night of the soul? It may be a sense of dryness, depression, even lostness. It strips us of overdependence on the emotional life. The notion, often heard today, that such experiences can be avoided and that we should live in peace and comfort, joy and celebration, only betrays the fact that much contemporary experience is surface slush. The dark night is one of the ways God brings us to a hush, a stillness, so that He can work an inner transformation of the soul. . . . Recognize the dark night for what it is. Be grateful that God is lovingly drawing you away from every distraction so that you can see Him.[22]

In his book, *That Incredible Christian*, A. W. Tozer has also described a similar experience, which he calls "the ministry of the night," as follows:

> To do His supreme work of grace within you, He will take away from your heart everything you love most. Everything you trust in will go from you. Piles of ashes will lie where your most precious treasures used to be. . . .

Slowly you will discover God's love in your suffering. Your heart will begin to approve the whole thing. You will learn from yourself what all the schools in the world could not teach you—the healing action of faith without supporting pleasure. You will feel and understand the ministry of the night; its power to purify, to detach, to humble, to destroy the fear of death, and what is more important to you at the moment, the fear of life. And you will learn that sometimes pain can do what even joy cannot, such as exposing the vanity of earth's trifles and filling your heart with longing for the peace of heaven.[23]

I have therefore previously written:

From a psychological perspective, Christian psychologists need to have a better acquaintance with such processes of the spiritual life as the dark night of the soul or the ministry of the night, so that they do not naively or prematurely attempt to reduce all painful symptoms, but rather to appropriate their meaning first. This will require not only psychological assessment skills but spiritual wisdom and discernment as well. Sometimes there is no easy solution or therapy or healing, but to trust God and His grace to help people grow through such deepening and painful spiritual experiences. The best therapy then is to provide understanding, support, and much prayer.[24]

What I have just cited applies not only to professional counselors or Christian psychologists, but also to lay Christian counselors.

Third, the model asserts that the *ultimate goal* of humanity is to know God and to enjoy him forever. For the Christian, the end goal in life is maturity in Christ or obedience to God's will (cf. Rom. 8:29). This may entail some suffering at times, as has already been pointed out, but God has promised he will provide sufficient grace (2 Cor. 12:7–9). Although mental-emotional health is a valid and worthwhile goal to attain in general, it is subordinate to the Christian's end goal. Happiness at all costs or the absence of troubling and painful emotions is therefore not the final goal of life for the Christian while on earth. The model therefore affirms scriptural perspectives on suffering, including the possibility of what C. Stephen Evans calls, "the blessings of mental anguish."[25] He has also emphasized that "the primary goal of a Christian counselor is not to help people become merely 'normal,' but to help them love God with all their hearts, minds, and souls."[26] The elimination of symptoms of mental-emotional suffering is therefore not always the most valid or appropriate goal in Christian counseling. The *ultimate goal* of Christian counseling, including lay counseling, should be holiness and not temporal happiness, spiritual health and not just mental-emotional or physical health.[27]

Fourth, the model does assume a basic cognitive-behavioral perspective by viewing problem feelings as *usually* due to problem behavior (cf. Gen. 4:3–7) and, more fundamentally, to problem thinking (cf. Prov. 23:7; John 8:32). Crabb, in particular, has emphasized that erroneous, unbiblical basic assumptions or beliefs (what Backus has called "misbeliefs") are at the root of nonorganically caused mental-emotional problems.[28] Hence, to change problem feelings, a counselor will focus on changing sinful, unbiblical thinking and behaviors where appropriate. The model views both insight and behavior change (cf. Eph. 4:22–24) as crucial factors in effective helping.

However, the model does *not* assume that problem feelings are *always* due to problem behavior and problem thinking. Collins has pointed out the need to focus equally on all three— feelings, behavior, and thoughts—and this is a good balance, since problem feelings may possibly be due to biological or physical factors at times, even if no specific organic cause can be located, especially with our present limited knowledge regarding such factors.[29] The model is therefore open to medical or psychiatric help if necessary. Furthermore, problem feelings (as well as behaviors and thoughts) may also at times be the result of demonic activity (demonization), whether demonic attack or oppression, or even demon possession. If so, prayer for deliverance, fasting, and exorcism may be necessary.[30]

It should be noted that most recently, Crabb himself has emphasized the need to attend to all four major circles or dimensions of a person's experience—the personal, rational, volitional, and emotional areas.[31]

The model I propose therefore espouses a biblical approach to human functioning and dysfunction, as well as to counseling, that is mainly cognitive-behavioral in orientation and practice, but more comprehensive and broad-based than secular cognitive-behavior therapy.[32] The finer points of such an approach will be covered in more detail under the section entitled "Basic Principles of Effective Counseling."

Finally, the model takes a holistic view of persons as physical, mental-emotional, social, and spiritual beings (cf. Luke 2:52). Hence, a mental-emotional problem should always be seen in the context of all the areas of a person's life. Adams' concept of Total Structuring, or looking at a client's problem in relation to all areas of his or her life, is an important one to use. More specifically, he advocates investigating and biblically restructur-ing the following major areas of a person's life, although he or she may present only one problem (e.g., depression): (1) church, Bible, prayer, witness; (2) work, school; (3) physical health, exercise, diet, sleep; (4) marriage, sex; (5) finances, budget; (6) family, children, discipline; (7) social activities, friends; (8) other (e.g., reading, etc.).[33]

A similar comprehensive and broad-based secular approach to therapy called Multimodal Therapy has been developed by Arnold Lazarus,[34] a psychologist who has done some significant clinical work and research previously in the areas of behavior therapy and cognitive-behavior therapy. Essentially, Lazarus has proposed that human functioning as well as problems can be best conceptualized under seven modalities with the acronym BASIC I.D. (B = Behavior, A = Affect, S = Sensation, I = Imagery, C = Cognition, I. = Interpersonal relationships, D. = Drugs/Biological factors). He describes his approach thus:

> We are beings who move, feel, sense, imagine, think, and relate to one another. At base, we are biochemical-neurophysiological entities. Our personalities are the products of our ongoing *b*ehavior, *a*ffective processes, *s*ensations, *i*mages, *c*ognitions, *i*nterpersonal relationships, and *b*iological functions. The first letters of each of these modalities form the acronym BASIC I.B. If we call the biological modality "D" for "Drugs," we have the more compelling acronym BASIC I.D. (It is most important to remember that "D" stands for much more than drugs, medication, or pharmacological intervention, but also includes nutrition, hygiene, exercise, and the panoply of medical diagnoses and interventions that affect personality). The BASIC I.D. (as in "identity") is an alternative and preferred acronym that represents "human person-ality."
>
> Multimodal Therapy involves the comprehensive assessment and treatment of the "BASIC I.D." By working in this manner, we do *not* fit clients to the "treatment"; we demonstrate instead precisely how to fit the therapy to the requirements of the client. The fundamental assumption is that BASIC I.D. comprises the entire range of human personality; that there is no problem, no

feeling, no accomplishment, no dream or fantasy that cannot be subsumed by BASIC I.D.[35]

Lazarus believes in "systematic eclecticism"[36] or technical eclecticism, using whatever counseling techniques that work or have received empirical or research support, but he still subscribes to a basically broad-based social learning, cognitive-behavioral theoretical framework. He uses over three dozen techniques drawn from different schools of psychotherapy or counseling, although many of them are cognitive-behavioral strategies.

While Multimodal Therapy has much to commend it, as a secular approach it is still inadequate and limited, for it ignores the crucial spiritual dimension of human life and experience. More specific limitations of secular approaches like Multimodal Therapy and Cognitive-Behavior Therapy will be delineated late in this chapter under "Basic Principles of Effective Counseling." Christian counselors who have adapted Lazarus' BASIC I.D. for use in Christian counseling usually add S for the spiritual dimension, so that the acronym reads BASIC I.D.S.

Basic View of Counseling

It is important at this point to further clarify the meaning of the term *counseling* as used in this book, and viewed by the model I am describing. Counseling was defined in the Introduction as "a caring relationship in which one person tries to help another deal more effectively with the stresses of life," according to Collins.[37]

The following is a more precise definition of counseling by Collins in an earlier book he wrote:

> Counseling can be defined as a relationship between two or more persons in which one person (the counselor) seeks to advise, encourage and/or assist another person or persons (the counselee[s]) to deal more effectively with the problems of life.[38]

Such counseling may have a number of goals, including "a changing of the counselee's behavior, attitudes or values; preventing more serious problems from developing; teaching social skills; encouraging expression of emotions; giving support in times of need; instilling insight; guiding as a decision is made; teaching responsibility; stimulating spiritual growth; and helping the counselee to mobilize his inner resources in times of crisis. Unlike psychotherapy, counseling rarely aims to radically alter or remold the personality."[39]

Collins has therefore differentiated "counseling" from "psychotherapy," although there is an implication that the two terms are really on a continuum. A number of other authors have similarly differentiated between the two terms, pointing out that "there is a continuum from the simplest form of counseling through to the deepest levels of psychotherapy," as Hurding has put it.[40] In fact, Hurding has outlined four levels of psychotherapy, following R. H. Cawley's classification: *psychotherapy 1,* which involves the provision of support and encouragement, and hence includes a great deal of what is usually described as counseling; *psychotherapy 2,* which involves the provision of deeper insight into causes of one's personal problems, including the challenging of defenses or psychological masks; *psychotherapy 3,* which refers to dynamic psychotherapy that deals with unconscious processes or phenomena and aims at the remolding of personality, and hence is usually seen as the province of the experienced professional therapist; and *psychotherapy 4,* which refers to behavioral psychotherapy or the application of behavioral therapy techniques to help a client to unlearn "bad habits" or maladaptive behaviors, and to relearn more appropriate and helpful patterns of behavior. Hurding suggests that counseling can be subsumed under psychotherapy 1 and the initial part of psychotherapy 2, while psychotherapy per se should be used to refer to the other levels.[41]

There are other authors, however, who disagree with such a differentiation between counseling and psychotherapy. For example, Truax and Carkhuff do *not* differentiate between these two terms, and use them interchangeably,[42] as have a number of other contemporary writers of textbooks on counseling and psychotherapy.[43]

My own view and the one assumed in the model I am describing is to use the terms *counseling* and *psychotherapy* somewhat interchangeably, recognizing that a continuum between them could be argued for, but only with somewhat arbitrary delineations that tend to blur easily.

Adams has listed twenty most frequent reasons why people seek help from counselors. They are:

1. Advice in making simple decisions

2. Answers to troublesome questions
3. Depression and guilt
4. Guidance in determining careers
5. Breakdowns
6. Crises
7. Failures
8. Grief
9. Bizarre behavior
10. Anxiety, worry, and fear
11. Other unpleasant feelings
12. Family and marital trouble
13. Help in resolution of conflicts with others
14. Deteriorating interpersonal relationships
15. Drug and alcohol problems
16. Sexual difficulties
17. Perceptual distortions
18. Psychosomatic problems
19. Attempted suicide
20. Difficulties at work/school.[44]

If these are the problems clients most often face, what then are some basic principles of effective counseling from a biblical perspective that lay Christian counselors can use to help their hurting clients? This is the focus of the next section.

Basic Principles of Effective Counseling

For the sake of conciseness and clarity, the model proposes thirteen basic principles of effective lay counseling from a biblical perspective.

1. *The Holy Spirit's ministry as counselor or comforter is critical in effective Christian counseling.* As Adams has pointed out, there are always at least three persons involved in every counseling situation: the client, the counselor, and the Holy Spirit.[45] Dependence on the Spirit and his work as counselor is therefore crucial (cf. John 14:16, 17). Recently, Marvin Gilbert and Raymond Brock have edited two volumes on the Holy Spirit and counseling. They emphasize the need to be aware of and depend on the Holy Spirit's presence, guidance, and ministry during counseling or therapy sessions, as well as in the personal life of the counselor, so that he or she can function as a "Spirit-filled" Christian counselor, fully open to the power and gifts of the Spirit.[46]

2. *The Bible is the basic guide for dealing with problems in living (cf. 2 Tim. 3:16–17).* God, through Scripture, has provided human beings with the means to deal with problems and to meet their basic needs or longings for meaning, hope, and love.[47] The Christian counselor must therefore have a good grasp of Scripture. Theology and Bible knowledge (especially in the areas of Old Testament, New Testament, Systematic Theology, Hermeneutics, Apologetics, and Christian Ethics) are key foundations for effective lay *Christian* counseling.[48] The Bible is a *comprehensive* guide to dealing with life's problems, or a *sufficient* guide for relational living, as Crabb puts it.[49] The Bible does speak meaningfully to every human problem, but only if we study and interpret it carefully in terms of its content, categories, implications, and images, including appropriate extended applications of scriptural truth to complex life situations and problems. In other words, we need to learn not only how to interpret the Scriptures accurately (exegesis and hermeneutics), but also how to apply them practically to life.[50] A number of authors have attempted to present fundamental doctrines of the Christian faith and how they apply to Christian counseling, emphasizing that good Christian or biblical theology is crucial for good Christian counseling.[51]

The model, however, does *not* assert that the Bible is an *exhaustive* guide to counseling. It affirms theologically God's general revelation and common grace, which allow truth to be discovered even by non-Christians, for example, through research. While Scripture does provide sufficient answers to life's major issues and problems, and serves as a comprehensive guide to counseling, it does not cover every detail involved. Hence, the model is open to the use of principles and strategies of counseling derived from psychology or psychiatry which do *not* contradict the Scriptures.[52] Implicit in this view is the assumption of the unity of truth, or "all truth is God's truth."

3. *Prayer is an integral part of biblical helping (cf. James 5:16).* At the very least, the Christian counselor should be praying for the client before and in between counseling sessions, and quietly during sessions. However, where appropriate, especially with Christian clients who are well motivated for help and growth, prayer should also be used explicitly during the counseling session. A specific kind of prayer called inner healing or the healing of memories from an emotionally

painful past may be particularly appropriate in certain cases.[53] It should be pointed out, however, that the *actual* use of prayer and the Scriptures *during* counseling sessions requires discernment and sensitivity on the part of the counselor, especially if the client is not a Christian or if the client is a Christian who is having significant struggles with the Lord and hence may not be ready to pray yet. There is a time and season for everything (Eccl. 3:1–8)—*proper timing* with regard to the use of prayer and Scripture, or anything else during counseling, is very important, and cannot be overemphasized. The discussion of spiritual issues and the use of spiritual resources in counseling should therefore be done in a caring and ethical way.[54]

4. *The ultimate goal of counseling is to make disciples or disciplers of clients.* If possible, counselors should fulfill the Great Commission, as Collins has pointed out.[55] Crabb takes a similar perspective when he states that the basic goal of counseling is to free people to better worship and serve God by helping them toward maturity in Christ.[56] This will involve helping clients to restore their personal identity in Christ and thus to live out an identity-based morality rather than a performance-based morality that is guilt-motivated and essentially one of self-atonement.[57]

5. *The personal qualities of the lay Christian counselor are important for effective counseling.*[58] More specifically, counselors should at least possess qualities like goodness, knowledge of God's Word, and wisdom in applying it in practical ways (Rom. 15:14; Col. 3:16), as Adams has emphasized.[59] Some may be especially gifted in people-helping.[60] Essentially, a lay Christian counselor must be a spiritually mature person to be effective (cf. Gal. 6:1, 2). Personal characteristics of the counselor which are important for effective counseling according to Collins include self-understanding; understanding of others; acceptance of others; appropriate social distance or ability to remain objective; ability to get along with people; experience; and the following spiritual characteristics: being a real believer or "born again" (John 3:3), capable, God-fearing, honest, available, willing to refer difficult cases (Ex. 18:21–22), thoroughly familiar with God's Word (2 Tim. 2:15), and a follower of Christ (1 Peter 2:2), who is the "Wonderful Counselor" (Isa. 9:6).[61]

6. *The client's attitudes, motivations, and desire for help are crucial factors for determining whether counseling will be*

helpful or not.[62] Several years ago Gomes-Schwartz reported results from a significant research study called the Vanderbilt Psychotherapy Study[63] which provide support for this point. She found that the process dimension that most consistently predicted therapy or counseling outcome was the degree of client involvement in therapy. In her own words:

> Patients who were not hostile or mistrustful and who actively contributed to the therapy interaction achieved greater changes than those who were withdrawn, defensive, or otherwise unwilling to engage in the therapy process.[64]

7. *The relationship between the counselor and the client is another significant variable affecting the effectiveness of counseling.* Good rapport and communication based on the so-called "core conditions" for therapeutic change, namely, the *facilitative* conditions of *empathy* (or understanding), *respect* (or caring for someone), and *concreteness* (or being specific), and the *action* conditions of *genuineness* (or being real), *confrontation* (or telling it like it is), and *immediacy* (or what's really going on between the two of you)[65] are important for effective counseling. Ephesians 4:15 seems to sum up this view quite well—speak the *truth* (e.g., covering the conditions of concreteness, immediacy, confrontation, and genuineness) in love (e.g., covering the conditions of respect or warmth, empathy, and genuineness).

However, the model does subscribe to Adams' assertion that talking alone is not enough in dealing with problems—it should lead eventually to definite decisions and actions which are in line with Scripture. For example, *confession,* while essential in dealing with problems involving obvious sins, is often *not* enough—it should lead to attempts at *reconciliation* and *restitution* where necessary (see Matt. 5:21–26; 18:15–20).[66] *Forgiveness* of others who may have hurt the client is also an important process for the client to work through, with God's grace and help.[67]

8. *Effective counseling is a process which unfolds cyclically, from exploration to understanding to action phases.* This point follows the views of Carkhuff as well as Egan.[68] The model therefore stresses the need to explore and understand adequately the client's problems before undertaking courses of action or giving directives to the client. Crabb has integrated such views

into a more comprehensive and biblical model of the counseling process in seven stages.

In *stage one,* the counselor helps the client to identify the client's problem (negative) feelings. In *stage two,* the counselor helps the client to identify his or her problem (negative) behaviors. In *stage three,* the focus is on identifying the client's problem (wrong) thinking. Such problem thinking often has to do with erroneous, irrational, unrealistic, and eventually unbiblical or sinful basic assumptions about how to meet the basic needs or longings for security and significance apart from the Lord. Examples of such unbiblical basic assumptions include: "I will be secure if I have a loving spouse," and "I will be significant if I excel and become the president of the company." In *stage four,* therefore, the counselor attempts to teach or clarify right, biblical thinking (basically, "I am secure and significant in Christ and his love for me") and in *stage five,* to secure a commitment on the part of the client to such biblical thinking in obedience to the Lord and his Word. In *stage six,* the client is encouraged to plan and carry out biblical or right behavior. Finally, in stage seven, the client can identify and enjoy Spirit-controlled feelings of security and significance.[69]

9. *Directive or nouthetic counseling is an important part of Christian counseling, but style or approach in counseling should be flexible.* The model incorporates Adams' nouthetic counseling as based mainly on New Testament passages. (In fact, a number of Old Testament passages relevant to a ministry of effective counseling [e.g., Ex. 18:5–26; Prov. 12:15; 13:10; 19:20, 20:18; 1 Kings 12:9, 28; Ps. 55:13–14] contain Hebrew words often translated as "counsel," with meanings associated with advice in the form of guidance or direction.[70]) However, the model does *not* take the view that nouthetic counseling is the only valid approach in biblical counseling. As pointed out earlier in chapter 2, the model accepts Carter's view that biblical counseling is more adequately based on *parakaleo* and *paraklesis* rather than only on *noutheteo* or *nouthesia*—Greek terms found in the New Testament which are most relevant to counseling from a biblical perspective.[71] Biblical counseling therefore includes not only the nouthetic or directive and confrontational approach, but also includes the other *parakaleo* functions of comforting, encouraging, and supporting, at appropriate times.

David Carlson has also similarly argued from Scriptures that Jesus' style of relating or helping was flexible, ranging from his prophetic, confrontational style to his priestly, accepting style, with his pastoral style in between, depending on the need of the person he was ministering to. Examples of the prophetic approach to Christian counseling include convicting, confronting, preaching, lecturing, thinking for, talking to, proclaiming the truth, and disturbing the comfortable. Examples of the priestly approach to Christian counseling include comforting, confessional, interviewing, listening, thinking with, talking with, affirming truth, and comforting the disturbed.[72]

10. *The model remains flexible with regard to specific techniques or methods to be used in counseling, at different stages or phases.* The Scriptures should be the ultimate screening device for accepting or rejecting particular techniques (cf. 1 Thess. 5:21), as several authors such as Crabb have emphasized. A number of cognitive-behavioral strategies or techniques may be particularly helpful and can be used by lay Christian counselors with some training and supervision. Examples of such techniques include the use of self-talk (cognitive restructuring), imagery, relaxation strategies, prayer in counseling (as described by Norman Wright[73]), and Misbelief Therapy methods (as described by William Backus[74]). Some useful secular books on basically cognitive-behavioral methods for helping people change include those by Cormier and Cormier, Lazarus, and Kanfer and Goldstein.[75]

The use of cognitive-behavioral methods in Christian counseling, however, should be qualified because of the limitations of such secular techniques. I have therefore suggested the following guidelines for a biblical approach to cognitive-behavior therapy:

a. Emphasize the primacy of agape love (1 Cor. 13), and the need to develop a warm, empathic, and genuine relationship with the client.

b. Deal more adequately with the past, especially unresolved developmental issues or childhood traumas, and use inner healing or healing of memories judiciously and appropriately.

c. Pay special attention to the meaning of spiritual, experiential, and even mystical aspects of life and faith, according to God's wisdom as revealed in Scripture and by the Holy Spirit's teaching ministry (John 14:26). Do not overemphasize the rational, thinking dimension, although biblical, propositional truth will still be given its rightful place of importance. The possibility of demonic involvement in some cases will also require serious consideration and appropriate action.

d. Focus on how problems in thought and behavior may often (*not* always, because of other factors, e.g., organic or biological) underlie problem feelings (Prov. 23:7; Rom. 12:1–2; Phil. 4:8; Eph. 4:22–24). Use biblical truth (John 8:32), not relativistic, empirically oriented values, to restructure thinking and change behavior.

e. Emphasize the Holy Spirit's ministry in bringing about inner healing as well as cognitive, behavioral, and emotional change. Using prayer and affirmation of God's Word to facilitate dependence on the Lord will produce deep and lasting personality change, and will not inadvertently encourage sinful self-sufficiency (cf. Phil. 4:13).

f. Pay more attention to larger contextual factors like familial, societal, religious, and cultural influences, and hence utilize appropriate community resources in therapeutic interventions, including the church as a body of believers and fellow "priests" to one another (1 Cor. 12; 1 Peter 2:5, 9).

g. Use only those techniques which are consistent with biblical truth; do not simplistically use whatever techniques work. This will reaffirm scriptural perspectives on suffering, including the possibility of the "blessings of mental anguish," with the ultimate goal of counseling being holiness or Christlikeness (Rom. 8:29), not necessarily temporal happiness. However, such a goal will include being more open to receiving God's love and grace, and growing thereby to be more Christlike, and overcoming mental anguish due to unbiblical, erroneous beliefs (i.e., misbeliefs).

h. Utilize rigorous outcome research methodology before making definitive statements about the superiority of cognitive-behavior therapy.[76]

11. *Effective counseling requires cultural sensitivity.* Some knowledge of *cross-cultural counseling* principles and methods, especially those written from a Christian perspective, is essential for effective counseling. American society is becoming even more pluralistic and multicultural in composition, particularly since many immigrants have entered the United States of America in recent years. In the light of such a development, the

following challenge put forth by Collins several years ago is even more pertinent: "Christian counselors have given very little consideration to cross-cultural counseling, and any approach to biblically based counseling in the future must not neglect this significant area."[77]

A good secular book on counseling the culturally different, including Asian-Americans, African-Americans, Hispanics, and Native Americans, has been written by Derald Sue.[78] A number of books and articles on cross-cultural counseling from a biblical perspective have also been published recently, notably David Hesselgrave's *Counseling Cross-culturally* and David Augsburger's *Pastoral Counseling Across Cultures.*[79]

12. *Outreach and prevention techniques are also important for effective lay Christian counseling.* Jeffrey Prater has pointed out that the church has historically provided prevention and community outreach services, and noted that most of the proposed biblically based models for lay Christian counseling have ignored this historical tradition of the church as a caring community, focusing instead on individual counseling based on the view that emotional problems are due to *individual* defect or deficits. He therefore made the following six proposals for including lay counselor training in interventions on a broader psychosocial level, so that such training is more integrated with the other outreach ministries of the church:[80]

The first proposal is that lay counselors should be trained to assess the role of environmental stressors in the development and maintenance of emotional problems. Examples of such stressors include poverty, unemployment, racism, sexism, and lack of social support, and they may need to be dealt with in counseling.

The second proposal is that lay counselors should be trained in the techniques of community outreach and empowerment. They should bring services directly to people where possible and appropriate, rather than merely waiting for people to come and use the services available.

The third proposal is that lay counselors should be trained in cultural awareness and sensitivity, so that lay counseling services will not be appropriate only for white, middle-class clients with problems in living. Cultural barriers actually represent a major obstacle to providing mental health services.

The fourth proposal is that lay counselors should be trained to be aware of and make use of existing support systems and services within churches. Collins, for example, has issued the following challenge: "We must learn to use worship, study programs, discussion groups, church socials, and other activities—whether religious or not—to help people avoid problems or show them how to cope more effectively with them."[81] Many churches provide informal services to the community which are not well publicized or known to the public. Examples of such services include pastoral visitation of the sick, provision of transportation to support meetings and other appointments, and friendly visitation of homebound elderly. Lay counselors need to be aware of these informal services and resources so that they can make appropriate referrals of needy people to them.

The fifth proposal is that lay counselors should be trained in how to develop new support systems within the church where needed. Some examples of these systems include small groups for individuals or families, regular breakfast or dinner meetings, Bible studies, and prevention-oriented training seminars on topics like stress management, parenting skills, and conflict resolution.

The sixth proposal is that lay counselors should be trained to communicate more actively and regularly with others, particularly the leaders involved in other outreach ministries of the church, so that a more coordinated and integrated package of ministries would result. Regular meetings could be arranged for the purpose of providing information, mutual encouragement, support, and prayer for one another's ministries.

13. *Lay Christian counselors must be aware of their limited knowledge and skill in helping people with needs and problems.* Lay counselors need to *be willing and able to make good referrals* in a supportive and sensitive way, steering their clients to other more experienced and better trained counselors or other appropriate professionals (e.g., lawyers, physicians, financial consultants, etc.) when necessary. Some helpful guidelines regarding when, where, and how to refer have been provided by Collins, and Grunlan and Lambrides.[82] William Oglesby has also written a helpful book entitled *Referrals in Pastoral Counseling*.[83]

Collins, for example, has suggested the following guidelines for deciding when referral is necessary:

Referral is necessary when the present helper lacks the time, emotional stamina or stability, and the skill, or experience to continue the counseling. As a general rule, we should refer whenever we don't seem to be helping someone deal with the problem of life or to grow as a whole person. More specifically, it is important to seek outside help for counselees who—

- are in legal difficulties
- have severe financial needs
- require medical attention
- are severely depressed or suicidal
- will require more time than we can give
- want to shift to another counselor
- show extremely aggressive behavior
- make excessive use of drugs or alcohol
- arouse strong feelings of dislike, sexual stimulation, or threat in the counselor
- appear to be severely disturbed.[84]

Concluding Comments

A biblical model for effective lay counseling has been described, and a summary of its main points is provided in Table 1. In concluding this chapter, I would like to emphasize again the primacy of agape love (1 Cor. 13) in the process of effective, biblical counseling. Such love will reveal itself in a warm, empathic, and genuine relationship with the client. By emphasizing love, I do not mean to say that techniques are not important, but only that they are not the most important factor in effective counseling. In fact, research has shown that *client* variables, then *therapist* variables, and finally, *technique* variables, in that order, are the most important or powerful predictors of counseling or psychotherapy effectiveness.[85]

Table 1: Summary of A Biblical Model for Effective Lay Counseling

Basic View of Humanity	Basic View of Counseling	Basic Principles of Effective Lay Counseling
1. Basic psychological and spiritual needs include needs for security (love), significance	Somewhat interchangeable with "psychotherapy"	1. The Holy Spirit's ministry as counselor is crucial—depend on him.

(meaning/impact), and hope (forgiveness).

2. Basic problem is sin—but not all emotional suffering is due to personal sin.

3. Ultimate goal of humanity is to know and enjoy God and spiritual health.

4. Problem feelings are usually due to problem behavior and, more fundamentally, problem thinking—however, biological and demonic factors should also be considered.

5. Holistic view of persons—with physical, mental/emotional, social, and spiritual dimensions.

2. The Bible is a basic and comprehensive (not exhaustive) guide for counseling.

3. Prayer is an integral part of biblical counseling.

4. Ultimate goal of counseling is maturity in Christ and fulfilling the Great Commission.

5. Personal qualities of the counselor are important, especially spiritual ones.

6. Client's attitudes, motivations, and desire for help are important.

7. Relationship between counselor and client is significant.

8. Effective counseling is a process involving exploration, understanding, and action phases, with a focus on changing problem thinking.

9. Style or approach in counseling should be flexible.

10. Specific techniques or methods of counseling should be consistent with Scripture—cognitive-behavioral ones may be especially helpful, with qualifications.

11. Cultural sensitivity and cross-cultural counseling skills are required.

12. Outreach and prevention skills in the context of a

caring community are
important.
13. Awareness of limitations
and referral skills are
also important.

I will end this chapter with the following note of appreciation
from a former client whom I saw in a local church lay counseling
service context. Her words, more so than mine, capture the
primacy of agape love and real caring in effective lay Christian
counseling:

> So many books
> with so many words
> yet so hard it is
> to say
> the things that touch
> a human breast
> in the passing
> of one day.
> Like a card
> or flower
> is a strength'ning hand
> like the warming
> of the sun
> is a list'ning ear, or
> the sharing of
> a battle
> fought, and won . . .
> a helper
> and a counsellor
> when days were hard
> and sad . . .
> a tender sympathizer
> in the sorrow
> that I had . . .
> a *stronger* arm to lean upon
> a voice
> that spoke of God
> *your* heart
> so full of hope
> I *knew He* knew the way
> I trod . . .
> and slowly
> an awareness

of the coming
of the morn
for as we spoke
within my soul
a greater hope
was born
until the colours,
red and gold
had filled
the eastern sky . . .
I mounted up
with eagles' wings
and felt
that I could FLY!
Someone who prayed,
someone who cared
in my life
as the course was run . . .
thank you for being
who you are . . .
a friend,
when I needed one.

NOTES

[1]L. J. Crabb, Jr., *Effective Biblical Counseling* (Grand Rapids: Zondervan, 1977), 31.

[2]See, e.g., J. D. Carter and B. Narramore, *The Integration of Psychology and Theology: An Introduction* (Grand Rapids: Zondervan, 1979); G. R. Collins, *The Rebuilding of Psychology: An Integration of Psychology and Christianity* (Wheaton, Ill.: Tyndale, 1977); G. R. Collins and H. N. Malony, *Psychology and Theology: Prospects for Integration* (Nashville: Abingdon, 1981); M. P. Cosgrove, *Psychology Gone Awry* (Grand Rapids: Zondervan, 1979); L. J. Crabb, Jr., *Effective Biblical Counseling* (Grand Rapids: Zondervan, 1977); W. J. Donaldson, ed., *Research in Mental Health and Religious Behavior* (Atlanta: Psychological Studies Institute, 1976); J. H. Ellens, *God's Grace and Human Health* (Nashville: Abingdon, 1982); C. S. Evans, *Preserving the Person: A Look at the Human Sciences* (Downers Grove, Ill.: InterVarsity Press, 1977); C. S. Evans, *Wisdom and Humanness in Psychology* (Grand Rapids: Baker, 1989);

Also, K. E. Farnsworth, *Wholehearted Integration: Harmonizing Psychology and Christianity Through Word and Deed* (Grand Rapids: Baker, 1985); J. R. Fleck and J. D. Carter, eds., *Psychology and Christianity: Integrative Readings* (Nashville: Abingdon, 1981); M. A.

Jeeves, *Psychology and Christianity: The View Both Ways* (Leicester, England: InterVarsity Press, 1976); S. J. Jones, ed., *Psychology and the Christian Faith* (Grand Rapids: Baker, 1986); W. K. Kilpatrick, *Psychological Seduction* (Nashville: Nelson, 1983); R. L. Koteskey, *Psychology from a Christian Perspective* (Nashville: Abingdon, 1980); H. N. Malony, ed., *Wholeness and Holiness: Readings in the Psychology/Theology of Mental Health* (Grand Rapids: Baker, 1983); J. M. McDonaugh, *Christian Psychology* (New York: Crossroad, 1982); P. D. Meier, F. B. Minirth, and F. B. Wichern, *Introduction to Psychology and Counseling: Christian Perspectives and Applications* (Grand Rapids: Baker, 1982);

Also, D. G. Myers, *The Human Puzzle: Psychological Research and Christian Belief* (New York: Harper & Row, 1978); M. S. Peck, *The Road Less Traveled: A New Psychology of Love, Traditional Values, and Spiritual Growth* (New York: Simon & Schuster, 1978); H. Vande Kemp, *Psychology and Theology in Western Thought, 1672–1965: A Historical and Annotated Bibliography,* in collaboration with H. N. Malony (Milwood, New York: Kraus International Publications, 1984); M. S. Van Leeuwen, *The Person in Psychology: A Contemporary Christian Approach* (Grand Rapids: Eerdmans, 1985); M. S. Van Leeuwen, *The Sorcerer's Apprentice: A Christian Looks at the Changing Face of Psychology* (Downers Grove, Ill.: InterVarsity Press, 1982); P. C. Vitz, *Psychology as Religion: The Cult of Self-Worship* (Grand Rapids: Eerdmans, 1977).

[3]See, e.g., numerous articles published in the following journals: *The Journal of the American Scientific Affiliation, Journal of Psychology and Christianity* (formerly *CAPS Bulletin*) and *Journal of Psychology and Theology.*

[4]Crabb, *Effective Biblical Counseling,* 31–56.

[5]Carter and Narramore, *Integration of Psychology and Theology,* 103–15.

[6]See, e.g., Ellens, *God's Grace and Human Health;* and Farnsworth, *Wholehearted Integration.*

[7]Ellens, *God's Grace and Human Health,* 99.

[8]For a discussion of these issues, see L. J. Crabb, Jr., "Biblical Authority and Christian Psychology," *Journal of Psychology and Theology* 9 (1981): 305–11, and the following responses: G. Breshears and R. E. Larzelere, "The Authority of Scripture and the Unity of Revelation: A Response to Crabb," *Journal of Psychology and Theology* 9 (1981): 312–17; J. H. Ellens, "Biblical Authority and Christian Psychology II," *Journal of Psychology and Theology* 9 (1981): 318–25; J. D. Guy, "Affirming Diversity in the Task of Integration: A Response to 'Biblical Authority and Christian Psychology'" *Journal of Psychology and Theology* 10 (1982): 35–39.

[9]E. L. Worthington, Jr., "Grace Theology" (featured review of J. H. Ellens, *God's Grace and Human Health*, Nashville: Abingdon, 1982), *Journal of Psychology and Theology* 12 (1984): 137–38.

[10]See S. Y. Tan, "Lay Counseling: The Local Church," *CAPS Bulletin* 7, no. 1 (1981): 15–20, for an earlier and briefer description of the model.

[11]W. Backus, *Telling the Truth to Troubled People* (Minneapolis: Bethany House, 1985); also see W. Backus and M. Chapian, *Telling Yourself the Truth* (Minneapolis: Bethany House, 1980); W. Backus and M. Chapian, *Why Do I Do What I Don't Want to Do?* (Minneapolis: Bethany House, 1984); and W. Backus, *Telling Each Other the Truth* (Minneapolis: Bethany House, 1985).

[12]E. L. Worthington, Jr., *When Someone Asks for Help: A Practical Guide for Counseling* (Downers Grove, Ill.: InterVarsity Press, 1982).

[13]R. R. Carkhuff, *Helping and Human Relations*, vols. 1 and 2 (New York: Holt, Rinehart and Winston, 1969); R. R. Carkhuff, *The Development of Human Resources* (New York: Holt, Rinehart and Winston, 1971); R. R. Carkhuff, *The Art of Helping* (Amherst, Mass.: Human Resources Development Press, 1972).

[14]G. Egan, *The Skilled Helper: A Systematic Approach to Effective Helping*, 3d ed. (Monterey, Calif.: Brooks/Cole, 1986).

[15]See W. H. Cormier and L. S. Cormier, *Interviewing Strategies for Helpers: Fundamental Skills and Cognitive Behavioral Interventions*, 2d ed. (Monterey, Calif.: Brooks/Cole, 1985), for a good description of the major cognitive-behavioral approaches and interventions, including Aaron Beck's "Cognitive Therapy," Albert Ellis' "Rational-Emotive Therapy," and Donald Meichenbaum's "Stress-Inoculation Training," and "Cognitive-Behavior Modification." See also S. Y. Tan, "Cognitive-Behavior Therapy: A Biblical Approach and Critique," *Journal of Psychology and Theology* 15 (1987): 103–12, for a biblical or Christian perspective on cognitive-behavior therapy, and F. Craigie and S. Y. Tan, "Changing Resistant Assumptions in Christian Cognitive-Behavioral Therapy," *Journal of Psychology and Theology* 17 (1989): 93–100.

[16]H. Norman Wright, *Self-Talk, Imagery, and Prayer in Counseling* (Waco, Tex.: Word, 1986).

[17]See J. E. Adams, *The Christian Counselor's Manual* (Grand Rapids: Baker, 1973).

[18]See Crabb, *Effective Biblical Counseling*.

[19]L. J. Crabb, Jr., *Understanding People: Deep Longings for Relationship* (Grand Rapids: Zondervan, 1987), 15. See also W. Kirwan, *Biblical Concepts for Christian Counseling* (Grand Rapids: Baker, 1984), for a description of the following similar, genuine needs of human beings since Adam fell into sin and the loss of personal identity occurred as a

consequence—the need to belong, the need for self-esteem, and the need for control (see 73–115).

[20]See J. E. Adams, *Competent to Counsel* (Grand Rapids: Baker, 1970), and Crabb, *Effective Biblical Counseling*. There have also been a number of publications in the secular literature dealing with how moral and spiritual decay may underlie many mental-emotional problems. See, e.g., K. Menninger, *Whatever Became of Sin?* (New York: Hawthorne Books, 1973), and G. Wood, *The Myth of Neurosis* (New York: Harper & Row, 1986). See also A. E. Bergin, "Psychotherapy and Religious Values," *Journal of Consulting and Clinical Psychology* 48 (1980): 95–105.

[21]See V. Grounds, *Emotional Problems and the Gospel* (Grand Rapids: Zondervan, 1976), 31–41, for an insightful discussion of the possibility of such anguish or deep distress experienced by Jesus as being equivalent to the emotion of anxiety or fear, and particularly the fear of death.

[22]R. Foster, *Celebration of Discipline* (New York: Harper & Row, 1978), 89–91.

[23]A. W. Tozer, *That Incredible Christian* (Beaverlodge, Alberta: Horizon House, 1977), 122, 124.

[24]S. Y. Tan, "Intrapersonal Integration: The Servant's Spirituality," *Journal of Psychology and Christianity* 6, no. 1 (1987): 34–39. Quotation is from p. 37. See also P. R. Welter, *Counseling and the Search for Meaning* (Waco, Tex.: Word, 1987).

[25]C. S. Evans, "The Blessings of Mental Anguish," *Christianity Today* 30, no. 1 (January 1986): 26–29.

[26]Ibid., 29.

[27]See Grounds, *Emotional Problems and the Gospel*, 105–11.

[28]See Crabb, *Effective Biblical Counseling*.

[29]See. G. R. Collins, *How to Be a People Helper* (Santa Ana, Calif.: Vision House, 1976).

[30]See R. K. Bufford, *Counseling and the Demonic* (Waco, Tex.: Word, 1988); K. Koch, *Christian Counseling and Occultism* (Grand Rapids: Kregel, 1972); and J. Wimber with K. Springer, *Power Healing* (New York: Harper & Row, 1987), 97–125, 230–35. See also M. I. Bubeck, *The Adversary: The Christian Versus Demonic Activity* (Chicago: Moody Press, 1975), and *Overcoming the Adversary* (Chicago: Moody Press, 1984); C. F. Dickason, *Demon Possession and the Christian: A New Perspective* (Chicago: Moody Press, 1987); J. W. Montgomery, ed., *Demon Possession* (Minneapolis: Bethany Fellowship, 1973), and M. Shuster, *Power Pathology Paradox: The Dynamics of Evil and Good* (Grand Rapids: Zondervan, 1987).

[31]Crabb, *Understanding People*.

[32]See Tan, "Cognitive-Behavior Therapy: A Biblical Approach and Critique."

[33]Adams, *Christian Counselor's Manual*, 409–12.

[34]See A. A. Lazarus, ed., *Multimodal Behavior Therapy* (New York: Springer, 1976); A. A. Lazarus, *The Practice of Multimodal Therapy* (New York: McGraw-Hill, 1981); A. A. Lazarus, ed., *Casebook of Multimodal Therapy* (New York: Guilford, 1985).

[35]Lazarus, *Practice of Multimodal Therapy*, 13–14.

[36]Ibid., 4.

[37]G. R. Collins, *Innovative Approaches to Counseling* (Waco, Tex.: Word, 1986), 73.

[38]G. R. Collins, *Effective Counseling* (Carol Stream, Ill.: Creation House, 1972), 13.

[39]Ibid., 13–14.

[40]R. F. Hurding, *The Tree of Healing: Psychological and Biblical Foundations for Counseling and Pastoral Care* (Grand Rapids: Zondervan, 1988), 22.

[41]Ibid., 24–25.

[42]C. Truax and R. Carkhuff, *Toward Effective Counseling and Psychotherapy* (Chicago: Aldine, 1967).

[43]See, e.g., G. Corey, *Theory and Practice of Counseling and Psychotherapy*, 3d ed. (Monterey, Calif.: Brooks/Cole, 1986); and A. Ivey and L. Simek-Downing, *Counseling and Psychotherapy: Skills, Theories, and Practice* (Englewood Cliffs, N.J.: Prentice-Hall, 1980).

[44]Adams, *Christian Counselor's Manual*, 277–78.

[45]Ibid., 4–8.

[46]M. G. Gilbert and R. T. Brock, eds., *The Holy Spirit and Counseling: Theology and Theory* (Peabody, Mass.: Hendrickson, 1988); and *The Holy Spirit and Counseling: Principles and Practice* (Peabody, Mass.: Hendrickson, 1985). See also John White, *When the Spirit Comes With Power* (Downers Grove, Ill.: InterVarsity Press, 1988); and J. P. Ozawa, "Power Counseling: Gifts of the Holy Spirit and Counseling," and "Prayer and Deliverance in the Healing of Chronic Disorders: Hope for the Hopeless," papers presented at the International Congress on Christian Counseling, November 1988, in Atlanta, Georgia.

[47]See Adams, *Christian Counselor's Manual;* and Crabb, *Effective Biblical Counseling.*

[48]See G. R. Collins and L. M. Tournquist, "Training Christian People Helpers: Observations on Counselor Education," *Journal of Psychology and Theology* 9 (1981): 69–80.

[49]Crabb, *Understanding People.*

[50]Ibid. See also J. E. Adams, *What to Do on Thursday: A Layman's Guide to the Practical Use of the Scriptures* (Grand Rapids: Baker,

1982); J. E. Adams, *The Use of the Scriptures in Counseling* (Grand Rapids: Baker, 1975); and W. O. Ward, *The Bible in Counseling* (Chicago: Moody Press, 1977). For two good books on basic principles of biblical interpretation, see G. D. Fee and D. Stuart, *How to Read the Bible for All Its Worth* (Grand Rapids: Zondervan, 1982), and H. A. Virkler, *Hermeneutics: Principles and Processes of Biblical Interpretation* (Grand Rapids: Baker, 1981).

[51]See, e.g., J. E. Adams, *A Theology of Christian Counseling (More Than Redemption)* (Grand Rapids: Zondervan, 1979); D. Capps, *Biblical Approaches to Pastoral Counseling* (Philadelphia: Westminster, 1981); Crabb, *Understanding People;* W. Hulme, *Counseling and Theology* (Philadelphia: Fortress, 1967); Kirwan, *Biblical Concepts for Christian Counseling;* S. B. Narramore, *No Condemnation* (Grand Rapids: Zondervan, 1984); S. Southard, *Theology & Therapy: The Wisdom of God in a Context of Friendship* (Dallas: Word, 1989); and R. S. Anderson, *Christians Who Counsel: The Vocation of Wholistic Therapy* (Grand Rapids: Zondervan, 1990).

[52]For a helpful and well-written book on such principles and strategies, see W. R. Miller and K. A. Jackson, *Practical Psychology for Pastors* (Englewood Cliffs, N.J.: Prentice-Hall, 1985). See also E. Kennedy, *On Becoming a Counselor: A Basic Guide for Non-Professional Counselors* (New York: Seabury, 1977).

[53]See Wright, *Self-Talk, Imagery, and Prayer;* and D. Seamands, *Healing of Memories* (Wheaton, Ill.: Victor, 1985).

[54]See A. A. Nelson and W. P. Wilson, "The Ethics of Sharing Religious Faith in Psychotherapy," *Journal of Psychology and Theology* 12 (1984): 15–23.

[55]Collins, *How to Be a People Helper.*

[56]Crabb, *Effective Biblical Counseling.*

[57]See J. D. Carter, "Toward a Biblical Model of Counseling," *Journal of Psychology and Theology* 8 (1980): 45–52; Narramore, *No Condemnation;* and D. C. Needham, *Birthright: Christian, Do You Know Who You Are?* (Portland, Ore.: Multnomah Press, 1979).

[58]Collins, *How to Be a People Helper.*

[59]Adams, *Christian Counselor's Manual.*

[60]P. D. Morris, *Love Therapy* (Wheaton, Ill.: Tyndale, 1974).

[61]Collins, *Effective Counseling,* 17–20.

[62]Collins, *How to Be a People Helper.*

[63]H. H. Strupp and S. W. Hadley, "Specific vs. Non-specific Factors in Psychotherapy: A Controlled Study of Outcome," *Archives of General Psychiatry* 36 (1979): 1125–36.

[64]B. Gomes-Schwartz, "Effective Ingredients in Psychotherapy: Prediction of Outcome from Process Variables," *Journal of Consulting and Clinical Psychology* 46 (1978): 1023–35. Quotation is from p. 1032.

[65]Carkhuff, *Development of Human Resources,* 170–71.

[66]Adams, *The Christian Counselor's Manual.*

[67]See L. Smedes, *Forgive & Forget: Healing the Hurts We Don't Deserve* (New York: Pocket Books, 1984); and R. P. Walters, *Forgive and Be Free: Healing the Wounds of Past and Present* (Grand Rapids: Zondervan, 1983).

[68]See Carkhuff, *Helping and Human Relations* and *Development of Human Resources;* and Egan, *The Skilled Helper.*

[69]See Crabb, *Effective Biblical Counseling;* and L. J. Crabb, Jr., "Biblical Counseling: A Basic View," *CAPS Bulletin* 4 (1978): 1–6. See also Crabb, *Understanding People,* and Kirwan, *Biblical Concepts for Christian Counseling,* for further insights into how to understand and help people at deeper levels, including unconscious processes.

[70]H. N. Wright, *Training Christians to Counsel: A Resource Curriculum Manual* (Eugene, Oreg.: Harvest House, 1977), 22.

[71]J. Carter, "Adams' Theory of Nouthetic Counseling," *Journal of Psychology and Theology* 3 (1975): 143–55.

[72]See D. E. Carlson, "Jesus' Style of Relating: The Search for a Biblical View of Counseling," *Journal of Psychology and Theology* 4 (1976): 181–92.

[73]Wright, *Self-Talk, Imagery and Prayer.*

[74]Backus, *Telling the Truth to Troubled People.*

[75]Cormier and Cormier, *Interviewing Strategies for Helpers;* Lazarus, *The Practice of Multimodal Therapy;* F. H. Kanfer and A. P. Goldstein, eds., *Helping People Change,* 3d ed. (New York: Pergamon, 1985). For a broader based book on teaching a number of psychological and counseling skills not limited to the cognitive-behavioral approaches, with particular relevance to lay counselors, see D. Larson, ed., *Teaching Psychological Skills: Models for Giving Psychology Away* (Monterey, Calif.: Brooks/Cole, 1984).

[76]Tan, "Cognitive-Behavior Therapy," 108–9.

[77]G. R. Collins, ed., *Helping People Grow: Practical Approaches to Christian Counseling* (Santa Ana, Calif.: Vision House, 1980), 342.

[78]D. W. Sue, *Counseling the Culturally Different* (New York: Wiley, 1981). A second edition of this book is to be published by Wiley in 1991. See also L. Comas-Dias and E. E. H. Griffith, eds., *Clinical Guidelines in Cross-Cultural Mental Health* (New York: Wiley, 1988).

[79]D. Hesselgrave, *Counseling Cross-Culturally* (Grand Rapids: Baker, 1984); D. Augsburger, *Pastoral Counseling Across Cultures* (Philadelphia: Westminster, 1986). See also C. R. Ridley, "Cross-Cultural Counseling in Theological Context," *Journal of Psychology and Theology* 14 (1986): 288–97; J. M. Uomoto, "Delivering Mental Health Services to Ethnic Minorities: Ethical Considerations," *Journal of Psychology and Theology* 14 (1986): 15–21; and S. Y. Tan, "Psycho-

pathology and Culture: The Asian-American Context," *Journal of Psychology and Christianity* 8, no. 2 (1989): 69–80.

[80]J. S. Prater, "Training Christian Lay Counselors in Techniques of Prevention and Outreach," *Journal of Psychology and Christianity* 6, no. 2 (1987): 30–34.

[81]G. R. Collins, "Psychology Is Not a Panacea But . . ." *Christianity Today* (November 16, 1979), 22–25. Quotation is from p. 25.

[82]See Collins, *How to Be a People Helper*, 108–15; and S. Grunlan and D. Lambrides, *Healing Relationships* (Camp Hill, Pa.: Christian Publications, 1984), 14.

[83]W. B. Oglesby, Jr., *Referrals in Pastoral Counseling*, rev. ed. (Nashville: Abingdon, 1978).

[84]Collins, *How to Be a People Helper*, 113.

[85]See A. E. Bergin and M. J. Lambert, "The Evaluation of Therapeutic Outcomes," in *Handbook of Psychotherapy and Behavior Change*, 2d ed., eds. S. L. Garfield and A. E. Bergin (New York: Wiley, 1978), 139–89.

4

The Literature of Lay
Counseling

The literature on lay counseling, both secular and Christian, has mushroomed in recent years. This chapter will review some of the vast literature that is now available.[1] We will look first at the secular sources and then at the Christian literature.

Secular Literature

We have seen that lay counseling has become a significant part of the contemporary mental health scene. There are a number of reasons for this, many of which are found in secular books and journals.

Reasons for Using Lay Counselors

First, the shortage of mental health professionals to meet the ever-increasing demand for their services has already been pointed out earlier. Second, many writers have described the national survey conducted in 1957 in the U.S. which found that when people had personal problems and sought help for them, only about 27 percent of them went to psychiatrists, psychologists, and other professional mental health sources (e.g., specialists or agencies). About 29 percent consulted their family physician, and 42 percent sought help from the clergy.[2] Gurin, Veroff, and Feld concluded: "These findings underscore the crucial role that nonpsychiatric resources—particularly clergymen and physicians—play in the treatment process. They are the major therapeutic agents."[3] A similar national survey was conducted in 1976, and again it revealed that a significant number of people who sought help for their personal problems consulted lay helpers like the clergy (39 percent) and their family physician (21 percent).[4] However, a significantly greater percentage of people—49 percent—now seek help from psychiatrists, psychologists, and other professional mental health sources (specialists or agencies). Thus it appears that Americans are more willing now to consult mental health professionals, since we are living today in what one author has called "the psychological society."[5] Nevertheless, a significant number of people still seek help from nonprofessional or paraprofessional counselors like the clergy and family physicians, and hence the continued interest in developing such helping resources.

Third, a closely related reason for developing lay counseling has to do with the phenomenon of "spontaneous remission," referring to the finding that a good number of patients with emotional disorders seem to recover over a two-year period without any professional treatment.[6] Estimates of such spontaneous recovery rates vary from 43 percent to 65 percent of "untreated" patients. However, "spontaneous remission" is really a misleading term, since many of such patients obtained counsel, advice, and support from a variety of helping persons, e.g., spouses, friends, teachers, physicians, and clergy—"persons untrained in formal psychotherapy but who practice a kind of natural therapy."[7] Lay counselors such as the clergy and physicians are, therefore, most sought after by people who have personal problems, and they seem to succeed quite well in helping such people, based on indirect evidence bearing on spontaneous recovery rates.

Fourth, more direct evidence supporting the effectiveness of lay or paraprofessional counseling is also available from the research literature which has compared the effectiveness of lay counseling with that of professional counseling. Earlier reports often quoted in this regard are Poser's study on group therapy conducted by untrained female college students with schizophrenics,[8] and Carkhuff and Truax's study on lay group counseling involving minimal training.[9] Since then, many more studies have been conducted. In a widely cited review published in 1979 of 42 comparative studies, Durlak concluded that paraprofessionals or lay counselors were generally as effective as, and sometimes even better than, professional helpers, especially when the counseling involved more specific target problems presented by college students or adults.[10] However, little information is available on the factors which may account for the effectiveness of such lay counselors, untrained or minimally trained, although some have suggested that "naive enthusiasm"[11] and "flexible attitudes"[12] may be important ones. Since Durlak's review was published, Strupp and Hadley have reported the results of their important Vanderbilt study,[13] which essentially showed that untrained college professors did as well as professionally trained expert therapists in helping neurotic college students, thus giving further support to Durlak's findings and conclusion that "professional mental health education, training, and experience do not appear to be necessary prerequisites for an effective helping person."[14] It should be pointed out that more recent reviews of the secular literature have included critiques of Durlak's findings, but the most recent statistical reanalyses of the research evidence from the more reliable studies have supported Durlak's major findings and conclusion.[15] For example, Berman and Norton asked the key question, "Does professional training make a therapist more effective?" Their answer, after further review and statistical reanalysis of the better studies conducted to date comparing the effectiveness of lay counselors with that of professional helpers, is still no.[16]

Other acknowledged leaders in the mental health field have expressed similar views based on their own experience and research. For example, after twenty-five years of practicing and researching psychotherapy, Dr. Joseph Matarazzo concluded that

> with the exception of that very small percentage—those, for example, who are severely disturbed by a severe life-crisis, depression or immobilizing anxiety and need the services of a highly trained, licensed psychologist—what I, and the majority of talking psychotherapists, accomplish in psychotherapy cannot be distinguished from what is accomplished between very good friends over coffee every morning in neighborhoods and in countless work settings anywhere.[17]

Similarly, Dr. Jerome Frank has said, "Anyone with a modicum of human warmth, common sense, some sensitivity to human problems, and a desire to help, can benefit many candidates for psychotherapy."[18]

It should be pointed out, however, that the debate over the research data apparently supporting the effectiveness of lay or paraprofessional counselors, and the interpretation of such data, is still not settled. In a more recent review of the literature on the effectiveness of psychotherapy or counseling, Lambert, Shapiro, and Bergin summarized the major findings from studies comparing lay or paraprofessional helpers and professional helpers. They drew this cautious conclusion:

> Although the failures of this literature generally to show unique therapeutic effectiveness for trained professionals are sobering, these studies are flawed in several respects. Many of the studies deal with types of cases that are not typical of those treated in the outcome studies reported in this chapter. Controls, criteria, and follow-up are often not rigorous; and frequently we seem to be observing improvements in morale of schizophrenics or mildly distressed persons due to attention and support. We are not observing substantial therapeutic effects in the usual kinds of cases. This is not to downgrade the importance of the effects observed but to suggest that they have some limitations. They may not generalize to representative patient populations or less selective groups of paraprofessionals. On the other hand, the studies do suggest that common therapeutic factors are not the sole domain of formal therapy and that they may be useful in many cases or settings. Definitive studies are yet to be done on this matter.[19]

Lorion and Felner recently viewed a similar literature and came to this somewhat more optimistic though still cautious conclusion:

> The 42 studies in question have been examined with a degree of intensity rarely found in the behavioral sciences. In spite of repeated analyses of their methodological soundness, the reported findings and resulting conclusions are unlikely to be accepted without further debate and question. The issue of concern is too central to be considered closed at this point. If the thrust of this set of reviews is indeed justified, one must, at the very least, consider paraprofessional resources as a legitimate factor in planning mental health services. . . . That they can contribute cannot be discounted. What remains unclear, however, are the conditions under which their contributions can be maximized—the types of interventions and patients for which this resource is most appropriate.[20]

Furthermore, there are two very recent studies not covered by the reviews cited so far, which appear to support the comparative effectiveness of professional therapists over lay or paraprofessional helpers. In one study, Brigham Young University psychologists Gary Burlingame and Sally Barlow found that group therapy clients led by both professionals and nonprofessionals improved significantly more than clients assigned to a waiting-list control group. At the midpoint of the fifteen-week group therapy series, clients seen by professionals had actually deteriorated, whereas those seen by nonprofessionals had improved significantly. At the end of therapy, there were no significant differences between clients seen by professionals and those seen by nonprofessionals. However, at a six-month follow-up, clients seen by professionals maintained and even built on their gains, whereas those seen by nonprofessionals had gotten worse.[21] The results of this study, therefore, raise some questions about the long-term therapeutic effects of counseling conducted by nonprofessionals, and point to the need for more long-term follow-up studies.

In a second study, Carey and Burish provided relaxation training to cancer chemotherapy patients, using three delivery techniques: professionally administered, paraprofessionally administered (by a trained volunteer), and audiotaped administered.[22] Professionally administered relaxation training was found to be significantly more effective than paraprofessionally administered and audiotaped administered relaxation training in reducing specific symptoms like physiological arousal and emotional distress. It should be noted, however, as Carey and Burish pointed out, that the hospital setting in which the study was conducted may have been more difficult or troublesome for the paraprofessionals than the professionals, who were also more technically skilled in relaxation training and more clinically experienced in general. Nevertheless, this study did find professionals to be more effective than paraprofessionals or audiotapes in providing relaxation training to cancer chemotherapy patients seen in a hospital setting.

Despite the results of these two more recent studies, the weight of the research data, however, still favors the conclusion that lay or paraprofessional counselors are generally as effective as professional counselors, although the debate over this issue will continue.

Dr. Bernie Zilbergeld, in a significant but somewhat controversial book, recently asserted that people would solve most problems better by talking to friends, spouses, relatives, or anyone else who appears to be doing well what the people believe they themselves are doing poorly! He made this assertion, however, only after carefully reviewing numerous research studies, and coming to the conclusion that professional psychotherapy or counseling is often of little or no help, and at times it can even make people worse.[23] His views and conclusions reflect the growing emphasis in the secular literature on using lay counselors, as well as the growing disillusionment with professional counseling, since there is still no agreement or consensus concerning its effectiveness despite a significant increase in research studies in recent years.[24]

Several researchers, after reviewing psychotherapy versus placebo studies, have even concluded that for real patients there is no evidence that the benefits of professional counseling or psychotherapy are greater than those of placebo treatment, although the shortcomings of such a review based on statistical reanalyses of the data have been pointed out,[25] and hence not everyone agrees with this conclusion. In fact, other researchers have actually concluded that the benefits of psychotherapy are now well supported and beyond doubt.[26] However, there are others who strongly disagree, pointing out the weaknesses of statistical reanalyses of data on the outcome or effects of psychotherapy, and emphasizing the superiority of behavior therapy over traditional psychotherapy, for certain problems like phobic and obsessive-compulsive disorders, and some sexual dysfunctions.[27] There is thus at present still no general agreement regarding the overall effectiveness of psychotherapy or professional counseling, except that many will agree that psychotherapy is more effective than no therapy. Some authors, like Garfield,[28] have therefore contended that for research studies to yield more meaningful data on the effectiveness of therapeutic interventions, more specific and refined questions should be asked, for example: What counseling or therapeutic interventions will be most effective with what clients? What kind of therapist will work best with what interventions and with what clients? Therapeutic interventions or counseling procedures should therefore be tailor-made or individualized, and their effectiveness for specific problems can then be more systematically evaluated.

Finally, Dr. Sheldon Korchin has listed several other arguments or reasons which have been used to justify the training and use of lay counselors.[29] First, he emphasizes the unique abilities of lay indigenous helpers in understanding and working effectively with clients from their own cultures. The assumption behind this argument is that such helpers may be more effective because they understand better, if not share, the cultural values and world views of such clients. Second, he mentions the positive effects on the lay counselor himself or herself of being involved in lay counseling. Such positive effects include the psychological growth and increased competence of the lay counselor. It seems that the person who benefits as much as the client (if not more) in lay counseling is the lay counselor! Reissman has referred to this as the "helper therapy" principle.[30]

Third and last, Korchin argues that nonprofessional or lay counseling serves as an effective means for recruiting lay counselors into professional counseling careers. Several lay counselors may end up pursuing professional training and becoming professional counselors eventually, as a result of their doing lay counseling.

Problems with Using Lay Counselors

Korchin, however, has also noted some problems related to the use of lay counselors or nonprofessionals in a variety of helping roles.[31] First, there may be problems related to the nonprofessional role. Role boundaries and limits are sometimes unclear, and lay counselors may try to do more than they are capable of doing, or end up confused at times. For example, should they remain "professionally objective" in their helping endeavors, precluding friendships with clients, or could they be friends with their clients to a greater extent than professional counselors, since lay counselors often provide friendship or peer counseling? Second, there may be problems related to the background and personal qualities of the nonprofessional. The lay counselor may feel insecurity because of lack of experience. Third, there may be problems related to professional values. Many professional counselors may be unwilling to support more nonprofessional or lay involvement in people-helping because of their own vested interests in and concern for prestige, social status, and income as professionals. Finally, there may be problems related to program organization, training, and career development. Academic leaders in universities and professional training centers may resist having to train more lay counselors, preferring to concentrate instead on the training and education of professional counselors. Lay counselors may also not have secure job opportunities, thus facing limited career development and transient, temporary roles as nonprofessional helpers. There may therefore be a need to create new teaching or training institutions and job opportunities for lay counselors.

In particular, the possibility of negative effects on clients due to lay counseling (perhaps because of factors like the lack of experience and insecurity or unclear role boundaries on the part of the lay counselor) should be of real concern, since research has shown that psychotherapy or counseling provided even by professionals tends to hurt some clients.[32]

Examples of How Lay Counselors Are Used

Korchin has also described a number of nonprofessional programs using lay counselors.[33] They include the use of student volunteers in mental hospitals, mature women as mental health counselors, college students as companion-therapists to troubled boys, and indigenous nonprofessionals in dealing with the problems of poverty communities. A well-known prevention program known as the Primary Mental Health Project, conducted by psychologist Emory Cowen and his colleagues in Rochester, New York, has also used lay counselors (housewives as nonprofessional child aides) to work directly with high-risk children in the schools.[34]

Selection and Training of Lay Counselors

In reviewing the selection of lay counselors, Korchin noted that there is usually a formal assessment phase which may involve interviews, psychological tests, and observation, but focuses mainly on personal attributes (e.g., warmth, compassion, general human-relations skills, a lack of personal defensiveness, and "positive mental health") rather than intellectual skills, experience, or formal training. In training lay counselors, emphasis has been given to learning both general human-relations skills as well as particular psychological techniques that may be of special relevance to the specific role of the lay counselor.[35] The literature on selection and training of lay counselors will be covered in greater detail in later chapters of this book.

The secular literature on the whole, therefore, seems to justify the need for, and support the effectiveness of, lay counseling in its various forms, but there are some problems or dangers which should still be borne in mind.

Christian Literature

In the last two decades, there has been a spate of publications by Christian authors on lay counseling, especially within the context of the local church. This may be partly due to a growing dissatisfaction with, and even an outright rejection of, secular counseling and psychotherapy.[36] Many Christian authors have, therefore, affirmed and advocated a scriptural or biblical approach to counseling, with a special focus on the spiritual dimension so often neglected by secular approaches. Such authors also maintain that biblically based counseling can be conducted by lay Christians (who are not ordained pastors or mental health professionals), especially those who are specially gifted for a counseling ministry,[37] or those who at least possess the personal qualities (e.g., goodness, knowledge, and wisdom) and grasp of the Scriptures which are seen to be essentials.[38]

Many years ago, psychologist Hobart Mowrer raised the question, "Has evangelical religion sold its birthright for a mess of psychological pottage?"[39] Today, evangelical leaders have begun to reclaim that birthright in a very definite way. Many of them are realizing that Christian or biblically based pastoral and lay counseling are better and more valid alternatives to the mess of psychological pottage. Not all leaders in the evangelical, Christian counseling field reject secular clinical psychology and psychiatry completely—however, most, if not all of them, advocate going beyond the pottage to sound scriptural principles for wholesome living, and for dealing with personal problems and the stresses of life.

Books on Biblically Based Approaches to Lay Christian Counseling

Several biblically based approaches to effective lay Christian counseling have been proposed. Dr. Jay Adams has advocated

nouthetic counseling as the unique scriptural approach, emphasizing the need to be directive, to confront the client with the
issue of sin, using the Bible as the basic helping manual.[40] He
has also rejected as unbiblical the prescriptive aspects of secular
professional counseling and psychotherapy, a view which has
been widely challenged, and which definitely needs further
qualification and clarification.

Dr. Gary Collins has helped to train Christians to become
effective lay "people-helpers" through his people-helping approach and training program, using what is valid and acceptable
from psychology and the behavioral sciences from a biblical
perspective, and consulting Scripture as the ultimate authority.
More specifically, he has emphasized that effective people-
helping requires a warm, empathic, and genuine helper who has
good rapport with an open and motivated client. The effective
helper focuses on the emotions, thoughts, and behavior of the
helpee, using a variety of helper skills, with the ultimate goal of
making disciples and disciplers.[41] Dr. Collins has also written a
widely used and comprehensive guide to Christian counseling[42]
and edited a helpful book on practical approaches to Christian
counseling.[43] At present he is involved as General Editor for a
series of books called "Resources for Christian Counseling,"
and has written the first volume.[44] Dr. Collins, therefore, has
made tremendous contributions to the development of Christian
counseling, including lay counseling.

Dr. Lawrence Crabb, Jr., another well-known Christian psychologist, has proposed a significant model for effective biblical
counseling. Also based on an integration of psychology and
Christianity that gives Scriptures final authority, Crabb's model
can be used by lay Christians, especially within the local church
context.[45] Essentially, Dr. Crabb views sinful, unbiblical thinking to be at the root of most problem behavior and problem
feelings (i.e., those that are nonorganically caused). More
specifically, such thinking involves trying to meet personal
needs for security (love) and significance (meaning) apart from
one's relationship with Jesus Christ. Dr. Crabb has also proposed three levels of lay counseling ministry for Christians:
level I is counseling by encouragement, involving all believers;
level II is counseling by exhortation, involving mature Christians with some basic counseling training; and level III is

counseling by enlightenment, involving a few gifted Christians with more advanced training in biblical counseling.

In my opinion, Adams' "Nouthetic Counseling," Collins' "People-Helping," and Crabb's "Biblical Counseling" have been the three most influential approaches to Christian counseling in the literature, and they have had significant impact, especially on lay Christian counseling. The finer points of their approaches have been incorporated in the integrated, biblical model for effective lay Christian counseling presented in chapter 3 of this book. Their approaches, while biblically based, do of course have their strengths and weaknesses.

Other important books in the area of lay Christian counseling or caregiving include those by William Arnold and Margaret Fohl, William Backus, Carol Baldwin, Martin Bobgan and Deidre Bobgan, Duncan Buchanan, John Drakeford, John Drakeford and Claude King, Timothy Foster, Stephen Grunlan and Daniel Lambrides, Kenneth Haugk, Selwyn Hughes, Isaac Lim and Shirley Lim, Stanley Lindquist, Paul Miller, Paul Morris, Evelyn Peterson, Harold Sala, Abraham Schmitt and Dorothy Schmitt, Charles Solomon, Robert Somerville, Melvin Steinbron, Joan Sturkie and Gordon Bear, Barbara Varenhorst with Lee Sparks, Richard Walters, Waylon Ward, Paul Welter, Everett Worthington, and H. Norman Wright.[46] The more general field of "Christian counseling" from an evangelical perspective is also growing rapidly, with so many books being published that it is difficult for anyone to keep up with the latest ones.[47]

Journal Articles on Lay Christian Counseling

In addition to the plethora of books now available in the literature on lay Christian counseling, numerous journal articles have also been published recently. They cover a broad range of topics, including literature reviews on lay counseling within the local church; the selection, training, supervision, and evaluation of lay counselors; and lay counseling models and programs.[48] The relevant literature on each of these topics will be covered in more detail in later chapters of this book. A special issue of the *Journal of Psychology and Christianity*, official publication of the Christian Association for Psychological Studies, has been devoted to lay Christian counseling.[49] It contains twelve articles covering a number of perspectives, programs, and proposals related to lay Christian counseling, which are briefly described in my guest editorial preceding them.

Research on Lay Christian Counseling

Unfortunately, little research has been done evaluating the effectiveness of training programs for lay Christian counselors, as well as the counseling provided by such counselors. Collins, in an earlier book, briefly mentioned that the preliminary results of a research project conducted to evaluate the effectiveness of his people-helper training program seem to indicate that it increased both the sensitivity and effectiveness of those who wanted to be people-helpers, but he did not specify the measures used in the project.[50]

I have also reported preliminary results using a self-report measure of knowledge of counseling and Christian counseling, competence in counseling and Christian counseling, and confidence in one's competence, which showed that lay counseling trainees improved significantly more than a control group of students who took a Bible course at Ontario Bible College.[51] The need for more sophisticated measures for evaluating the effectiveness of lay counselor training was obvious. Therefore, in a later study, Tan and Sarff used a more comprehensive set of evaluation measures and administered them before and after a lay Christian counselor training program conducted in a Chinese evangelical local church context. The results showed that the lay counseling trainees rated themselves to be more knowledgeable and more competent in both counseling and Christian counseling, chose more understanding and less evaluative and supportive response styles, and were rated as being more empathic, respectful, and genuine based on an audiotaped role-play counseling situation, after the training. However, no control group was employed in this study.[52] Schaefer, Dodds, and Tan also recently found positive changes in attitudes toward peer counseling and several scales on the Personal Orientation Inventory (POI) in a small number of subjects who received growth facilitator training for cross-cultural ministry, but no control group was used.[53]

Boan and Owens found peer ratings of lay counselor skill to be useful measures which are related to client satisfaction, but they did not directly evaluate the effectiveness of their training program, and no control group was used.[54]

Welter also used a comprehensive package of evaluation measures to assess the effectiveness of a lay counselor training program for retirement center and nursing home staff and residents. At the end of training, he administered a variety of measures, including an external evaluation of concepts learned, evaluations by the leader and the participants, and evaluation of the trainers, with generally positive findings. However, no comparison or control group was used, and the measures were all administered only at the end of training.[55]

Jernigan, Tan, and Gorsuch, in a more recent study using evaluation measures similar to those employed by Tan and Sarff, included a comparison group of subjects. This group participated in weekly Bible study classes at the same local church as the lay counseling trainees. They found some positive results: when posttraining scores were compared to pretraining scores, the lay counseling trainees improved significantly more than the comparison group of Bible study students on self-ratings of knowledge about counseling and Christian counseling, competence in counseling and Christian counseling, and confidence about competence in counseling and Christian counseling, as well as on ratings of genuineness in a videotaped role-play counseling situation, by two independent raters.[56]

A crucial test of the effectiveness of any lay Christian counselor training program must eventually involve the evaluation of the counseling effectiveness of such trained lay counselors in terms of therapeutic outcome. Evaluation research on the effectiveness of lay Christian counseling per se is even more scarce.

Richard and Flakoll noted several years ago that two formal but unpublished studies had been conducted to evaluate the effectiveness of lay counselors providing counseling services through the New Directions Counseling Center.[57] One study by Corcoran investigated client satisfaction and found that on most measures client satisfaction was at least 80 percent.[58] Another study by Cuvelier examined counselor satisfaction and also concluded that it was high.[59] However, no control or comparison group was apparently employed, and it is not clear whether the evaluation measures used were adequate and whether they were administered before and after counseling or only at the end of counseling.

Harris more recently found that the use of nonpaid, nonprofessional lay helpers in combination with professional pastoral counseling led to a more favorable increase in self-esteem for clients, compared to private professional pastoral counseling only.[60]

Most recently, Walters reported that lay counselors in a local church context compared favorably with Family Service Association (FSA) professionals on measures of client change and client satisfaction, using mail survey evaluations (FSA questionnaires) sent out to clients six months or more after termination of counseling.[61] His study therefore provides some encouraging but still tentative outcome findings because of methodological flaws obvious in such a retrospective evaluation study which did not employ control groups.

Controlled outcome studies that compare the effectiveness of lay Christian counseling with no counseling and/or a "placebo" intervention are lacking in the literature. This is not surprising, since good outcome studies evaluating the effectiveness of more *professional* Christian counseling approaches are also scarce.[62] Collins has suggested that the paucity of Christian counseling research may be due to a lack of time, energy, money, and expertise to do competent evaluative studies.[63] Nevertheless, such studies need to be done, hopefully in the near future, so that the data base supporting lay Christian counselor training programs as well as lay Christian counseling can be strengthened. Evaluative research issues will be discussed further in chapter 9 of this book.

Concluding Comments

Almost two decades ago, Thomas Oden, a well-known theologian who has written extensively on the integration of Christian theology and counseling or psychotherapy, issued a strong call for the laicization of counseling and psychotherapy. He affirmed the use of lay therapeutic resources, especially within a religious context, and he critiqued the overprofessionalization, pointing out the limitations of the helping professions.[64] Jay Adams, a little earlier than Oden, also made a similar call to all Christians to be involved in a biblical lay counseling ministry, contending from Scriptures that Christians are competent to counsel.[65] Such calls have not gone unheeded. In fact, they have been prophetic of what has occurred in the last two decades in the field of lay Christian counseling.

It is clear from the above review of both the secular and Christian literature on lay counseling that the field has grown tremendously in recent years. Lay counseling in general has received consistent research support for its effectiveness, although there are still potential problems with using lay counselors which should be borne in mind. Much more research remains to be done on lay Christian counseling in particular. Also required are attempts at evaluating, and if possible, integrating the various approaches to effective lay Christian counseling currently available. My attempt to do this and hence develop a biblical model for effective Christian counseling as well as lay counseling was the focus of the previous chapter. However, much work remains to be done in more sophisticated theological, ethical, and philosophical analyses of current biblical models of Christian counseling. These models need to be tested to determine how *biblical* they are, how *consistent* they are with Christian tradition and theology, and how *effective* they are in helping clients.[66]

NOTES

[1]This chapter will serve as an updated version of the literature review provided in S. Y. Tan, "Lay Counseling: The Local Church," *CAPS Bulletin* 7, no. 1 (1981): 15–20, and in S. Y. Tan, "Lay Christian Counseling: Present Status and Future Directions," invited paper presented at the International Congress on Christian Counseling, Lay Counseling Tack, November 1988, in Atlanta, Georgia.

[2]See Joint Commission on Mental Illness and Health, *Action for Mental Health* (New York: Science Editions, 1961).

[3]G. Gurin, J. Veroff, and S. Feld, *Americans View Their Mental Health* (New York: Basic Books, 1960), 341.

[4]See J. Veroff, R. A. Kulka, and E. Douvan, *Mental Health in America: Patterns of Help-Seeking from 1957 to 1976* (New York: Basic Books, 1981).

[5]M. L. Gross, *The Psychological Society* (New York: Random House, 1978).

[6]See Bergin and Lambert, "The Evaluation of Therapeutic Outcomes," in *Handbook of Psychotherapy and Behavior Change*, 2d ed., ed. S. L. Garfield and A. E. Bergin (New York: Wiley, 1978), 139–89.

[7]Ibid., 150.

[8]E. G. Poser, "The Effect of Therapists' Training on Group Therapeutic Outcome," *Journal of Consulting Psychology* 30 (1966): 283–89.

[9]R. R. Carkhuff and C. B. Truax, "Lay Mental Health Counseling: The Effects of Lay Group Counseling," *Journal of Consulting Psychology* 29 (1965): 426–31.

[10]J. A. Durlak, "Comparative Effectiveness of Paraprofessional and Professional Helpers," *Psychological Bulletin* 86 (1979): 80–92.

[11]See Poser, "Effect of Therapists' Training."

[12]See M. J. Rioch, "Changing Concepts in the Training of Psychotherapists," *Journal of Consulting Psychology* 30 (1966): 290–92.

[13]H. H. Strupp and S. W. Hadley, "Specific vs. Nonspecific Factors in Psychotherapy: A Controlled Study of Outcome," *Archives of General Psychiatry* 36 (1979): 1125–36.

[14]Durlak, "Comparative Effectiveness of Paraprofessional and Professional Helpers," 80.

[15]See, e.g., N. T. Nietzel and S. G. Fisher, "Effectiveness of Professional and Paraprofessional Helpers: A Comment on Durlak," *Psychological Bulletin* 89 (1981): 555–65; J. A. Durlak, "Evaluating Comparative Studies of Paraprofessional and Professional Helpers: A Reply to Nietzel and Fisher," *Psychological Bulletin* 89 (1981): 566–69; A. Hattie, C. F. Sharpley, and H. J. Rogers, "Comparative Effectiveness of Professional and Paraprofessional Helpers," *Psychological Bulletin* 95 (1984): 534–41; J. S. Berman and N. C. Norton, "Does Professional Training Make a Therapist More Effective?" *Psychological Bulletin* 98 (1985): 401–7. For other reviews of the research literature with similar conclusions, see R. P. Lorion and J. Cahill, "Paraprofessional Effectiveness in Mental Health: Issues and Outcomes," *The Paraprofessional Journal* 1, no. 1 (1980): 12–38; and D. M. Stein and M. J. Lambert, "On the Relationship Between Therapist Experiences and Psychotherapy Outcome," *Clinical Psychology Review* 4 (1984): 1–16.

[16]See Berman and Norton, "Does Professional Training Make a Therapist More Effective?" 407.

[17]J. Matarazzo, "Comment on Licensing," *A.P.A. Monitor* 10 (September–October 1979): 36.

[18]J. D. Frank, *Persuasion and Healing*, 2d ed. (New York: Schocken Books, 1974), 167.

[19]See M. J. Lambert, D. A. Shapiro, and A. E. Bergin, "The Effectiveness of Psychotherapy," in S. L. Garfield and A. E. Bergin, eds., *Handbook of Psychotherapy and Behavior Change*, 3d ed. (New York: Wiley, 1986), 157–211, p. 175.

[20]See R. P. Lorion and R. D. Felner, "Research on Mental Health Interventions with the Disadvantaged," in S. L. Garfield and A. E.

Bergin, eds., *Handbook of Psychotherapy and Behavior Change*, 3d ed. (New York: Wiley, 1986), 739–75, p. 763.

[21]See S. Bergin, "Therapy: Beyond 'Warm Fuzziness,' " *Psychology Today* (April 1988): 14.

[22]See M. P. Carey and T. G. Burish, "Providing Relaxation Training to Cancer Chemotherapy Patients: A Comparison of Three Delivery Techniques," *Journal of Consulting and Clinical Psychology* 55 (1987): 732–37.

[23]B. Zilbergeld, *The Shrinking of America: Myths of Psychological Change* (Boston: Little, Brown, 1983).

[24]See S. L. Garfield, "Effectiveness of Psychotherapy: The Perennial Controversy," *Professional Psychology: Research and Practice* 14 (1983): 35–43.

[25]See L. Prioleau, M. Murdock, and N. Brody, "An Analysis of Psychotherapy Versus Placebo Studies," *The Behavioral and Brain Sciences* 6 (1983): 275–310; and a "Continuing Commentary" on this article published in *The Behavioral and Brain Sciences* 7 (1984): 756–62. See also *Journal of Consulting and Clinical Psychology* 51 (1983): 3–74 (special section: "Meta-Analysis and Psychotherapy"); J. S. Searles, "A Methodological and Empirical Critique of Psychotherapy Outcome Meta-Analysis," *Behavior Research and Therapy* 23 (1985): 453–63; and D. A. Shapiro, "Recent Applications of Meta-Analysis in Clinical Research," *Clinical Psychology Review* 5 (1985): 13–34.

[26]See M. L. Smith, G. V. Glass, and T. I. Miller, *The Benefits of Psychotherapy* (Baltimore: Johns Hopkins University Press, 1980).

[27]See S. J. Rachman and G. T. Wilson, *The Effects of Psychological Therapy*, 2d enlarged ed. (New York: Pergamon, 1980).

[28]S. L. Garfield, *Psychotherapy: An Eclectic Approach* (New York: Wiley, 1980).

[29]See S. J. Korchin, *Modern Clinical Psychology* (New York: Basic Books, 1976), 519–21.

[30]F. Reissman, "The 'Helper Therapy' Principle," *Social Work* 10 (1965): 27–32.

[31]Korchin, *Modern Clinical Psychology*, 530–33.

[32]See, e.g., A. E. Bergin and M. J. Lambert, "The Evaluation of Therapeutic Outcomes," D. Mays and C. M. Franks, eds., *Negative Outcome in Psychotherapy and What to Do About It* (New York: Springer, 1985); H. H. Strupp, S. W. Hadley, and B. Gomes-Schwartz, *Psychotherapy for Better or for Worse: An Analysis of the Problem of Negative Effects* (New York: Jason Aaronson, 1977).

[33]Korchin, *Modern Clinical Psychology*, 523–28. See also introduction, n. 6.

[34]See E. L. Cowen, M. A. Trost, D. A. Dorr, R. P. Lorion, L. D. Izzo, and R. V. Isaacson, *New Ways in School Mental Health: Early*

Detection and Prevention of School Maladaptation (New York: Human Sciences Press, 1975).

[35]Korchin, *Modern Clinical Psychology,* 528–29; for two well-known models or programs for training lay counselors, see: R. R. Carkhuff, *Helping and Human Relations,* vols. 1 and 2 (New York: Holt, Rinehart and Winston, 1969); G. Egan, *The Skilled Helper,* 3d ed. (Monterey, Calif.: Brooks/Cole, 1986).

[36]See, e.g., J. E. Adams, *Competent to Counsel* (Grand Rapids: Baker, 1970); M. Bobgan and D. Bobgan, *The Psychological Way/The Spiritual Way* (Minneapolis: Bethany House, 1979); *How to Counsel From Scripture* (Chicago: Moody Press, 1985).

[37]See P. D. Morris, *Love Therapy* (Wheaton, Ill.: Tyndale House, 1974).

[38]J. E. Adams, *The Christian Counselor's Manual* (Grand Rapids: Baker, 1973).

[39]O. H. Mowrer, *The Crisis in Psychiatry and Religion* (Princeton, N.J.: D. Van Nostrand, 1961), 60.

[40]Adams, *Competent to Counsel,* and *The Christian Counselor's Manual.* See also Adams, *Ready to Restore* (Grand Rapids: Baker, 1981).

[41]G. R. Collins, *How to Be a People Helper* (Santa Ana, Calif.: Vision House, 1976), and *People Helper Growthbook* (Santa Ana, Calif.: Vision House, 1976).

[42]G. R. Collins, *Christian Counseling: A Comprehensive Guide* (Waco, Tex.: Word, 1980). A revised, updated, and expanded edition was published in 1988.

[43]G. R. Collins, ed., *Helping People Grow: Practical Approaches to Christian Counseling* (Santa Ana, Calif.: Vision House, 1980).

[44]Collins, *Innovative Approaches to Counseling* (Waco, Tex.: Word, 1986).

[45]L. J. Crabb, Jr., *Basic Principles of Biblical Counseling* (Grand Rapids: Zondervan, 1975), and *Effective Biblical Counseling* (Grand Rapids: Zondervan, 1977). See also L. J. Crabb, Jr., and D. B. Allender, *Encouragement: The Key to Caring* (Grand Rapids: Zondervan, 1984); Crabb, *Understanding People: Deep Longings for Relationship* (Grand Rapids: Zondervan, 1987), and *Inside Out* (Colorado Springs: NavPress, 1988).

[46]W. V. Arnold and M. A. Fohl, *Christians and the Art of Caring* (Philadelphia: Westminster, 1988); W. Backus, *Telling the Truth to Troubled People* (Minneapolis: Bethany House, 1985); C. L. Baldwin, *Friendship Counseling: Biblical Foundations for Helping Others* (Grand Rapids: Zondervan, 1988); Bobgan and Bobgan, *How to Counsel From Scripture;* D. Buchanan, *The Counseling of Jesus* (Downers Grove, Ill.: InterVarsity Press, 1985); J. W. Drakeford, *People*

to People Therapy (New York: Harper & Row, 1978); J. W. Drakeford
and Claude V. King, *WiseCounsel: Skills for Lay Counseling* (Nashville: The Sunday School Board of the Southern Baptist Convention,
1988); T. Foster, *Called to Counsel* (Nashville: Oliver Nelson, 1986); S.
Grunlan and D. Lambrides, *Healing Relationships* (Camp Hill, Pa.:
Christian Publications, 1984); K. C. Haugk, *Christian Caregiving*
(Minneapolis: Augsburg, 1984); S. Hughes, *A Friend in Need* (East-
bourne, England: Kingsway, 1982); I. Lim and S. Lim, *Comfort My
People: Christian Counseling—A Lay Challenge* (Singapore: Methodist Book Room, 1988);

   Also, S. E. Lindquist, *Action Helping Skills* (Fresno, Calif.: Link-
Care Foundation Press, 1976); P. M. Miller, *Peer Counseling in the
Church* (Scottdale, Pa.: Herald, 1978); Morris, *Love Therapy;* E.
Peterson, *Who Cares? A Handbook of Christian Counseling* (Wilton,
Conn.: Morehouse-Barlow, 1980); H. Sala, *Coffee Cup Counseling:
How to Be Ready When Friends Ask for Help* (Nashville: Nelson,
1989); A. Schmitt and D. Schmitt, *When a Congregation Cares*
(Scottdale, Pa.: Herald, 1984); C. R. Solomon, *Counseling With the
Mind of Christ* (Old Tappan, N.J.: Revell, 1977); R. B. Somerville, *Help
for Hotliners: A Manual for Christian Telephone Crisis Counselors*
(Phillipsburg, N.J.: Presbyterian and Reformed, 1978); M. J. Steinbron,
*Can the Pastor Do It Alone? A Model for Preparing Lay People for Lay
Pastoring* (Ventura, Calif.: Regal, 1987);

   Also, J. Sturkie and G. Bear, *Christian Peer Counseling: Love in
Action* (Dallas: Word, 1989); B. B. Varenhorst, with L. Sparks, *Training
Teenagers for Peer Ministry* (Loveland, Colo.: Group, 1988); R. P.
Walters, *The Amity Book: Exercises in Friendship Skills* (Grand
Rapids: Christian Helpers, 1983); W. O. Ward, *The Bible in Counseling*
(Chicago: Moody, 1977); P. Welter, *How to Help a Friend* (Wheaton,
Ill.: Tyndale, 1978), and *Connecting With a Friend: Eighteen Proven
Counseling Skills to Help You Help Others* (Wheaton, Ill.: Tyndale,
1985); E. L. Worthington, Jr., *When Someone Asks for Help: A Practical
Guide for Counseling* (Downers Grove, Ill.: InterVarsity Press, 1982),
and *How to Help the Hurting: When Friends Face Problems With Self-
Esteem, Self-Control, Fear, Depression, Loneliness* (Downers Grove,
Ill.: InterVarsity Press, 1985); H. N. Wright, *Training Christians to
Counsel* (Eugene, Oreg.: Harvest House, 1977).

   [47]See, e.g., volumes in the ongoing *Resources for Christian Counseling* series (Dallas: Word), G. R. Collins, gen. ed.; and G. R. Collins,
Helping People Grow. Also, for a recent comprehensive review and
critique of both secular and Christian counseling approaches, see R. F.
Hurding, *The Tree of Healing: Psychological and Biblical Foundations
for Counseling and Pastoral Care* (Grand Rapids: Zondervan, 1988),

published in Great Britain as *Roots and Shoots: A Guide to Counseling and Psychotherapy.*

[48]See, e.g., W. W. Becker, "A Delivery System Within the Church: The Professional Consultant and the Laity," *CAPS Bulletin* 7, no. 4 (1981): 15–18; D. M. Boan and T. Owens, "Peer Ratings of Lay Counselor Skill as Related to Client Satisfaction," *Journal of Psychology and Christianity* 4, no. 1 (1985): 79–81; G. L. Cerling, "Selection of Lay Counselors for a Church Counseling Center," *Journal of Psychology and Christianity* 2, no. 3 (1983): 67–72; Collins, "Lay Counseling Within the Local Church," *Leadership* 1 (1980): 78–86; J. Harris, "Nonprofessionals as Effective Helpers for Pastoral Counselors," *The Journal of Pastoral Care* 39, no. 2 (1985): 165–72; H. C. Lukens, Jr., "Training Paraprofessional Christian Counselors: A Survey Conducted," *Journal of Psychology and Christianity* 2, no. 1 (1983): 51–61; H. C. Lukens, Jr., "Training of Paraprofessional Christian Counselors: A Model Proposed," *Journal of Psychology and Christianity* 2, no. 3 (1983): 61–66;

Also, E. B. Osborn, "Training Paraprofessional Family Therapists in a Christian Setting," *Journal of Psychology and Christianity* 2, no. 2 (1983): 56–61; R. C. Richard and D. A. Flakoll, "Christian Counseling Centers: Two Effective Models," *CAPS Bulletin* 7, no. 4 (1981): 12–15; R. C. Richard and D. A. Flakoll, "Integration in Action: The Use of Lay Counselors," *Theology News and Notes* 21, no. 4 (1975): 14–16;

Also, S. Y. Tan, "Lay Counseling: The Local Church," *CAPS Bulletin* 7, no. 1 (1981): 15–20; S. Y. Tan, "Training Paraprofessional Christian Counselors," *The Journal of Pastoral Care* 40, no. 4 (1986): 296–304; S. Y. Tan, "Training Lay Christian Counselors: A Basic Program and Some Preliminary Data," *Journal of Psychology and Christianity* 6, no. 2 (1987): 57–61; S. Y. Tan, "Care and Counseling in the 'New Church Movement,'" *Theology, News and Notes* 33, no. 4 (1986): 9–11, 21; S. Y. Tan, "Lay Counseling (An Interview)," *Christian Journal of Psychology and Counseling* 4, no. 2 (1989): 1–5; S. Y. Tan, "Lay Christian Counseling: The Next Decade," *Journal of Psychology and Christianity* 9, no. 3 (1990): 59–65; S. Y. Tan, "Religious Values and Interventions in Lay Christian Counseling," *Journal of Psychology and Christianity* 10, no. 2 (1991).

[49]*Journal of Psychology and Christianity* 6, no. 2 (1987): 1–84, on "Lay Christian Counseling," S. Y. Tan, guest ed.

[50]Collins, *People Helper Growthbook,* 7.

[51]Tan, "Training Paraprofessional Christian Counselors," and "Training Lay Christian Counselors: A Basic Program and Some Preliminary Data."

[52]See S. Y. Tan and P. Sarff, "Comprehensive Evaluation of a Lay Counselor Training Program in a Local Church," invited paper pre-

sented at the International Congress on Christian Counseling, Lay Counseling Track, November 1988, in Atlanta, Georgia.

[53]See C. A. Schaefer, L. Dodds, and S. Y. Tan, "Changes in Attitudes Toward Peer Counseling and Personal Orientation Measured During Growth Facilitator Training for Cross-Cultural Ministry," unpublished manuscript, 1988.

[54]Boan and Owens, "Peer Ratings of Lay Counselor Skill."

[55]P. R. Welter, "Training Retirement Center and Nursing Home Staff and Residents in Helping and Counseling Skills," *Journal of Psychology and Christianity* 6, no. 2 (1987): 45–56.

[56]R. Jernigan, S. Y. Tan, and R. L. Gorsuch, "The Effectiveness of a Local Church Lay Christian Counselor Training Program: A Controlled Study," paper presented at the International Congress on Christian Counseling, Lay Counseling Track, November 1988, in Atlanta, Georgia.

[57]Richard and Flakoll, "Christian Counseling Centers: Two Effective Models," 14.

[58]J. Corcoran, "Effectiveness of Paraprofessional Counselors at a Community Counseling Center: The Client's Perspective," unpublished manuscript, 1979.

[59]B. Cuvelier, "A Needs Assessment and Evaluation Plan of Lay Counselors for New Directions Counseling Center," unpublished manuscript, 1980.

[60]J. Harris, "Non-professionals as Effective Helpers for Pastoral Counselors," *The Journal of Pastoral Care* 39, no. 2 (1985): 165–72.

[61]R. P. Walters, "A Survey of Client Satisfaction in a Lay Counseling Program," *Journal of Psychology and Christianity* 6, no. 2 (1987): 62–69.

[62]See E. L. Worthington, Jr., "Religious Counseling: A Review of Published Empirical Research," *Journal of Counseling and Development* 64 (1986): 421–31.

[63]Collins, *Innovative Approaches to Counseling* (Waco, Tex.: Word, 1986), 178.

[64]T. C. Oden, N. C. Warren, K. B. Mulholland, C. R. Schoonhoven, C. H. Kraft, and W. Walker, *After Therapy What? Lay Therapeutic Resources in Religious Perspective* (Springfield, Ill.: Charles C. Thomas, 1974).

[65]J. E. Adams, *Competent to Counsel.*

[66]For an incisive theological, philosophical, and ethical analysis and critique of several secular modern psychologies, with relevance to Christian counseling approaches as well, see D. S. Browning, *Religious Thought and the Modern Psychologies* (Philadelphia: Fortress, 1987). See also Hurding, *The Tree of Healing.*

5

Building a Ministry of Lay Counseling

Bill is a committed Christian who has served for several years in his church as a Sunday school teacher and chairperson of one of the adult fellowships. After attending a weekend seminar on lay Christian counseling, he saw again the great need for a ministry of lay counseling from a biblical perspective, in both local church and parachurch contexts. During the seminar he had been exposed to the biblical basis for such a ministry. He also learned the basics of a biblical model for effective lay counseling and people-helping. He had been presented with material similar to what has been covered in the preceding chapters of this book.

Bill returned home from the seminar excited about the possibility of starting a lay counseling ministry in his own local church. He has a real burden for people struggling with personal problems and needs, and has done his best to reach out to them in the fellowship group he is chairing. However, he has often felt inadequate in his knowledge of and skills in people-helping, and hence signed up immediately when he heard about the special weekend seminar on lay Christian counseling. He did this also out of concern for his pastor, who has been carrying a heavy load of pastoral care and counseling, often seeing twenty to thirty people each week. Bill was interested in learning more about lay caring and counseling so that he could help shoulder some of his pastor's load. He therefore thought seriously of talking to his pastor about the possibility of beginning and building a ministry of lay Christian counseling in their local church. However, Bill was not sure what to say or where to start. The seminar schedule was so tight that the seminar leader was able only to spend a few minutes on the practical steps necessary to start a ministry of lay counseling in a local church.

In the past fourteen years of my ministry in different local churches and parachurch organizations, I have met many people who have echoed sentiments similar to Bill's. These were warm and caring people who had a deep desire to reach out and help others in need. They have often asked for some practical guidelines and more specific information on how to establish a lay helping or counseling ministry in their local churches.

The purpose of this chapter is, therefore, to provide such information, so that people like Bill will be able to realize their vision of building a ministry of lay counseling. I believe we need to start by choosing an appropriate *model* for a lay Christian counseling ministry for a particular type of local church.

Models for a Ministry of Lay Christian Counseling

For the sake of simplification, there are at least three major models available for establishing a ministry of lay Christian counseling: Informal, Spontaneous; Informal, Organized; and Formal, Organized.

1. The Informal, Spontaneous Model

This model assumes that lay Christian counseling should occur spontaneously and informally in interactions and relationships already present or possible through the existing structures of the church. Such structures normally include fellowships (e.g., for youth, adults, seniors, singles, etc.), Bible study or discipleship groups, outreach or evangelism programs, visitation of church members by pastors or other church leaders, and Sunday school classes, to name a few. Leaders in these ministries may be given some basic training in how to care for or counsel with people, but they do not usually receive regular, ongoing, and close supervision of their caring and counseling ministry. This first model is a common one found in many evangelical churches. It makes use of many gifted laypeople and leaders to care and counsel with one another in informal settings and spontaneous ways.

2. The Informal, Organized Model

This model assumes that lay Christian counseling should be an organized and well-supervised ministry which nevertheless should still occur in informal settings as far as possible. Lay Christian counselors are therefore carefully selected, trained, and supervised, but they are used in a ministry of lay caring and counseling through structures similar to the ones mentioned in the first model, and hence in relatively informal settings in comparison to a counseling center or a pastor's office. These lay counselors are given systematic training in helping skills and receive regular, ongoing, and relatively close supervision of their counseling ministry, usually by a pastor or director of counseling and care in a particular local church.

An excellent example of the second model is the Stephen Series system of lay caring ministry, founded by Dr. Kenneth Haugk, a pastor and clinical psychologist.[1] The Stephen Series enables a pastor of a local church to use a team of lay Stephen ministers to carry out a lay caring ministry to the whole congregation. These lay Stephen ministers receive systematic training in lay Christian caregiving and are then used to reach out to or visit with people in and around their congregation who need some pastoral care or help. Lay Stephen ministers care and counsel in an organized way but often in informal settings, including people's homes, nursing homes, and hospitals.

Some of the areas that lay Stephen ministers have been involved in include people who are hospitalized; the terminally ill and their families; people going through separation or divorce; those experiencing an unwanted pregnancy and their families; people in trouble with the law; parents who have children leaving home for various reasons; people who are lonely, depressed, or bereaved; new members of the congregation and/or community; those who are shut in or in a nursing home and their families; those who are inactive in church and in need of pastoral visitation; parents and families with handicapped children; single parents; people convalescing at home or in an institution; those who have suffered a significant financial setback or who have lost their job; people in the process of moving out of town; people going through retirement or forced early retirement; those who are struggling with their faith in God; and persons affected by natural disasters.

This is not an exhaustive list, but it does give an accurate picture of the comprehensive ministry that lay Stephen ministers can have in lay caring and counseling. It should be pointed out that the Stephen Series is meant primarily to train lay Stephen ministers in lay pastoral caregiving, but I believe that lay Christian counseling is a part of such caregiving.

3. The Formal, Organized Model

This model assumes that lay Christian counseling should not only be an organized and well-supervised ministry, but should occur in a formal way, in the context of a lay counseling center or service within the local church. Such a well-structured and formalized center or service can stand on its own or be a part of a larger counseling center of the church, staffed by professional counselors and therapists and directed by a licensed mental health professional, whether psychiatrist, psychologist, social worker, counselor, marriage and family therapist, psychiatric nurse, or pastoral counselor. Lay Christian counselors for such a formal, organized ministry are therefore carefully selected, trained, and closely supervised on a regular, ongoing basis. Such lay counselors see people or clients in church offices, with formal appointments set up. They usually keep specific hours for counseling at the church, whether for a few hours in the afternoon or evening, oftentimes for one particular day per week. They meet regularly for staff meetings as well as for supervision sessions. Staff meetings are often held monthly, whereas supervision sessions (one-on-one, in dyads, or in small groups) are usually held on a weekly or biweekly basis, with a licensed, professional counselor or a pastor of lay counseling serving as the supervisor.

In this third model, much formal organizational structure is required. A number of variations of this formal, organized model are available, and several churches have already put together very practical and helpful manuals on policies and procedures for implementing such a lay counseling service or center in a local church context.[2]

Five Steps for Building a Lay Counseling Ministry

People like Bill who are interested in building a ministry of lay counseling should consider the following steps for establishing a lay counseling ministry.

1. *Become familiar with the three models for counseling ministry.* Assess your congregation and discuss these options thoroughly with your pastor. Would your church be better served by a formal or informal, spontaneous or organized ministry? Or would some combination of models work best? These three models are *not,* after all, necessarily mutually exclusive. For example, in a large church of a thousand or more people, all three models could be employed at the same time, resulting in three different levels of caring and helping ministries in the church. After discussing the models with the pastor or pastoral staff, one or more of the models should be selected as most suitable for the particular church in question.

2. *Garner support for the idea of lay counseling from the pastor, pastoral staff, and church board.*[3] The leaders of your church should view such a lay counseling ministry as an extension of pastoral care and counseling and as an essential ministry by the priesthood of all believers (1 Peter 2:5, 9). If such support theologically and personally is not forthcoming from some or all of the church board and pastoral staff, then it will be difficult, if not impossible, to establish a more organized lay Christian counseling ministry.

3. *Screen potential lay Christian counselors from the congregation.* Using appropriate spiritual and psychological criteria, select the best qualified people for the role of lay counselor. The next chapter spells out these criteria in more detail. Initially, the pastor or pastoral staff could recommend people from the congregation who may be good prospects to serve as lay counselors.

4. *Provide a training program for lay counselors.* The program should focus on basic counseling skills within a biblical framework. It should include material from earlier chapters of this book on the biblical basis for lay counseling and a biblical model for effective lay counseling. Consult chapter 7 for different models of training and further details of an effective training program.

5. *Develop programs or ministries where the trained lay counselors can be used.* As the program gets underway, continue to provide training and supervision to the lay counselors. The programs you develop will, of course, depend on which model you chose for your ministry in step one.

Every local church is unique, and therefore different churches may choose different models to implement lay caring and counseling ministries.

The Choice of Models

The *informal, organized* model is particularly appropriate for churches that want to be involved in outreach and ministry through lay caring and counseling. It may also be especially suitable to certain ethnic churches, like some Chinese churches whose congregations may still have a strong stigma against seeking help or counseling for personal problems. In such churches a formal lay counseling center (patterned somewhat after a professional counseling center) using only lay counselors may not be as acceptable for reasons like stigma and fear of "losing face" for those who seek help from such counselors. Also, in certain church contexts, the credentials of the counselors are of critical importance, and *lay* counselors without professional credentials and degrees may not be as respected or accepted. Hence both *counseling per se* as well as *lay* or *nonprofessional* counseling may not be as acceptable in certain churches, including some ethnic churches. The *informal, organized* model for lay caring and counseling ministries can, however, still be used in such churches because it avoids the formal aspects of a lay counseling center or service. The Stephen Series is a good example of the application of this model, having been successfully used in over 2,500 congregations throughout the country.

For a number of other churches, however, especially larger ones, the *formal, organized* model may also be appropriate. In fact, a number of churches and congregations have effectively employed this model and established successful lay counseling centers or services. Several of them are described in more detail in chapter 10, which gives examples of local churches which have set up good programs for lay caring and counseling ministries, using appropriate models.

Ten Guidelines for Establishing a Lay Counseling Center

In order to apply the *formal, organized* model in building a ministry of lay counseling in a local church, several practical guidelines should be followed. Trevor Partridge has delineated ten helpful considerations in establishing a professional Christian Counseling Center.[4] I have adapted them for application to the context of a *lay* counseling center or service.

1. *Determine clear objectives for the counseling service.* Your main objective should be to provide distinctively biblical, Christian counseling services. The counseling center should deal explicitly with spiritual issues and use spiritual resources like prayer and the Scriptures where appropriate. The goal of such counseling should be ultimately to grow in holiness or Christlikeness, and not simply to bring about temporal happiness. The center may also be a place for evangelism conducted in a sensitive and appropriate way with non-Christian clients who are open and interested in hearing more about the gospel.

2. *Establish the "ethos" or distinctive character of the lay counseling center by giving it an appropriate name.* In a local church context, the counseling ministry often, but not always, will include the name of the particular church. Some churches prefer to call the center by a more general name so that it will be perceived more as a community counseling service rather than one catering only to the needs of a particular congregation. However, a number of lay counseling centers named after their sponsoring churches have successfully ministered to the needs of their communities as well as to their own congregations.

3. *Carefully select, train, and supervise the counseling personnel.* The director of the center should either be a licensed professional counselor, or a pastor or church leader with some training and experience in counseling who also has access to a licensed professional counselor as a consultant. Provide ongoing, regular meetings (weekly, biweekly, or monthly) for further training and supervision of the lay counselors. Weekly meetings usually last an hour; biweekly meetings, two hours; and monthly meetings from three to four hours. Preferably, supervision sessions should be held weekly or biweekly. Some churches also organize special weekend retreats once or twice a year for the lay counselors, for further spiritual growth as well as the development of counseling knowledge and skills. To further encourage their development, provide good training materials to the lay counselors, developing a small library of journals, articles, books, manuals, audiotapes, and videotapes pertaining to counseling skills, especially from a biblical perspective.

4. *Arrange for suitable facilities for the counseling center.*

Lay counselors will need comfortable rooms where they can meet with their clients or counselees. If possible, such facilities should include a reception area and at least two or three counseling rooms. It would be ideal for training and supervision purposes if one-way observation mirrors and audiotape as well as videotape equipment can be made available as well.

5. *Establish the operating hours of the counseling center.* Some churches have operated lay counseling centers that are open two nights a week, from 7:00 to 10:00 p.m. The length or duration of counseling sessions should also be determined. Usually they would be about an hour for individuals and an hour and a half to two hours for couples, families, or groups.

A particular center may also need to decide whether to have a telephone counseling service or "hotline," and, if so, whether it should be a twenty-four-hour emergency phone-in service. I recommend that such a service *not* be attempted unless there are sufficient numbers of trained lay counselors who can staff the telephones, with adequate supervision and back-up services by licensed professional counselors.

Partridge has suggested that a counseling center will need a "council of reference." This referral network should consist of Christian doctors, psychiatrists, accountants, psychologists, professional counselors, attorneys, and so forth. Counselors can then refer clients who need further help to such professionals.

6. *Establish a structure within which the lay counseling center will function.* Appoint a director who has appropriate training or experience. The director will run the center, coordinating the selection, training, and supervision of the lay counselors. The director also usually screens all potential clients either by a telephone interview or an initial intake interview, and then assigns them to appropriate lay counselors, depending on the needs or problems presented. There may be occasions when the director refers a potential client to a professional counselor because the presenting problem is deemed too complex or severe for a lay counselor to handle.

An alternative approach to having the director screen potential clients is to have the lay counselors themselves conduct the initial intake interview, by telephone or in person, but preferably in person. The lay counselors will then report their assessments or findings to the director of the center, who will decide whether to assign the client to a lay counselor or refer the client to a professional.

It is also a good idea to establish a church board or committee to oversee the ministry of the center. This committee provides accountability, support, and guidance to the director. Some churches have a small committee consisting of the pastor and one or two elders or deacons of the church, whereas other churches appoint a larger committee by adding a couple of lay counselors and several professional counselors as well. In relatively small churches, however, it is not uncommon for the director of the center to be accountable to the pastor of the church, so that the pastor functions essentially as a one-person "committee." It would be preferable even in such churches to have one or two more members on the committee.

Besides appointing a director and establishing a committee, the church should also provide secretarial support, as well as office supplies, needed by the center.

7. *Spread the word about the counseling center.* Publicity for the center can be handled in various ways: word of mouth, informational brochures, announcements in the church bulletin or from the pulpit, and advertising in the local newspapers.

The following is an example of a four-page publicity brochure designed for a lay counseling center I set up and directed at North Park Community Chapel, a nondenominational, evangelical local church in London, Ontario, which had about 1000 members and adherents. The first page of the brochure simply had in bold letters the name of the service/center (The Counseling Service), the times of its operation (Tuesdays and Wednesdays, 7–10 p.m.), a key verse (Gal. 6:2), and the name of the church, its address, and telephone number.

The second page provided an introduction to the service/center. It read:

AN INTRODUCTION:
THE COUNSELING SERVICE AT
NORTH PARK COMMUNITY CHAPEL

The Counseling Service at North Park Community Chapel exists to meet the spiritual and emotional needs of people in our congregation and in the larger community of London. It functions on a voluntary basis, and should not be considered as a Professional Counseling Service. As such, no fees are charged.

The Service aims to provide:
a) friendship and fellowship on a one-to-one basis for those who may need someone to talk to;
b) counseling and supportive help for those who may be facing some life crisis or emotional/spiritual problems;
c) guidance and growth experiences for those who may be searching for practical ways to grow spiritually and mature as a human person;
d) referrals to professionals or appropriate agencies for those who may seek or need further help.

The Counseling Service operates within a Biblical, Christian framework, and exists to fulfill the Scriptural injunctions to "bear one another's burdens" (Gal. 6:2), and to "love one another as Christ loved us" (John 13:34, 35). We do care about you and your needs. Call us or speak to us about an appointment. The Service is open on Tuesdays and Wednesdays from 7–10 p.m.

Our telephone number is _____.

The third page contained this introductory paragraph:

Let us introduce ourselves:
It is important to notice that many of us are not professional counselors, although we all have had some basic training in helping people with their needs or problems. We do care about you as a person and will spend time to talk and help as we are able to do so.

The rest of the third page and most of the fourth page had brief biographical sketches of the director of the service and nine other counselors (most of them lay counselors), and a consultant psychiatrist who was also a deacon of the church. The last part of the fourth page of the brochure read:

COUNSELING IS BY APPOINTMENT ONLY. To make an appointment phone the chapel secretary at the office Monday to Friday from 9:00 a.m. to 4:00 p.m.

or

phone The Counseling Service Tuesday or Wednesday from 7:00 to 10:00 p.m.

Telephone _____

Pulpit announcements inviting people to use the counseling center should be made in as nonthreatening a way as possible to reduce the stigma often associated with seeking help from counselors. Emphasize that one does *not* have to experience severe problems before using the services of the center. Present the counseling service as a burden-bearing and lay-caring ministry, outlining the diversity and range of its services, and stressing that it can meet a variety of needs.

8. *Clarify what specific services the lay counseling center will offer.* The brochure on the lay Counseling Service at North Park Community Chapel listed four basic services provided. To expand on those services, you may consider adding a telephone hotline, premarital and marital counseling, and vocational guidance and counseling to the unemployed. However, some of these areas of counseling (e.g., vocational counseling and counseling the unemployed) may be more appropriate for a professional Christian counseling center to handle than a lay counseling service, because they may require specialized professional skills like vocational testing and assessment. If possible, consider arranging special one-day or weekend seminars on particular topics of interest for the benefit of the local community.

Some lay counseling centers do use personality or vocational tests as part of the services they offer. However, lay counselors, in using such tests, should be closely supervised by licensed, professional counselors, or, at the very least, by a pastor who has had sufficient training and experience with the particular tests involved (e.g., the widely used Taylor-Johnson Temperament Analysis, or TJTA). My own recommendation is that testing should either not be provided at all by lay counselors, or be provided only minimally and always under careful supervision and guidance by licensed professional counselors or experienced and trained pastors. There are dangers associated with the abuse or misuse of tests, not only by lay counselors, but even by professional counselors. The best way to avoid such dangers for lay counselors, in my opinion, is for them *not* to provide testing services at all but to refer any need for testing to qualified professional counselors.

However, if the director of the center is a licensed professional counselor or someone qualified to conduct such testing and interpret the results of the tests given, then he or she may, of course, provide such services through the center. There is usually a fee charged for testing services.

A related issue has to do with whether notes or files should be kept on clients seen in a lay counseling center. Some churches have decided *not* to keep notes or files on clients, but instead to simply keep a record in a book of those who have used the services of the center, recording their names or first names or initials only, their sex and age, and the dates when they were seen. Many centers, however, keep very brief notes and files on the clients seen to document the work done by the lay counselors. These records may be of critical importance if a malpractice suit is ever filed against the center or a lay counselor.

Potential clients who call in for appointments should also be told of the limits to confidentiality in the counseling situation at the beginning of the intake interview, and should then sign an informed consent form. California law, for example, requires professional counselors to report incidences of reasonably suspected child abuse or elder abuse (physical or sexual), and to warn appropriate individuals if the client intends to take harmful, dangerous, or criminal action against another human being or against himself or herself. Many lay counseling centers in California have decided to follow such laws even for lay counselors. The director of the center, therefore, should be familiar with the specific laws of the state he or she is working in, pertaining to the practice of professional counseling, and decide whether to follow them for lay counselors, preferably after consulting with an attorney regarding potential risks for litigation. Useful forms for keeping brief notes on clients, obtaining informed consent including information on limits of confidentiality, informed consent for release of information, etc., can be found in Appendix F of this book (reprinted with permission). Client files containing confidential information should be kept under lock and key in a safe and secure place or office.

9. *Carefully consider the financing for the lay counseling center.* Be sure that the counseling center is included in the annual budget of the church. A number of churches have succeeded in operating effective lay counseling centers with relatively small budgets (several hundred dollars a year), using mainly volunteer lay counselors or staff who are unpaid. Nevertheless, some financial support is still needed for a number of items like office supplies, books, journals, audio- or videotape equipment, publicity costs, and so forth. Some churches ask clients for voluntary donations to help defray

expenses incurred in the operation of such centers. Since you are not offering professional services, however, it would be wise to avoid asking for donations or charging any fees for lay counseling services, especially to minimize the risk of litigation or malpractice suits.

With regard to possible malpractice suits,[5] a particular church with a lay counseling center needs to decide whether to obtain malpractice insurance for its lay counselors (which can be very expensive or not easily available), or to have an "emergency fund" for securing legal counsel in the event of a malpractice suit being filed against a lay counselor or the lay counseling center. A number of churches with lay counseling centers have actually functioned without any malpractice insurance or emergency fund, but they have tried to minimize the risk of litigation by following community standards for the ethical practice of counseling.

10. *Determine the church affiliation of the lay counseling center.* I have written this chapter mainly from the perspective of a lay counseling center being operated by one local church. However, it is possible for a number of local churches in a particular community to collaborate together and establish a lay counseling center which will serve the needs of their respective congregations as well as those of the wider community in which they live. Such a center should still be church oriented so that clients can be channeled to appropriate churches for further spiritual nurture and growth where necessary.

These ten considerations are helpful ones for people like Bill to think through and discuss with their pastors and church leaders if there is interest in setting up a more formal lay counseling center or service.

With some adaptation and modification, the models and guidelines I have described and delineated in this chapter can also be applied in parachurch contexts and missionary work where lay caring and counseling ministries are also greatly needed. With much prayer, careful planning, and wise decision-making, building or establishing a lay counseling ministry can become a reality in many more churches, parachurch organizations, and missions, for the helping and healing of more persons, to the greater glory and honor of God.

NOTES

[1]For further information about the Stephen Series, contact: Stephen Ministries, 1325 Boland, St. Louis, MO 63117 (Tel. 314-645-5511). See also K. C. Haugk, *Christian Caregiving* (Minneapolis: Augsburg, 1984).

[2]For copies of helpful manuals on policies and procedures, write to the following two churches which have set up formal lay counseling centers: Creative Counseling Center (Hollywood Presbyterian Church), 1763 North Gower, Hollywood, CA 90028; and Counseling Resource Center of First Presbyterian Church, 1820 15th Street, Boulder, CO 80302. There will be a charge for the manuals.

[3]See G. R. Collins, "Lay Counseling Within the Local Church," *Leadership* 1 (1980): 78–86, in which several of the steps mentioned in this chapter were first suggested.

[4]Trevor J. Partridge, "Ten Considerations in Establishing a Christian Counselling Centre," *The Christian Counsellor's Journal* 4, no. 4 (1983): 31–33. For more information on the establishment of professional counseling centers, see John C. Carr, John E. Hinkle, and David M. Moss III, eds., *The Organization and Administration of Pastoral Counseling Centers* (Nashville: Abingdon, 1981); and H. Wahking, "A Church-Related Professional Counseling Service," *Journal of Psychology and Christianity* 3, no. 3 (1984): 58–64. See also T. J. Sandbeck and H. N. Malony, "The Church Counseling Center: A Modern Expression of an Ancient Profession," *CAPS Bulletin* 7, no. 4 (1981): 9–12; and R. C. Richard and D. A. Flakoll, "Christian Counseling Centers: Two Effective Models," *CAPS Bulletin* 7, no. 4 (1981): 12–15.

[5]For a helpful book on the subject of malpractice as related to the church and clergy, see H. Newton Malony, Thomas L. Needham, and Samuel Southard, *Clergy Malpractice* (Philadelphia: Westminster, 1986). See also T. L. Needham, ed., *New Challenges in Church Liability: The Post-Nally Years,* forthcoming.

6

Selection of Lay Counselors

"In the next few months we will be starting a new lay counseling service in our church in order to extend and expand our pastoral care and counseling ministries. As you know, this project has been approved by our church board and pastoral staff. We will be starting a three-month intensive training program for about a dozen lay counselors, once they have been selected. If you are interested and feel you have relevant gifts or experience in helping people with their problems and needs, please fill in an application form available at the church office, to be considered for selection as a lay counselor for our new lay counseling service. Thank you."

After Pastor Smith made this announcement during a Sunday morning worship service, Bob, a faithful member of the church for many years, said to his wife: "I guess it's time for me to get more involved in the church—like you've been nagging me to do for years! I have a stable personality and years of management experience, so I should be able to help quite a few of those poor souls with their problems. I'll get an application form from the pastor today and fill it in. He'll be glad to see me volunteer, and happier still to have me as one of the lay counselors!"

Another member of the church, Alice, thought to herself: "I wonder if I should apply to be a lay counselor? I'm not sure if I am qualified, and I don't know what the exact requirements or criteria are. But lots of people pour out their hearts and their struggles to me. All I do is listen, try to understand, and pray with them, but apparently it helps, because they usually come back to talk some more with me, and quite a few have told me I've been really helpful. Some even suggested I should consider being a counselor! I guess I should ask Pastor Smith for an application form and discuss this further with him before making up my mind about whether to apply. But I do want to serve the Lord more in church."

This fictitious scenario raises two important questions: (1) What criteria should be used to select lay counselors? and (2) What are the best methods for screening lay counselors? This chapter will attempt to answer these questions.

Criteria for the Selection of Lay Counselors

Everyone agrees that the careful selection of lay counselors is a crucial step in the development of an effective lay counseling ministry. However, there is less agreement and little research on what specific criteria should be used to select counselors.

Lorraine Hart and Glen King have pointed out: "Another approach to enhance the effectiveness of paraprofessionals is that of adequate selection. From this perspective a desirable paraprofessional could be chosen on the basis of some criteria that would help assure that they would be effective. In spite of the fact that selection is a reasonably well-accepted idea, little concerted research has defined what selection criteria should be."[1] They also note that the following psychological tests or measures of personality characteristics have been used to select most telephone counselors who are paraprofessionals or lay volunteers: California Psychological Inventory, Personality Research Form, Omnibus Personality Inventory, Edwards Personal Preference Schedule, Minnesota Multiphasic Personality Inventory, and the Internal-External Locus of Control Scale.[2]

Most of the research that has been conducted on selection criteria for lay counselors has been on the characteristics of volunteers versus those of nonvolunteers. Hart and King, in reviewing the research, conclude that "volunteers have been found to score higher in nurturance, affiliation and empathy, . . . to be more idealistic and generous, . . . and to be higher in flexibility, achievement via independence, and maturity and sensitivity. . . . These differences do not imply correlation with counseling effectiveness, of course, and there is little research to show that selecting counselors in this way is helpful."[3]

They therefore suggest that instead of using personality characteristics to select paraprofessionals, to use the initial level of their facilitative or helping skills, since Robert Carkhuff has found that persons with high initial levels of helping skills improved more with training than those with low levels initially.[4] In their own study, however, Hart and King did not find selection based on high levels of initial facilitative or helping skills to be a more potent factor than training, and concluded that their data provide strong support for the gross screening methods that are presently being used in many telephone counseling centers. Nevertheless, they also noted that during training, the experimenter observed that persons who were initially high in facilitative or helping skills were instrumental in producing a better quality of training.[5] More specifically, progress was limited or slow in a group which consisted only of those functioning at a low level, whereas progress in learning helping skills was much quicker in a group which had several people already functioning at a high level of facilitative skills, who may have served as good models for others in the group. Hence, both adequate selection (based on high initial levels of helping skills) and adequate training probably contribute to the development of effective paraprofessionals or lay counselors.

One well-known procedure for assessing facilitative skills or interpersonal skills is the Group Assessment of Interpersonal Traits (GAIT).[6] Dooley has described it thus: "The GAIT procedure consists of a series of five-minute discloser-understander dyads followed by evaluations by the participants (peer ratings) or by observers (in person or subsequently from audio or video recordings). Each participant takes each role once. The discloser role entails sharing an authentic present concern about the person's relationships while the understander is asked to show understanding to the discloser. . . . In the GAIT, participants are judged on the Rogerian . . . constructs of Empathy (accurate understanding), Acceptance (warmth or unconditional positive regard), and Openness (emotional honesty or genuineness)."[7] In his study on selecting nonprofessional counselor trainees with the GAIT, Dooley used the following measures to determine which ones would be significantly related to a scale of counseling readiness: pre-GAIT first impression peer ratings, GAIT Empathy, Acceptance, and Openness ratings by peers and by trained audiotape judges, and staff ratings based on written applications submitted by the trainees. After nine months of training, twenty-six trainees were evaluated on the criterion scale of counseling readiness. Pre-GAIT first impression peer ratings and GAIT Empathy, Acceptance, and Openness ratings by peers did not predict counseling readiness. Only the GAIT Empathy rating by trained audiotape judges, as well as the staff ratings, were significantly related to the criterion measure of counseling readiness.[8] The GAIT procedure may therefore be potentially useful for screening lay counselors, but only to a limited degree.

Geraldine Cerling has reviewed a number of important characteristics for counselors to possess,[9] including the following description of an effective helper taken from Gerard Egan's book *The Skilled Helper:*

> First of all committed to his own growth, physical, intellectual, social-emotional, (spiritual) . . . he shows respect for his body through proper exercise and diet. . . . He has adequate basic intelligence, is aware of his own intellectual possibilities, respects the world of ideas. . . . He has good common sense and good social intelligence. . . . He knows that helping is a great deal of work. . . . He is concrete in his expressions, dealing with actual feelings and actual behavior rather than vague formulations or generalities. . . . His speech, while caring and human, is also lean and to the point. . . . He is an integrator (uses data from the client to help the client understand himself better). . . . He is active, capable of helping his client elaborate actions, programs that lead to constructive behavioral change. . . . He is at home with people. . . . He is not a man who has never known problems, but does not retreat from the problematic in his own life. . . . He is living more effectively than the client, at least in the area the client is having trouble.[10]

This is quite a formidable list of characteristics of a good and effective helper, but Egan's book has been widely read and used in many counselor training programs.

Cerling also summarized the views of Paul Miller, who wrote a book on peer counseling in the church several years ago.[11] According to Miller, four essential characteristics of a counselor are: mature attitudes, capacity for sustained and perceptive listening, skills of tactful intervention, and a deep grasp of human nature. He also described ten essential attitudes and skills for counselors to have: personal warmth, trustworthiness, accurateness in empathy, unconditional positive regard, confidence in counselee's ability to change, inner consistency, growth in personal maturity, appropriate self-disclosure, training in counseling, and a professional stance.

Cerling therefore concluded: "While cited sources showed differences, there appeared to be a consensus that characteristics and qualities enabling a person to be aware of, open to, and available for interaction with other human beings were prized in a helper. Also valued were the individual's capacity and desire for personal growth and development throughout his/her life."[12] She conducted her own study, using a structured questionnaire to survey eighty-one church counseling centers across the United States in order to determine their criteria for selecting lay counselors. However, only twenty-eight (34.6%) of the centers used lay counselors, reflecting a general reluctance to utilize lay counselors in such centers. The respondents in her study used two different definitions of "lay" counselors—"lay" as referring to nonprofessional or paraprofessional counselors (as Cerling intended) and "lay" as referring to nonordained but professional trained counselors (this was not Cerling's intended meaning). The major selection criteria used by the church counseling centers, together with their frequency and percentage, are shown in her table on page 101.[13] In general, they reflect the criteria already mentioned earlier by other authors in the counseling field.

The specific criteria for the selection of lay counselors may therefore differ from church to church or center to center. However, in my opinion, from both a biblical perspective and a sound psychological perspective, the following criteria should be used to select lay Christian counselors for a lay counseling ministry:

1. *Spiritual maturity*—the counselor should be a Spirit-filled, mature Christian (cf. Gal. 6:1) who has a good knowledge of Scripture, wisdom in applying Scripture to life, and a regular prayer life;

2. *Psychological stability*—the counselor should be psychologically stable, not emotionally labile or volatile, but open and vulnerable. He or she should not be suffering from a serious psychological disorder;

3. *Love for and interest in people*—the counselor should be a

Selection Criteria from Cerling's Study

Number	Percentage	
26	17.4	Personal and spiritual maturity [printed response]
24	16.1	Interest in people [printed response]
22	14.8	Willingness to make a commitment to a counseling ministry [printed response]
17	11.4	Graduate level training in a professional field, MA or higher
11	7.4	Commitment to Christ as Savior and Lord [printed response]
8	5.4	Personal Integrity (i.e., dependability, reliability, standing in the community)
7	4.7	Certification by a professional organization, and/or state licensure
5	3.4	Counseling skills (i.e., empathy, acceptance, self-disclosure)
5	3.4	Value commitments (i.e., religious, moral, personal, social)
3	2.0	Ongoing supervision
3	2.0	Personal therapy
3	2.0	Training program within the counseling center
2	1.3	Clinical competence (directly stated; inferred in professional training and certification)
2	1.3	Continued personal growth
2	1.3	Recommendation by pastor and/or faith group
2	1.3	Stable marital relationship
1	0.7	Emotional and psychological stability as determined by MMPI and POI [Personal Orientation Inventory]
1	0.7	Interest in community and parish systems
1	0.7	Interview by executive director
1	0.7	Rich life experience and rewarding personal life
1	0.7	Transportation
1	0.7	Willingness to work for little, if any, financial compensation
1	0.7	Works well in group setting
149	100.1%	

warm, caring, and genuine person with a real interest in people
and their welfare;

4. *Spiritual gifts*—the counselor should possess appropriate
spiritual gifts like exhortation (other examples may include
wisdom, knowledge, discerning of spirits, mercy, and healing);

5. *Some life experience*—the counselor should have had some
life experience and hence not be too young;

6. *Previous training or experience in helping people*—experience would be helpful but not necessary for the counselor to
have;

7. *Age, sex, education, socioeconomic status, and ethnic/
cultural background*—it would be helpful to have a variety of
counselors from different backgrounds, ages, and from both
sexes;

8. *Availability and teachability*—the counselor should have
the time to be trained, supervised, and involved in a lay
counseling ministry, and should be teachable and open to
learning a biblical approach to helping people;

9. *Ability to maintain confidentiality*—the counselor should
be able to maintain confidentiality and protect the privacy of
clients.[14]

With these nine basic, specific selection criteria in mind, what
are the best methods or ways to screen potential lay counselors
so that only those who possess all or a majority of such criteria
will be chosen for a lay counseling ministry? Should both Bob
and Shirley, mentioned in the opening scenario in this chapter,
be selected? Or should only one of them be chosen? If so, which
one? How can we tell? The following section should answer
these questions.

Methods for the Screening of Lay Counselors

Gary Collins has proposed the following helpful requirements
in the screening of potential lay counselors or applicants.[15] First,
solicit a brief written statement from the potential lay counselor
affirming his or her adherence to your church's statement of faith
or doctrinal positions, in addition to a testimony of his or her
personal Christian experience. A statement of reasons for
wanting to be involved in a lay counseling training program and
ministry is also helpful. Second, require two or three letters of
recommendation from different people who know the potential

lay counselor or applicant well. Third, the director and another church leader should interview the applicant to assess his or her spiritual maturity, stability, and motivation. Fourth and finally, do psychological testing of the potential lay counselor (e.g., using the 16PF or the Taylor-Johnson Temperament Analysis), if possible. A trained psychologist or other appropriately competent person should obtain and interpret the psychological tests. Other tests that have been used include the Minnesota Multiphasic Personality Inventory or MMPI, the Personal Orientation Inventory or POI, and the Myers-Briggs Temperament Type Indicator. Although Collins does not mention the use of measures other than psychological or personality tests, there are tests which are helpful for assessing applicants' spiritual qualities (e.g., spiritual well-being, spiritual life and maturity, and spiritual leadership) and spiritual gifts.[16] Some of these tests include the Shepherd Scale, developed by Rodney Bassett and his colleagues, which is a measure of orthodox Christian belief and adherence to a Christian lifestyle; Craig Ellison's Spiritual Well-Being Scale; Paul Schmidt's Character Assessment Scale, which is a measure of Christian character or maturity; Peter Wagner's Wagner-Revised Houts Questionnaire, which is a spiritual gifts inventory; Dennis Wayman's Spiritual Life Check-Up Questionnaire; and Frank Wichern's Spiritual Leadership Qualities Inventory. A trained psychologist is usually not required to administer such measures of spirituality, which are briefly described below.

1. The Shepherd Scale

Developed by Rodney Bassett and his colleagues, this test is an instrument designed to differentiate Christians from non-Christians, using items based on New Testament texts. It has two components: a thirteen-item *Belief Component* which measures orthodox Christian belief (e.g., "I believe I can have the personal presence of God in my life [John 14:16]," and "I believe that it is possible to have a personal relationship with God through Christ [Romans 14:22, Ephesians 2:14–17, Colossians 1:19–20]")[17] and a twenty-five-item *Christian Walk Component,* which measures the extent to which a person adheres to a Christian lifestyle (e.g., "I do kind things regardless of who's watching me [Matt. 6:1–6, 25:31–46, Ephesians 6:5–9]," and "Status and material possessions are not of primary importance to me [Matthew 6:16–21, 25–33, Luke 12:13–21, I Corinthians 1:26–31, Philippians 4:10–13].")[18] For each item on the scale, a person is to choose one of the following four possible responses: (1) true, (2) generally true, (3) generally not true, and (4) not true.

2. The Spiritual Well-Being Scale

Developed by Craig Ellison and his colleague Raymond Paloutzian, this measure is composed of twenty items, ten of which assess *religious well-being* (e.g., "I don't find much satisfaction in private prayer with God," and "I believe that God loves me and cares for me"), and the other ten of which assess *existential well-being* (e.g., "I don't know who I am, where I came from, or where I'm going," and "I feel that life is a positive experience").[19] A six-point scale is used, ranging from Strongly Agree to Strongly Disagree, for each of the items. Ellison has pointed out that the *Spiritual Well-Being Scale* measures an individual's personal experience or sense of well-being, and this may not be the same as his or her state of spiritual health or spiritual maturity. While a spiritually mature or healthy person would be expected to have a positive sense of spiritual well-being, someone with a positive sense of spiritual well-being may not be spiritually mature (e.g., a young Christian).[20]

3. The Character Assessment Scale

Developed by Paul Schmidt, this is a personality test with 225 items assessing a number of morally relevant character traits based on the Bible. It is therefore a measure of Christian character or maturity. An individual taking this Scale has to answer each item as either applicable (true) or nonapplicable (false). The Scale has eight research scales for measuring the following character traits, each of which has its corresponding strength and weakness components: (1) *Truth* (with Denial as weakness and Honesty as strength); (2) *Respect* (with Vanity as weakness and Humility as strength); (3) *Concern* (with Envy as weakness and Compassion as strength); (4) *Anger* (with Resentment as weakness and Peacemaking as Strength); (5) *Money* (with Greed as weakness and Resourcefulness as strength); (6) *Time/Energy* (with Laziness as weakness and Enthusiasm as strength); (7) *Sexuality* (with Lust as weakness and Sexual

Integrity as strength); (8) *Body Health* (with Gluttony as weakness and Physical Fitness as strength).[21]

4. The Wagner-Revised Houts Questionnaire

Revised by Peter Wagner, this is an inventory designed to help a person discover his or her spiritual gifts. It consists of 125 items to be answered on a 4 point scale as to what extent each item/statement is true of an individual's life (3 = much; 2 = some; 1 = little; and 0 = not at all). A total of 25 spiritual gifts are assessed by this measure, with 5 items for each of the spiritual gifts. For example, the item/statement, "I have a desire to speak direct messages from God that edify, exhort, or comfort others" is relevant to the spiritual gift of prophecy.[22] The 25 spiritual gifts covered by this questionnaire are: prophecy, pastor, teaching, wisdom, knowledge, exhortation, discerning of spirits, giving, helps, mercy, missionary, evangelist, hospitality, faith, leadership, administration, miracles, healing, tongues, interpretation, voluntary poverty, celibacy, intercession, exorcism, and service.[23]

5. The Spiritual Life Check-Up Questionnaire

Developed by Dennis Wayman, this test is a measure for determining the present state of a person's spiritual health or spiritual life, using a physical check-up analogy. There are six major sections to the questionnaire. Section I covers *Blood Type*, and the key questions are, "Are you now a Christian?" and "Have you been baptized?" Section II covers *Red Blood Cells* (oxygen carriers that prevent anemia), with questions on one's devotional life (e.g., "How meaningful is Sunday morning worship to you?" and "How meaningful is private worship to you?"), and one's intellectual life (e.g., "Are your doubts and questions being answered?" and "Do you feel you know your Bible and what help you need?" Section III covers *White Blood Cells* (disease fighters for inner spiritual cleansing and renewing), and includes questions like "Do you feel you are a more accepting, forgiving, loving person than you have been?" and "Do you feel you are stronger against temptations (to be impatient, angry, greedy, lustful, etc.)?" Section IV covers *Platelets* (blood clotters that stanch the wounds of living in a hurting world), and includes questions like "Have you found someone to help bear the burdens of life?" and "When you fail (or succeed), what happens within you?" Section V covers *Blood Pressure* (hypertension and exercise), and includes questions like "Are you able to turn your finances over to God and tithe, trusting Him to supply?" and "How concerned are you with injustices and other social evils?" The final section, Section VI, is on *Tired Blood* (from imbalanced spiritual diet), and key questions here are "Is your life balanced?" and "Do you feel you have a balance of worship, study, and service to stay in shape?"[24]

6. The Spiritual Leadership Qualities Inventory

Developed by Frank Wichern, this test is a measure that assesses a person's attitudes, beliefs, and values pertaining to qualities desired in Christian leaders according to 1 Timothy 3:1–7 and Titus 1:5–9. It contains a total of 222 items measuring the following nineteen qualities of a spiritually mature leader: (1) upright; (2) good reputation; (3) above reproach; (4) respectable; (5) desire to be an overseer; (6) holy; (7) able to teach; (8) temperate; (9) prudent; (10) able to manage family; (11) husband of one wife; (12) gentle; (13) not quick-tempered; (14) self-controlled; (15) not addicted to wine; (16) not greedy; (17) lover of good; (18) not self-willed; (19) hospitable.[25]

There are other measures of spirituality which have not been mentioned,[26] but the ones I have just briefly described are, in my opinion, potentially helpful ones to use in the screening of lay counselors.

The methods for screening potential lay counselors as proposed by Collins are therefore comprehensive and somewhat stringent. Some churches may not use all of them (e.g., psychological testing may not be easily available in some rural church communities or may be too costly), while other churches may use all these methods and a couple more.

The Example of La Canada Presbyterian Church

La Canada Presbyterian Church in Southern California is an example of a local church that has developed a comprehensive and stringent screening process for the selection of lay counselors, consisting of three major phases.[27] In *Phase One*, all applicants are required to complete a *written questionnaire or application form* with the following nine items (after the name, address and telephone number(s), of the applicant have been filled in):

1. What do you believe constitutes effective counseling?
2. What does being a Christian mean to you personally?
3. What does it mean to you to counsel others as a Christian?
4. If you have had previous counseling experiences (either as a counselor *or* counselee) that may be helpful for us to know, please describe them and their significance to you.
5. What (if any) prior training or education have you had that may help you to be a counselor?
6. Prior work experience (list most recent first).
7. Would you please list as references the names, addresses, and phone numbers of two people who would be willing and able to affirm and endorse your participation in this ministry.
8. Why do you want to be a lay counselor?
9. Within the last two years have you experienced (or are you currently experiencing, or expect to experience) any significant life changes, e.g., separation, divorce, death in the family, job change, critical illness, etc.? Please explain.

The written responses of the applicant plus the recommendations of the two references listed in the application form serve as the basis upon which applicants are selected for continuation on to Phase Two of the selection process.

In *Phase Two*, selected applicants are *interviewed* by the church's Lay Counseling Task Force of five members, which includes two supervising consultants who are licensed mental health professionals, the Lay Counseling Ministry Coordinator/Director, and two Lay Counselors. Each year, whenever possible, a total of sixteen applicants are usually selected for two group interviews of eight applicants at one time. The following ten basic questions are asked of the applicants in the group interview process:

1. Please tell us your name and something about your current work situation.
2. What do you understand to be the purpose of the Lay Counseling Ministry?
3. What to you are some of the more important ingredients of effective counseling?
4. What does it mean to you to be a Christian?
5. Admittedly, the Lay Counseling Ministry requires a significant commitment of time and effort, perhaps 6–10 hours

per week. How do you see yourself meeting such a demanding responsibility?

6. Being a La Canada Presbyterian Church Lay Counselor means more than counseling counselees. It involves being a part of a team of Lay Counselors who can be at some times intensely earnest and serious while at other times free and frivolous. How might you "fit in" among such a group?

7. How do you see yourself already or currently involved in the "counseling" of friends or colleagues?

8. How do you think being a Lay Counselor will meet *your* needs?

9. How have you felt about this interviewing experience today?

10. Do you have any questions for us?

The interviewers evaluate the answers given by each applicant to each of the ten basic questions, using a scale of 1–10 (1 = Unsatisfactory Response: Seemingly without thought; presented uncomfortably; not coincident with the direction of the Lay Counseling Ministry; 5 = Mediocre Response: Somewhat thoughtful; presented somewhat comfortably; practically coincident with the direction of the Lay Counseling Ministry; 10 = Excellent Response: Thoughtful, presented comfortably; coincides with the direction of the Lay Counseling Ministry).

Each interviewer then rates each applicant as to his or her *personal sense of the applicant as a counselor,* on a 1–10 scale as follows:

1. Would be psychologically/relationally dangerous.
2. Would probably make most people uneasy.
3. Would probably make many people uneasy.
4. Makes me moderately uneasy.
5. Makes me slightly uneasy.
6. Blah, but not dangerous.
7. Certain others might benefit from this person.
8. I would enjoy time with this person but don't know if it would be beneficial.
9. I might benefit by seeing this person.
10. I would benefit by seeing this person.

Each interviewer also rates each applicant as to his or her *personal sense of the applicant's benefit to the Lay Counseling Ministry,* on a 1–10 scale as follows:

1. Ministry must not have him/her.
2. Ministry would rarely benefit from him/her.
3. Ministry would seldom benefit from him/her.
4. Ministry would infrequently benefit from him/her.
5. Ministry would sporadically benefit from him/her.
6. Ministry would occasionally benefit from him/her.
7. Ministry might benefit a little from him/her.
8. Ministry would probably benefit some from him/her.
9. Ministry would definitely benefit from him/her.
10. Ministry must have him/her.

A final part of the Phase Two interview process is a unique one that involves the eight *applicants ranking themselves and each other in terms of their potential of helping or counseling ability*. An *Applicant Feedback Sheet* is used with the following major question: " 'Accurate perception of self and of others' is a criterion often used in assessing potential counselor ability. To help us with this process, then, we would like you to consider the following.

Imagine someone in need of counseling. Imagine that he or she had somehow been able to observe our interview session here today. Based on our time together, which person of these applicants do you believe the observer would be most likely to select for help? (Please include yourself in the ranking which goes from First to Eighth)."

A final group of applicants (usually 8–10) is selected from Phase Two interviews. They go on to *Phase Three* of the process, the *Lay Counseling Initial Intensive Training Program,* which usually begins in March and ends in August of each year. Applicants who successfully complete Phase Three training are then selected to become Lay Counselors for a required minimum time commitment of one year.

Concluding Remarks

I have described in some detail the methods used by La Canada Presbyterian Church in the selection and screening of lay counselors because they are helpful examples of systematic, comprehensive, stringent screening methods, which can and should be used by local churches wanting to be involved in lay counseling ministries. However, such stringent and comprehensive screening methods could be adapted and modified where

necessary without compromising the need to conduct a careful
and thorough selection process. For example, some churches
may prefer to conduct personal rather than group interviews of
applicants, and make the final selection of lay counselors after
the interviews rather than after the initial intensive lay counselor training program. Other churches may allow any interested
Christian first to sign up for and go through a Basic Lay
Counseling Skills Training program (usually a 10–12 week
course) and subsequently ask those who have completed the
basic training program to apply more formally for possible
selection as lay counselors, if they are interested, willing, and
able. A selection interview process can then be conducted after
applications have been made.

The process of selecting and screening lay counselors is not
only an important and time-consuming one; it can also lead to
misunderstanding and disappointment for those applicants who
are not selected. Therefore, be sure to state clearly at the outset
the applicant requirements, and explain that not all who apply
will be selected. La Canada Presbyterian Church states clearly
that they are looking for Christians who are regular participants
in the life of the church, believe God has gifted them for a
counseling ministry, would be willing to participate in a
rigorous counselor training program, and are able to volunteer
six to eight hours a week of involvement in the lay counseling
ministry for at least one year. Their Lay Counseling Ministry
Coordinator, Chuck Osburn, also explains in a letter to potential
applicants: "We sincerely regret to have to say that not everyone
who applies to this Ministry can become a Lay Counselor. We
can only select a limited number of participants who we believe
will most appropriately meet our current counselor needs. It is
our hope and prayer that this selection process will help us
discern God's best for you as well as for the Lay Counseling
Ministry."

The lay counselors finally selected should be those who
possess the kinds of characteristics or criteria described earlier
in this chapter, including being spiritually mature and specially
gifted by God to engage in a lay counseling ministry that is
equivalent to Crabb's Level III Counseling by Enlightenment,
requiring some intensive training. Since all Christians are called
to counsel or help others at some basic level (e.g., what Crabb
has called Level I Counseling by Encouragement), basic

training in encouragement or helping skills should be provided to as many interested Christians as possible, through different means like a Sunday school class, retreat or workshop on "Basic Caring" or "The Ministry of Encouragement," etc.[28] Periodic sermons from the pulpit on this theme of caring for each other or burden bearing would also be helpful. I therefore agree with Gary Sweeten's proposal that the church should be viewed as a "therapeutic growth community" in which "the general level of personal and interpersonal functioning" can be raised "by adapting a lay helper training strategy to the whole congregation, and then selecting those who are properly talented, skilled, gifted, and called, to enter the specific ministry of helping and pastoral care" or lay counseling.[29]

The screening methods described in this chapter are most appropriate for churches interested in starting more organized (whether formal or informal) lay counseling services or ministries. Some churches may prefer to provide basic training in lay pastoral care and counseling skills to *all* their church leaders who provide such care more informally through, for example, small discipleship groups, home fellowships or Bible studies, prayer teams, and visitation programs. However, even in such cases, careful selection of *church leaders* is needed, and some of the screening methods mentioned may still be helpful and appropriate ones to use for this purpose.

Let me end this chapter by returning to our potential lay counselors, Bob and Alice. It should be quite clear by now that Alice rather than Bob appears to be a better choice for selection as a lay counselor. However, the final decision should involve at least a careful and thorough interview process. Bob will probably not be selected because of his arrogant, condescending, and insensitive attitude and stance. Alice has a good chance of being selected because she seems to possess humility and a genuine caring attitude toward people. She also probably has spiritual gifts like exhortation and appropriate personality characteristics that have already resulted in several people coming back to her repeatedly for help in an informal way. Her spiritual life and maturity (as well as Bob's) should be more thoroughly explored during the interview process, which could include the use of Wayman's Spiritual Life Check-Up Questionnaire.[30] While all of the basic selection criteria that I have delineated should be kept in mind, the criterion of spiritual maturity—including a serious commitment to Jesus Christ as Lord and Savior, and to seeking God and his kingdom first (Matt. 6:33)—should be a foundational and essential one for any lay Christian counselor or church leader to fulfill.

NOTES

[1]See L. E. Hart and G. D. King, "Selection Versus Training in the Development of Paraprofessionals," *Journal of Counseling Psychology* 26 (1979): 235–41. Quotation is from p. 236.

[2]See I. N. Sandler, "Characteristics of Women Working as Child Aides in a School-Based Preventive Mental Health Program," *Journal of Consulting and Clinical Psychology* 39 (1972): 56–61.

[3]See Hart and King, "Selection Versus Training," 236.

[4]R. R. Carkhuff, *Helping and Human Relations: A Primer for Lay and Professional Helpers* (vols. 1, 2) (New York: Holt, Rinehart and Winston, 1969).

[5]See Hart and King, "Selection Versus Training," 239.

[6]See G. Goodman, *Companionship Therapy: Studies in Structured Intimacy* (San Francisco: Jossey-Bass, 1972).

[7]D. Dooley, "Selecting Nonprofessional Counselor Trainees with the Group Assessment of Interpersonal Traits (GAIT)," *American Journal of Community Psychology* 3 (1975): 371–83. Quotation is from p. 372.

[8]Ibid., 371, 379–80.

[9]G. L. Cerling, "Selection of Lay Counselors for a Church Counseling Center," *Journal of Psychology and Christianity* 2, no. 3 (1983): 67–72.

[10]Ibid., 68. See also G. Egan, *The Skilled Helper* (Monterey, Calif.: Brooks/Cole, 1975), 22–24.

[11]Ibid., 69. See also P. Miller, *Peer Counseling in the Church* (Scottdale, Pa.: Herald, 1978).

[12]Ibid., 69.

[13]Ibid., 71; reprinted by permission.

[14]S. Y. Tan, "Care and Counseling in the 'New Church Movement,'" *Theology, News and Notes* 33, no. 4 (1986): 9–11, 21. See p. 11.

[15]See G. R. Collins, "Lay Counseling Within the Local Church," *Leadership* 1 (1980): 81.

[16]See R. L. Bassett, R. D. Sadler, E. E. Kobishen, D. M. Skiff, I. J. Merrill, B. J. Atwater, and P. W. Livermore, "The Shepherd Scale: Separating the Sheep from the Goats," *Journal of Psychology and Theology* 9 (1981): 335–51; C. W. Ellison, "Spiritual Well-Being: Conceptualization and Measurement," *Journal of Psychology and Theology* 11 (1983): 330–40; P. F. Schmidt, *Manual for Use of the Character Assessment Scale*, 2d ed. (Shelbyville, Ky.: Institute for Character Development, 1983), available from the Institute for Charac-

ter Development, 1109 Main Street, Shelbyville, KY 40065; C. Peter Wagner, *Wagner-Modified Houts Questionnaire for Discovering Your Spiritual Gifts* (Pasadena, Calif.: Fuller Evangelistic Association, 1989), available from Charles E. Fuller Institute of Evangelism and Church Growth, P.O. Box 91990, Pasadena, CA 91109-1990;

Also, D. L. Wayman, "A Spiritual Life Check-Up," *Leadership* 4, no. 4 (1983): 88–92; F. B. Wichern, *Spiritual Leadership Qualities Inventory* (Richardson, Tex.: Believer Renewal Resources, 1980), and *The Spiritual Leadership Qualities Inventory Instruction Manual* (Richardson, Tex.: Believer Renewal Ministries, 1980), with *Scoring Sheets* and *Scoring Key*, and J. S. Townsend II and F. B. Wichern, "The Development of the Spiritual Leadership Qualities Inventory," *Journal of Psychology and Theology* 12 (1984): 305–13, all available from Dr. Frank B. Wichern, 600 West Campbell Road, Richardson, TX 75080.

[17]See Bassett et al., "The Shepherd Scale," 349.

[18]Ibid., 350.

[19]See Ellison, "Spiritual Well-Being," 340.

[20]Ibid., 332.

[21]See Schmidt, *Manual for Use of the Character Assessment Scale;* and J. H. Elzerman and M. J. Boivin, "The Assessment of Christian Maturity, Personality, and Psychopathology Among College Students," *Journal of Psychology and Christianity* 6, no. 3 (1987): 50–64, esp. 53–54.

[22]See Wagner, *Wagner-Modified Houts Questionnaire,* 3, 13.

[23]Ibid., 14–17.

[24]See Wayman, "Spiritual Life Check-Up," 90–92.

[25]See Wichern, *Spiritual Leadership Qualities Inventory Instruction Manual,* 2–4, and appendix D, 14ff.

[26]For other examples of measures of different dimensions of spirituality, see R. E. Butman, "The Assessment of Spiritual and Psychological Well-Being," paper presented at the National Convention of the Christian Association for Psychological Studies (CAPS), April 1987, in Memphis, Tennessee (available from the author, who is a faculty member of the Psychology Department of Wheaton College, Wheaton, IL 60187) as well as R. E. Butman, "The Assessment of Religious Development: Some Possible Options," *Journal of Psychology and Christianity* 9, no. 2 (1990): 14–26; and D. E. Smith, "The Christian Life Assessment Scales: Christian Self-Perception," *Journal of Psychology and Christianity* 5, no. 3 (1986): 46–61.

[27]See *La Canada Presbyterian Church Lay Counseling Ministry Information Packet,* available from Chuck Osburn, D. Min., Lay Counseling Ministry Coordinator, La Canada Presbyterian Church, 626 Foothill Boulevard, La Canada, CA 91011.

28Some useful books for this purpose of equipping all the saints for the basic ministry of caring or encouraging one another include G. R. Collins, *The Joy of Caring* (Waco, Tex.: Word, 1980): L. J. Crabb, Jr., and D. Allender, *Encouragement: The Key to Caring* (Grand Rapids: Zondervan, 1984); K. C. Haugk, *Christian Caregiving* (Minneapolis: Augsburg, 1984); M. Slater, *Stretcher Bearers* (Ventura, Calif.: Regal, 1985).

29G. R. Sweeten, "Lay Helpers and the Caring Community," *Journal of Psychology and Christianity* 6, no. 2 (1987): 14–20. Quotations are from the abstract on p. 14.

30See Wayman, "Spiritual Life Check-Up."

7

Training of Lay Counselors

Once a local church or parachurch organization has decided to begin a lay counseling ministry, as well as selected the lay counselors for such a ministry, the crucial task of putting together an adequate and biblically based *training* program remains. There is some evidence, though still somewhat inconclusive, that lay counselors are more effective if they have received some training or have had some experience in helping people.[1] In the field of professional counseling and psychotherapy there has been a recent surge of interest in developing more systematic training programs that focus on improving the actual competency of the trainees in such programs.[2] The research literature showing that lay counselors are generally as effective as professional counselors in helping people with different types of problems actually challenges the very essence of professional therapist training. However, as Dr. Brian Shaw and Dr. Keith Dobson, two well-known psychologists and researchers in the area of developing counselor competence, have recently pointed out, none of the studies reviewed in the research literature reported on the actual levels of skillfulness or competency of the professional versus the lay counselors. The question of how counselor competence affects the outcome of the counseling provided is therefore still an open and unanswered one.[3] Such negligible differences between professional and lay counselors may mean that existing programs of professional training are not particularly effective in producing competent professional counselors who consistently do better

115

counseling than lay counselors. As efforts increase to improve professional training programs in order to raise the levels of competence of professional counselors, efforts to adequately train lay counselors must also continue to be made. What kinds of training programs are best suited for lay counselors is a question, however, which will require further research to answer more definitively. Training programs for lay counselors are usually of much shorter duration and are more focused on a simpler set of helping skills than professional training programs.

Three Phases of Training

Dr. Gary Collins has suggested that it may be helpful to divide training for lay counselors into *three phases:* pretraining, training, and posttraining.[4]

1. The Pretraining Phase

This phase usually includes selecting training materials, publicizing the training program, selecting participants (open or by invitation only), and possibly conducting an initial course on caring and the discovery of spiritual gifts. Collins suggests his book *The Joy of Caring* or Rick Yohn's *Discover Your Spiritual Gift and Use It* (Tyndale, 1982) for reading and discussion in such a basic course.

2. The Training Phase

Actual training should provide opportunities for the lay trainees to learn counseling skills by listening to lectures, reading, observing, and experience (for example, through role-plays or use of an "experimental client" or friend, or use of real-life cases). Most programs include a minimum of 40–50 hours of training over a period of several months. In this phase of training, the training groups are usually kept small, with 10–15 lay trainees who meet on a regular basis, usually weekly or biweekly for 2–3 hours each time. Collins further suggests that training should include the following: (1) basic biblical knowledge, particularly that which is relevant to people-helping, personal problems, and the person and ministry of the Holy Spirit; (2) knowledge of counseling skills, with opportunity to practice them; (3) understanding of common problems people face (e.g., discouragement, anxiety, excessive stress, or spiritual dryness); (4) awareness of ethics and dangers in counseling; and (5) knowledge of the importance and techniques of referral. Several good programs incorporating these components are already available for the training of lay Christian counselors and they will be briefly reviewed later in this chapter.

3. The Posttraining Phase

This is a follow-up phase which should provide further learning opportunities, discussion and supervision of cases seen by the newly trained lay counselors, and encouragement for the lay counselors to continue in their new ministry of people-helping.

Models of Lay Christian Counselor Training

Several models of lay Christian counselor training are currently available,[5] but only four of the more significant or well-known models will now be briefly reviewed.

Lawrence Crabb's Model

Dr. Lawrence Crabb has proposed a model for the training of lay Christian counselors following his biblical counseling approach.[6] He describes three levels of biblical counseling and suggests different training requirements for each level. Level I is Counseling by Encouragement, and Dr. Crabb believes that every Christian should be trained in Level I counseling, which involves learning how to be more sensitive, how to listen, and how to communicate care. With his colleague Dan Allender, he has also written a book, *Encouragement: The Key to Caring,* which is relevant to Level I Counseling.[7]

Level II is Counseling by Exhortation. Dr. Crabb suggests 35–40 hours of classroom training for mature believers in Level II Counseling. Finally, Level III is Counseling by Enlightenment, and Dr. Crabb recommends that only a few selected Christians in each local church be trained in Level III Counseling, using a six-month to a year-long training program of weekly classes. He has used his model in training lay Christian counselors through the Institute of Biblical Counseling which he founded and still directs.

While Dr. Crabb's model is a helpful one in delineating different levels of biblical counseling requiring different types and amounts of training, it is not always easy or possible to keep the three levels of counseling so distinct. Level II and Level III Counseling in particular are difficult to keep separate. I therefore suggest that it may be more helpful to train specially selected, mature Christians in effective biblical counseling which actually involves all three levels of counseling. All Christians, however, should have some training in basic listening and caring skills (i.e., Level I Counseling) as Dr. Crabb has recommended. This can be done through the pulpit or preaching ministry of the church and supplemented by Sunday school classes and other special workshops.

Gary Sweeten's Model

Dr. Gary Sweeten, formerly Minister of Christian Growth (nonclergy) at College Hill Presbyterian Church in Cincinnati, Ohio, has developed a model for the training of lay Christian counselors. The model begins by adapting a lay helper training strategy and applying it to the total congregation of a local church in order to raise its general level of personal and interpersonal functioning so that such a church can become a therapeutic growth community. Those who are properly talented, skilled, gifted, and called are then selected to be involved in the specific ministry of helping and pastoral care or lay counseling.[8]

Dr. Sweeten's discipleship counseling approach to lay counselor training attempts to integrate psychology, Christian theology, and the power of the Holy Spirit, and makes use of a variety of training materials like books, audiotapes, and videotapes. Special training seminars—called "Counseling with Power" seminars—that cover this approach are conducted by Dr. Sweeten and his colleagues periodically in different parts of the country and even abroad.

The training program has four major components or courses. The first course, "Apples of Gold I," is a competency-based interpersonal skills program focused on developing empathy, warmth, and respect in the helper toward the helpee or counselee. The second course, "Apples of Gold II," teaches the helper the skills of concreteness, genuineness, self-disclosure, confrontation, and immediate feedback to facilitate speaking the truth in love with accountability. Both these courses are taught sequentially over an eight-week period for two and a half hours each session, with homework assignments given. The third course, "Rational Christian Thinking," integrates principles of rational-emotive therapy with Scripture, and seeks to help people in the process of "renewing their minds." It is a six-week long course of two and a half hours per session, also with homework assignments. The fourth and final course, "Breaking Free from the Past," is the most intense one, requiring some fifty hours of preparation, dealing with past traumas, generational blessings and curses, and personal sins and character defects in the context of self-disclosure and prayer in a supportive small group. Two facilitators lead group members through this process, which also includes some didactic teaching.

Horace Lukens' Model

Dr. Horace Lukens has described a model for the training of lay or paraprofessional Christian counselors in which he proposes six sequential levels of training in the curriculum.[9]

Level 1, called "Body Life Skills I," is for all Christians and focuses on basic skills of living in Christian community. It includes skills for entering and building relationships, listening skills, and Carkhuff's core conditions. Dr. Lukens recommends that specific criteria for defining and measuring such skills be used.

Level 2, called "Theory and Theology," is for Christian leaders and teachers, covering the integration of Christianity and psychology, developmental psychology, and abnormal psychology as specific knowledge areas they need to be exposed to.

Level 3, called "Personal Awareness," is for lay counselor trainees only. In this segment of the training curriculum, the trainees examine their personal needs, issues, and motives as they relate to becoming a counselor. Their gifts and talents, strengths and weaknesses, and temperament or personality characteristics are also explored, with the help of psychological testing.

Level 4, called "Body Life Skills II," is for lay counselor trainees only. It focuses on further development and refinement of counseling skills for the trainees, and includes training in action, sharing and teaching responses, interviewing skills, problem definition, and the process of counseling. Dr. Lukens emphasizes once more that specific criteria for defining and assessing such skills should be used, and he notes that such criteria needed for evaluating Level 1 and Level 4 Body Life Skills can be found in a book written by William H. Cormier and L. Sherilyn Cormier entitled *Interviewing Strategies for Helpers: A Guide to Assessment, Treatment, and Evaluation*. There is also a second edition of this helpful book entitled *Interviewing Strategies for Helpers: Fundamental Skills and Cognitive Behavioral Interventions*.[10]

Level 5, called "Practicum," involves counseling supervision for lay counselor trainees who have demonstrated competence in all previous levels of training. Dr. Lukens suggests a minimum of forty client hours and ten supervision hours for each trainee.

Level 6, called "Advanced Training," is for lay counselor trainees who have successfully completed the previous five levels of training, and who show an interest in, as well as appropriate talents or gifts for, further advanced training. Areas of such training may include marital and family therapy, vocational evaluation or counseling, financial counseling, and inner healing and deliverance.

Dr. Lukens proposes that each level of training be limited to eight or ten weeks in duration. In his training model, he also addresses the development of goals and objectives, counselor selection, skill development, curriculum goals, the scriptural principle of multiplication (i.e., training trainees to become effective trainers), supervision, evaluation of counselor readiness and effectiveness, program evaluation, and the need to establish standard acceptable criteria and levels of training for all paraprofessional Christian counselors.

Kenneth Haugk's Model and the Stephen Series

Dr. Kenneth Haugk founded the Stephen Series of lay caring ministry in 1975. He is a pastor, clinical psychologist, author, and educator, as well as the Executive Director of Stephen Ministries, a transdenominational, international, nonprofit caring ministry organization based in St. Louis, Missouri. Although Dr. Haugk's model applies more generally to a lay caring ministry in the local church context and *not* to lay counseling per se, much of the lay caring ministry covered by the Stephen Series also involves some level of lay Christian counseling, as I have defined it. He developed the Stephen Series with the following steps or components: (1) a congregation should enroll in the Stephen Series by contacting the Stephen Ministries office in St. Louis, Missouri, and by paying a one-time enrollment fee; (2) a congregation should select leaders such as the pastor, other church staff, and gifted lay leaders to be involved in leadership for the Stephen Series; (3) selected leaders should attend a twelve-day Leader's Training Course; (4) the congregation should be prepared for the Stephen Series about to be implemented; (5) lay caregivers should be recruited and selected to be trained as Stephen ministers by the Stephen leaders; (6) lay caregivers or Stephen ministers should be trained for fifty hours; (7) Stephen leaders should find and prepare those with particular needs to receive care from the trained Stephen ministers; (8) trained Stephen ministers should be appropriately assigned to people with particular needs which match the gifts and skills of the Stephen ministers; (9) helping relationships between Stephen ministers and those who are receiving care from them should continue to be supervised on a regular basis. Stephen ministers have to make a two-year commitment to such a lay caring ministry, which includes fifty hours of training, an average of one one-hour visit each week, and meeting for supervision and support twice a month.

The twelve-day Leader's Training Course is an intensive and comprehensive one which covers three main areas: (1) administrative resources; (2) training topics/presentations; and (3) implementing and maintaining Stephen Ministry in the congregation. The training topics/presentations are also the same ones that Stephen leaders will use to provide the fifty hours of training needed by selected Stephen ministers.

The training topics/presentations include the following: what to do during the first helping contact; feelings: yours, mine, and ours; the art of listening; telecare: the next best thing to being there; effective use of the traditional resources of Christianity; assertiveness: relating gently and firmly; being "professional"; confidentiality; relationship exercise; the "small step" approach; utilizing community resources; when and how to terminate a caring relationship; crisis theory and intervention; stress of hospitalization; ministry to those experiencing grief; ministry to the dying, their family and friends; ministering to depressed persons; ministering to suicidal persons and family and friends; ministering to older persons; ministering to shut-in persons; ministering to those experiencing divorce; ministering to inactive members; childbirth as a family crisis; Jo-Hari window; everything Stephen Ministers wanted to know about caring but were afraid to ask; and supervision: a key to quality Christian care. Available separately is training on ministering to chemically dependent individuals and their families.

In addition to receiving training on the comprehensive and important topics just listed, Stephen leaders also receive training in implementing and maintaining Stephen Ministry in the congregation. Topics covered include: preparing the congregation as a whole for Stephen Ministry; recruiting, selecting, and training Stephen Ministers; commissioning Stephen Ministers; generating and making referrals to Stephen Ministers; supervising Stephen Ministry; and recognizing and affirming the work of Stephen ministers.

Dr. Haugk's model and Stephen Series are most applicable to the "informal, organized" model of lay counseling ministry which I described in an earlier chapter of this book. The other models of lay Christian counselor training proposed by Crabb, Sweeten, and Lukens contain different levels of training, and therefore they are applicable to all three models of lay counseling ministry that I have described—the *informal, spontaneous; informal, organized;* and *formal, organized.* However, such models, including Collins' delineation of the phases of lay Christian counselor training, are most applicable to the *informal, organized* and the *formal, organized* models of lay counseling ministry. There are, of course, other models of lay Christian counselor training, but the ones I have just described are among the most significant or well-known ones. There are many more *specific programs* available for lay Christian counselor training, and several of the better known or widely used ones will now be briefly reviewed.

Examples of Lay Christian Counselor Training Programs

Dr. Gary Collins is the author of a number of helpful training programs or materials for lay Christian counselors. In 1976, Dr. Collins put together the "People Helper Pak" containing a text, a growthbook, and audiotapes for training lay Christians in basic people-helping skills in twelve sessions.[11] His widely used classic textbook, *Christian Counseling: A Comprehensive Guide,* was first published in 1980 and recently expanded, updated, and completely revised in 1988.[12] There is also a Christian Counselor's Library (revised edition) that contains forty audio cassettes, a counselor's manual, counselee worksheets, and a copy of the 1988 revised edition of the textbook, available from the Educational Products Division of Word, Inc. (5221 N. O'Connor Blvd., Suite 1000, Irving, TX 75039). The library or textbook can be used in an extensive program of lay Christian counselor training. Part of the first edition of the library, including the 1980 textbook, was used in a one-year, part-time training course for lay or paraprofessional Christian counselors at the Institute of Christian Counseling which I set up and directed at Ontario Bible College in Toronto in September 1984.[13]

Dr. Lawrence Crabb has written a number of helpful books which can be used in a lay counselor training program.[14] He has also authored a Training Manual that is available only through the Institute of Biblical Counseling and its seminars or workshops on biblical counseling.

Dr. Jay Adams has authored several books on nouthetic counseling which can be used in a training program for lay nouthetic counselors.[15] He has also put together a "Competent to Counsel" Training Kit that is available from the National Association of Evangelicals, 450 Gunderson Drive, Wheaton, IL 60187.

Dr. Gary Sweeten's materials for training lay counselors as well as the whole congregation in a local church context have already been mentioned earlier, and should be noted. Similarly, the Stephen Series developed by Dr. Kenneth Haugk has already been described. His book *Christian Caregiving: A Way of Life*[16] is a helpful guide for training lay caregivers and is used as a text in the Stephen Series.

Dr. William Backus has developed a Christian, biblical approach to cognitive therapy called Misbelief Therapy and has written a useful textbook, *Telling the Truth to Troubled People*, for training lay counselors in Misbelief Therapy.[17]

Dr. Charles Solomon originated "Spirituotherapy" and has written a couple of books relevant to the training of lay counselors, especially those interested in using his "Spirituotherapy" approach to helping people.[18] This approach is based on the "victorious life" or exchanged-life theology, focusing on

"How Can I Help? - Training in Friendship Counseling"

the need for a person to appropriate his or her identification with Christ.

William H. ("Skip") Hunt has more recently written a number of training courses for lay Christian counselors, including a relatively well-known one entitled "How Can I Help?" This college-level course in personal counseling and evangelism is used to train the ordinary layperson to help friends in crisis. It is also used by Christian crisis centers across the United States to train staff and volunteers. Hunt is president of Christian Helplines, Inc., a national association of Christian telephone counseling ministries, and can be contacted at P.O. Box 10855, Tampa, FL 33679, telephone (813) 874-5509.

A number of other significant training programs or materials available for lay Christian counselor training were mentioned in chapter 4.[19] Certain secular books on helping or counseling skills have also been used in lay Christian counselor training programs. They include Lawrence Brammer's *The Helping Relationship*, Robert Carkhuff's *The Art of Helping*, Gerard Egan's *The Skilled Helper*, and William Cormier and Sherilyn Cormier's *Interviewing Strategies for Helpers*.[20]

Also available are some specialized training programs for lay counselors interested in helping ministries with particular populations or groups of people. For example, Dr. Paul Welter has developed a specific program for training retirement center and nursing home staff and residents in lay helping and counseling skills. The Board of National Ministries of the American Baptist Churches funded and helped organize this lay counseling program in seven of their retirement centers/nursing homes over a seven-year period, with basically positive evaluations or results.[21] Dr. Welter's training program for lay counselors in long-term care settings includes the use of several helpful books he has written.[22]

Emily Osborn has developed a fifteen-week training program for lay or paraprofessional family counselors who specialize in helping families with problems or difficulties.[23] Her program was initially conducted at St. Matthew's Episcopal Church in Bellaire, Texas. Several other churches have also begun training their lay counselors in family counseling. For example, at La Canada Presbyterian Church, Rev. Chuck Osburn has included a special training program on family counseling for their lay counselors, using mainly books by Minuchin, Satir, an son.[24]

It is also important to include training in prevention and outreach services in any lay counselor training program, as Dr. Prater has strongly recommended.[25]

The rest of this chapter will focus on the details of a basic twelve-session training program as well as a one-year expanded and more intensive version of it which I have developed for lay Christian counselors.

A Basic Twelve-Session Lay Christian Counselor Training Program

The basic twelve-session training program I have developed was originally used in 1981 to train lay Christian counselors at North Park Community Chapel, a local church with about one thousand people in London, Ontario.[26] The training program met biweekly and therefore lasted six months. Each training session was about three hours in duration. The program can be shortened to three months by conducting weekly sessions of three hours each instead of biweekly sessions.

The model of Christian counseling used in the training program is a biblically based, largely cognitive-behavioral model I described in chapter 3. The major textbook I have chosen is Dr. Gary Collins' *Christian Counseling: A Comprehensive Guide* (Word, 1988), first published in 1980, but now available in a revised and updated 1988 edition. Other highly recommended or required readings include Jay Adams' *The Christian Counselor's Manual* (Baker, 1973), William Backus and Marie Chapian's *Telling Yourself the Truth* (Bethany House, 1980), Gary Collins' *How to Be A People Helper* (Vision House, 1976), and Lawrence Crabb's *Effective Biblical Counseling* (Zondervan, 1977). I would also highly recommend Everett Worthington's *When Someone Asks for Help: A Practical Guide for Counseling* (InterVarsity Press, 1982) or Carol Baldwin's *Friendship Counseling: Biblical Foundations for Helping Others* (Zondervan, 1988) as basic texts for teaching basic counseling or helping skills to lay Christian counselors. William Backus' *Telling the Truth to Troubled People* (Bethany House, 1985) is also a very helpful text for training lay counselors from a Christian cognitive-behavioral perspective. It includes an important section on the signs and symptoms of the major psychiatric disorders, which may be particularly helpful for teaching lay counselors appropriate referral of counselees to professional counselors.

The training sessions should include didactic teaching or lectures, demonstrations of specific counseling skills and techniques (through role-plays with the instructor as the counselor), discussion of issues, and role-playing in smaller groups (of three or five) with feedback and discussion, and sufficient opportunity for each trainee or lay counselor to role-play the counselor as well as the counselee.

The following topics were covered in the original training program, and are suggested as helpful and basic ones to cover in an initial training program:

Session 1: An Integrated, Biblically Based Model for Effective Christian Counseling (see chapters 3 and 4 of this book).

Session 2: Basic Interviewing Skills (e.g., building rapport, listening attentively, watching carefully, handling silence, questioning wisely, responding appropriately, using spiritual resources); Overview of the Counseling Process (exploration, understanding, action phases, and termination).

Session 3: Some Useful Counseling Methods (e.g., homework assignments, relaxation and coping techniques, imagery exercises, including stress-inoculation training, thought-stopping and cognitive restructuring, problem-solving, providing information on diet, exercise, and rest, making referrals, bibliotherapy, role-playing strategies and assertiveness or social skills training, meditation, prayer, and inner healing).

These first three sessions cover basic counseling skills and methods within a biblical framework, and such skills and methods are then applied in later sessions to specific problem areas. Required reading for these foundational sessions should include Worthington (1982) or Baldwin (1988), Crabb (1977), Backus (1985), and David Seamands' *Healing of Memories* (Wheaton, Ill.: Victor, 1985). Cormier and Cormier (1985) should be consulted by the trainer for helpful descriptions of several useful counseling methods, especially cognitive-behavioral interventions. Another helpful book for the trainer to consult is *Teaching Psychological Skills: Models for Giving Psychology Away* (Brooks/Cole, 1984), edited by Dale Larson.

In the remaining sessions, assign as required reading the following topics and chapters from Collins' textbook:

Session 4: Personal Growth of the Counselor and Prevention of Burnout (for sessions 1–4: Collins, 1980, chaps. 1–4; or Collins, 1988, chaps. 1–5).

Session 5: Depression (Collins, 1980, chap. 7; or Collins, 1988, chap. 8).

Session 6: Anger (Collins, 1980, chap. 8; or Collins, 1988, chap. 9).

Session 7: Anxiety (Collins, 1980, chap. 5; or Collins, 1988, chap. 6).

Session 8: Sexuality (Collins, 1980, chaps. 20–22; or Collins, 1988, chaps. 17–19).

Session 9: Marital and Family Problems (Collins, 1980, chaps. 13–15; or Collins, 1988, chaps. 11, 27–30).

Session 10: Spiritual Problems (Collins, chap. 29; or Collins, 1988, chap. 36).

Session 11: Referrals and Psychiatric Intervention.

Session 12: Using Your Counseling Skills; Setting Up a Counseling Service in a Local Church.

A One-Year, Part-Time Expanded Training Program for Lay Christian Counselors

I have expanded the basic twelve-session training program into a more intensive and comprehensive one-year, part-time training program for lay Christian counselors. This program was first taught at the Institute of Christian Counseling of Ontario Bible College in Toronto, with college credit given for three semesters of study and training totaling 108 hours.[27]

The format of the training sessions or classes is similar to that of the basic training program, with weekly meetings, each of three hours' duration. The training program includes didactic teaching or lectures, listening to selected cassette tapes taken from *The Christian Counselor's Library* edited by Dr. Gary Collins, discussion of issues, and demonstrations of counseling skills or methods through role-playing with the instructor as counselor. A significant portion of time should, however, be spent in practical counseling skills training, including role-playing and discussion with feedback in small groups of three to five trainees, using cases provided or those taken from the counseling ministries of the lay counselors or trainees. Audiotapes or videotapes of counseling situations should be used as often as possible. Trainees must, of course, obtain permission from their counselees before presenting and discussing them and their problem situations.

The expanded training program consists of three major parts, but I have revised the original curriculum to reflect the use of more recently published books, as well as to follow Collins' revised 1988 edition of the textbook chosen, *Christian Counseling: A Comprehensive Guide*. The revised curriculum is as follows:

> *Part I: Introductory and Personal Issues*
> (Total time: 12 weeks or 36 hours)

> *Topics:* A Biblical Model for Effective Counseling; Lay Counseling in the Local Church; Critical Issues in Christian Counseling (including ethical and legal issues and the need for referral); Basic Counseling Skills and Overview of the Counseling Process; Some Useful counseling Methods; Inner Healing; Personal Growth of the Counselor; Anxiety; Loneliness; Depression; Anger; and Guilt.

> *Required Reading:* Collins, 1988, chapters 1–10; Worthington, 1982, or Baldwin, 1988.

> *Recommended Reading:* Jay Adams, *Ready to Restore: The Layman's Guide to Christian Counseling* (Baker, 1981); *The Christian Counselor's Manual* (Baker, 1973); and *A Theology of Christian Counseling: More Than Redemption* (Zondervan, 1979); Samuel Southard, *Theology and Therapy: The Wisdom of God in a Context of Friendship* (Word, 1989); Ray Anderson, *Christians Who Counsel: The Vocation of Wholistic Therapy* (Zondervan, 1990); William Backus and Marie Chapian, *Telling Yourself the Truth* (Bethany House, 1980); William Backus, *Telling the Truth to Troubled People* (Bethany House, 1985); Lawrence Crabb, *Effective Biblical Counseling* (Zondervan, 1977);

Understanding People (Zondervan, 1987),
(NavPress, 1988); and David Seamands, .
Memories (Victor Books, 1985).

Part II: Singleness, Marriage, and Developmental
Family Issues
(Total time: 12 weeks or 36 hours)

Topics: Singleness, Choosing a Marriage Partner, Premarital
Counseling, Marital Problems, Pregnancy Issues,
Family Problems, Divorce and Remarriage, Child-
Rearing and Parental Guidance, Adolescence, Young
Adulthood, Middle Age, and the Later Years.

Required Collins, 1988, chapters 24–30 and 11–15; Norman
Reading: Wright, *Marital Counseling: A Biblical Behavioral,*
Cognitive Approach (Harper & Row, 1981), or Ever-
ett Worthington, *Marriage Counseling: A Christian*
Approach to Counseling Couples (InterVarsity Press,
1989); or Deloss and Ruby Friesen, *Counseling and*
Marriage (Word, 1989); and G. A. Rekers, *Counseling*
Families (Word, 1988).

Recommended Lawrence Crabb, *The Marriage Builder: A Blueprint*
Reading: *for Couples and Counselors* (Zondervan, 1982);
Keith Olson, *Counseling Teenagers: The Complete*
Christian Guide to Understanding and Helping
Adolescents (Group Books, 1984); and Norman
Wright, *Premarital Counseling: A Guidebook for the*
Counselor (Moody Press, 1981).

Part III: Sex and Interpersonal Issues and Other Issues
(Total time: 12 weeks or 36 hours)

Topics: Interpersonal Relationships, Sex Apart from Marriage, Sex Within Marriage, Homosexuality, Violence
and Abuse, Inferiority and Self-Esteem, Physical
Illness, Grief, Mental Disorders, Alcoholism, Addic-
tions, Financial Counseling, Vocational Counseling,
Spiritual Issues, Other Problems, Counseling the
Counselor.

Required Collins, 1988, chapters 16–23, 31–38; and William
Reading: Backus, *Telling the Truth to Troubled People.*

Recommended William Backus and Marie Chapian, *Why Do I Do*
Reading: *What I Don't Want to Do?* (Bethany House Pub-
lishers, 1984); Ed and Gaye Wheat, *Intended for*
Pleasure: Sex Technique and Sexual Fulfillment in
Christian Marriage, rev. ed. (Revell, 1981); Clifford

> and Joyce Penner, *The Gift of Sex: A Christian Guide to Sexual Fulfillment* (Word, 1981); and John White, *Eros Defiled: The Christian and Sexual Sin* (InterVarsity Press, 1977).

The one-year, part-time expanded training program or course for lay or paraprofessional Christian counselors just described can be completed in thirty-six weeks or less than a year if the three parts of the program are conducted sequentially, without a break in between parts. A lay counselor or trainee going through such a program will receive 108 hours of instruction and training on a comprehensive list of topics and problem areas covered in Collins' textbook, and hence will be more adequately prepared for a lay counseling ministry of helping others with problems in living. However, further training and ongoing supervision will still be needed by the trained lay counselor. The next chapter deals with the important topic of supervision of lay counselors.

Concluding Comments

In this chapter I have described several models of lay Christian counselor training, as well as examples of specific training programs. The choice of which model(s) or specific training program(s) to use will depend on at least the following factors: (1) the theoretical counseling preference and theological persuasion of the leader or trainer and the church or parachurch or missionary organization involved; (2) the model of lay counseling ministry chosen (i.e., whether it will be an "informal, spontaneous," or "informal, organized," or "formal, organized" model, or some combination of these models); and (3) the specific focus or clientele of the lay counseling ministry (e.g., focusing on individual counseling, or marital and family counseling, or group counseling, or a combination of these; focusing on helping adolescents, adults, or the elderly, etc.).

It is obvious, however, that several good, biblically based training models and programs for lay Christian counselors are now available and can be used with benefit to train lay Christian counselors for a helping ministry. Many local churches have actually developed their own versions of lay counselor training programs, incorporating the best components from several of the models and programs described in this chapter, and adding other material where necessary. However, no matter what specific training program is chosen, it should incorporate the five essential components of a biblically based training program for lay counselors suggested by Dr. Collins at the beginning of this chapter.

Further research is also needed to determine what components of a training program are particularly helpful or effective, as well as which specific training model and program is relatively more helpful or effective, or whether most training programs are comparable in effectiveness. The few research or evaluation studies that have been done so far and that were reviewed in chapter 4 have generally yielded favorable results supporting the effectiveness of some of the training programs I have described, including the basic twelve-session program I developed.[28] More evaluation studies are obviously needed.

NOTES

[1]See A. Hattie, C. F. Sharpley, and H. J. Rogers, "Comparative Effectiveness of Professional and Paraprofessional Helpers," *Psychological Bulletin* 95 (1984): 534–41, who concluded that paraprofessionals or lay counselors show greater therapeutic effectiveness the longer their training or the more experienced they are. However, see also Berman and Norton, "Does Professional Training Make a Therapist More Effective?" *Psychological Bulletin* 98 (1985): 401–7, who found that extensive preparation (training) or prior experience with the counseling task, or frequent supervision by a professional were factors that could not account for the lack of difference in therapeutic effectiveness between professionals and paraprofessionals or lay counselors. Further clarification of the role of training and supervision, as well as experience, on the therapeutic effectiveness of lay counselors is therefore needed. See also A. M. Graziano and J. N. Katz, "Training Paraprofessionals," in A. S. Bellack, M. Hersen, and A. E. Kazdin, eds., *International Handbook of Behavior Modification and Therapy* (New York: Plenum, 1982), 207–29.

[2]Series on "Training to Competence in Psychotherapy," *Journal of Consulting and Clinical Psychology* 56 (1988): 651–709.

[3]See B. F. Shaw and K. S. Dobson, "Competency Judgments in the Training and Evaluation of Psychotherapists," *Journal of Consulting and Clinical Psychology* 56 (1988): 666–72, p. 669.

[4]G. R. Collins, "Lay Counseling Within the Local Church," *Leadership* 1 (1980): 78–86.

[5]See S. Y. Tan, "Lay Christian Counseling: Present Status and Future Directions," invited paper presented at the International Congress on

Christian Counseling, Lay Counseling Track, November 1988, in Atlanta, Georgia.

6See L. J. Crabb, Jr., "Biblical Counseling" in G. R. Collins, *Helping People Grow* (Santa Ana, Calif.: Vision House, 1980), 165–85; and L. J. Crabb, Jr., *Effective Biblical Counseling* (Grand Rapids: Zondervan, 1977).

7L. J. Crabb, Jr., and D. Allender, *Encouragement: The Key to Caring* (Grand Rapids: Zondervan, 1984).

8G. R. Sweeten, "Lay Helpers and the Caring Community," *Journal of Psychology and Christianity* 6, no. 2 (1987): 14–20. Dr. Sweeten's training materials can be obtained or purchased by contacting Equipping Ministries International, 4015 Executive Park Drive, Suite 309, Cincinnati, OH 45241 (Tel. 513-769-5353). They are being used in forty states and twenty-five countries.

9Lukens, "Training of Paraprofessional Christian Counselors: A Model Proposed," *Journal of Psychology and Christianity* 2, no. 3 (1983): 61–66. He proposed this model after conducting a survey of Christian counseling and training programs, and finding that only eight out of seventy-seven programs provided training at the lay or paraprofessional level, with the length of training clustering between five months and two years. Few areas of consistency were found with regard to the nature and goals of training, the selection of lay counselors, the skills and knowledge taught, the length of training, the qualifications of the supervisors, the nature or type of supervision, and the criteria used for evaluating quality of training. See Lukens, "Training Paraprofessional Christian Counselors: A Survey Conducted," *Journal of Psychology and Christianity* 2, no. 1 (1983): 51–61.

10William H. Cormier and L. Sherilyn Cormier, *Interviewing Strategies for Helpers: A Guide to Assessment, Treatment, and Evaluation* (Monterey, Calif.: Brooks/Cole, 1979), and *Interviewing Strategies for Helpers: Fundamental Skills and Cognitive Behavioral Interventions* (Monterey, Calif.: Brooks/Cole, 1985).

11G. R. Collins, *How to Be A People Helper* and *People Helper Growthbook* (Santa Ana, Calif.: Vision House, 1976).

12G. R. Collins, *Christian Counseling: A Comprehensive Guide*, rev. ed. (Dallas: Word, 1988).

13S. Y. Tan, "Training Paraprofessional Christian Counselors," *The Journal of Pastoral Care* 40, no. 4 (1986): 296–304.

14See L. J. Crabb, Jr., *Basic Principles of Biblical Counseling* (Grand Rapids: Zondervan, 1975), and *Effective Biblical Counseling* (Grand Rapids: Zondervan, 1977). See also L. J. Crabb, Jr., and D. B. Allender, *Encouragement: The Key to Caring* (Grand Rapids: Zondervan, 1984); Crabb, *Understanding People: Deep Longings for Relationship* (Grand

Rapids: Zondervan, 1987), and *Inside Out* (Colorado NavPress, 1988).

[15]See J. E. Adams, *Competent to Counsel* (Grand Rapids ᴗaker, 1970), and *The Christian Counselor's Manual* (Grand Rapids: Baker, 1973).

[16]See e.g., D. Detwiler-Zapp and W. C. Dixon, *Lay Caregiving* (Philadelphia: Fortress, 1982); R. E. Grantham, *Lay Shepherding: A Guide for Visiting the Sick, the Aged, the Troubled, and the Bereaved* (Valley Forge, Pa.: Judson, 1980); K. C. Haugk, *Christian Caregiving— A Way of Life* (Minneapolis: Augsburg, 1984); S. J. Menking, *Helping Laity Help Others* (Philadelphia: Westminster, 1984); A. Schmitt and D. Schmitt, *When a Congregation Cares* (Scottdale, Pa.: Herald, 1984); S. Southard, *Comprehensive Pastoral Care* (Valley Forge, Pa.: Judson, 1975); S. Southard, *Training Church Members for Pastoral Care* (Valley Forge, Pa.: Judson, 1982); R. P. Stevens, *Liberating the Laity* (Downers Grove, Ill.: InterVarsity Press, 1985); H. W. Stone, *The Caring Church* (San Francisco: Harper & Row, 1983). See also K. C. Haugk and W. J. McKay, *Christian Caregiving—A Way of Life*, Leaders Guide (Minneapolis: Augsburg, 1986).

[17]See W. Backus, *Telling the Truth to Troubled People* (Minneapolis: Bethany House, 1985); also see W. Backus and M. Chapian, *Telling Yourself the Truth* (Minneapolis: Bethany House, 1980); W. Backus and M. Chapian, *Why Do I Do What I Don't Want to Do?* (Minneapolis: Bethany House, 1984); W. Backus, *Telling Each Other the Truth* (Minneapolis: Bethany House, 1985); and W. Backus, "A Counseling Center Staffed by Trained Christian Lay Persons," *Journal of Psychology and Christianity* 6, no. 2 (1987): 39–44.

[18]See C. R. Solomon, *Handbook to Happiness* (Wheaton: Tyndale, 1975), and *Counseling With the Mind of Christ* (Old Tappan, N.J.: Revell, 1977).

[19]See chap. 4, n. 46. It should also be noted that another recently developed lay Christian counselor training program, using videocassettes with accompanying leader's guide and learner's manual and textbooks, is available from Innovations in Learning, 7018 El Paseo St., Long Beach, CA 90815. It features four courses (Introduction, Relationship, Realization, and Responsibility), each involving eight weekly sessions, with homework. The videocassettes feature people such as Dr. Joyce Hulgus, H. Norman Wright, the Rev. Rex E. Johnson, and Richard J. Mohline.

[20]L. M. Brammer, *The Helping Relationship* (Englewood Cliffs, N.J.: Prentice-Hall, 1973); R. Carkhuff, *The Art of Helping* (Amherst, Mass.: Human Resources Development Press, 1972). G. Egan, *The Skilled Helper* (Monterey, Calif.: Brooks/Cole, 1986); Cormier and Cormier, *Interviewing Strategies for Helpers*.

21Welter, "Training Retirement Center and Nursing Home Staff and Residents in Helping and Counseling Skills," *Journal of Psychology and Christianity* 6, no. 2 (1987): 45–56.

22See P. Welter, *How to Help a Friend* (Wheaton, Ill.: Tyndale, 1978); *Connecting With a Friend* (Wheaton, Ill.: Tyndale, 1985); *The Nursing Home: A Caring Community, A Guide for Staff and Residents* (Valley Forge, Pa.: Judson, 1981); and *The Nursing Home: A Caring Community, Trainer's Manual* (Valley Forge, Pa.: Judson, 1981).

23E. Osborn, "Training Paraprofessional Family Therapists in a Christian Setting" *Journal of Psychology and Christianity* 2, no. 2 (1983): 56–61.

24See S. Minuchin, *Families and Family Therapy* (Cambridge, Mass.: Harvard University Press, 1974); V. Satir and M. Baldwin, *Satir Step by Step* (Palo Alto, Calif.: Science and Behavior Books, 1983); G. R. Patterson, *Families* (Champaign, Ill.: Research Press, 1977); V. D. Foley, "Family Therapy," in R. Corsini, ed. *Current Psychotherapies* (F. E. Peacock, 1979). See also H. A. Liddle, R. Schwartz, and D. Breunlin, eds., *Family Therapy Training* (New York: Guilford, 1985). For recent books on marital and family counseling written from a Christian perspective, see G. A. Rekers, *Counseling Families* (Dallas: Word, 1988); and J. C. Wynn, *The Family Therapist: What Pastors and Counselors Are Learning From Family Therapists* (Old Tappan, N.J.: Revell, 1987).

25Prater, "Training Christian Lay Counselors in Techniques of Prevention and Outreach," *Journal of Psychology and Christianity* 6, no. 2 (1987): 30–34.

26See S. Y. Tan, "Training Lay Christian Counselors: A Basic Program and Some Preliminary Data," *Journal of Psychology and Christianity* 6, no. 2 (1987): 57–61.

27See S. Y. Tan, "Training Paraprofessional Christian Counselors," *The Journal of Pastoral Care* 40, no. 4 (1986): 296–304.

28See chap. 4, nn. 51–52.

8

Supervision of Lay Counselors

Lay counselors who have completed a basic training program in lay Christian counseling and begun their lay counseling ministry (after being appropriately screened and selected) still need ongoing supervision as well as further training. The literature on supervision of lay *Christian* counseling is sparse and limited compared to that on training. In this chapter I will review the larger secular literature on clinical supervision of counselors or therapists (whether professional or nonprofessional) as well as the much smaller literature on supervision of Christian counselors, especially lay Christian counselors. From my review of the relevant literature I will glean practical guidelines for effective supervision of lay Christian counselors, and I will provide a hypothetical verbatim example of how to apply some of the guidelines in a supervision session.

Definition of Supervision

First, the term *supervision* needs to be defined more carefully. When used in the context of counseling or therapy, we are really referring to clinical supervision or supervision of clinical work like counseling or therapy. A widely accepted definition of *clinical supervision* is the following one proposed by Loganbill, Hardy, and Delworth: "an intensive, interpersonally focused, one-to-one relationship in which one person is designated to facilitate the development of therapeutic competence in the other person."[1] The clinical supervisor, or supervisor for short, is therefore the person responsible for overseeing and guiding the counselor in such a way as to further develop the counselor's skills, competence, and effectiveness.

The definition of clinical supervision just provided refers to the traditional one-on-one supervision relationship between a more experienced or trained supervisor and a less experienced or trained supervisee or trainee. Clinical supervision can also be conducted in other formats like the following: dyadic (one supervisor with two supervisees), group (one supervisor with a group of three or more supervisees), and peer (a group of two or more supervisees or peers providing supervision to one another). Because of limited time and supervisory resources, most lay Christian counseling centers provide supervision in dyadic, group, or peer formats, supplemented when necessary by one-on-one supervision.

Responsible, ongoing, regular supervision of lay Christian counselors is essential not only for ethical and legal reasons, but also because there is some evidence from a national survey reported by Wiley that counselors improved most when they received regular, face-to-face supervision. *Mere counseling experience did not help counselors improve their ability or competence.*[2] Professional circles typically expect regular supervision at least once a week, usually for an hour with a particular supervisor. A professional trainee in such a context of practicum training may see several counselees each week. Predoctoral interns in doctoral (Ph.D. or Psy.D.) programs in professional psychology (e.g., clinical or counseling psychology) doing their final year of full-time clinical internship training will often be involved in sixteen or more hours a week of clinical work and will therefore usually receive a few hours (e.g., up to five) of clinical supervision a week from different supervisors, in individual or group supervision formats.[3]

Lay Christian counselors do not usually see more than a few counselees a week. Regular supervision for them should therefore involve once-a-week supervision for an hour, whether in individual or group supervision formats. An alternative is to have supervision sessions conducted biweekly or once every two weeks but for up to 2 hours each time, with individual supervision provided on an "as needed" basis.

Supervision should not only be regular, but it should also be effective and helpful to the lay counselors. Good supervision should involve a balance between *skills training* (in terms of the supervisor teaching or modeling more refined and effective counseling skills and methods) and some focus on or discussion of *process issues or dynamics* (i.e., what is going on internally in the counselor as well as what is going on interpersonally between the counselor and the counselee). However, supervision sessions should *not* turn into therapy or counseling sessions for the supervisee (or lay counselor).

A number of helpful books and journals on clinical supervision of counselors or therapists are now available, and they can be consulted for the supervision of lay counselors as well. They include books by Ekstein and Wallerstein, Hart, Hess, Kaslow, Robbins, Stoltenberg and Delworth, and Estadt, Compton, and Blanchette.[4] Important publications on clinical supervision in the secular journals include two special issues of *The Counseling Psychologist* (in 1982 and 1983), and a special series on advances in psychotherapy supervision in *Professional Psychology: Research and Practice* (1987).[5] The special series on training to competence in psychotherapy published in the *Journal of Consulting and Clinical Psychology* (1988) referred to in the previous chapter on training of lay counselors, is also relevant to clinical supervision,[6] as is a significant review chapter on counselor training and supervision by Russell, Crimmings, and Lent in the *Handbook of Counseling Psychology* edited by S. D. Brown and R. W. Lent.[7] Finally, it should be noted that while the literature on supervision of *lay Christian counseling per se* is sparse, a helpful, key article by Worthington has recently been published.[8]

Practice Models of Supervision

How is supervision practiced or conducted in real life? In his article, Worthington has briefly described four main practice models of supervision as follows:

1. The Minimum Intervention Model

In this model of supervision, brief training is provided to lay counselors without any direct supervision of actual counseling done by lay counselors.

2. *The Vertical Supervision Model*

In this model, which is advocated by Jay Adams for the training and supervision of nouthetic counselors, there are usually four levels of trainees (supervisees) or lay counselors. The first level of trainees are those who attend classes and receive didactic teaching. The second level of trainees are those who observe more experienced counselors doing actual counseling, and then participate in case discussions. The third level of trainees are those who are involved in doing actual counseling but as junior counselors on a team, and therefore they function as junior co-counselors following the lead of more experienced or senior co-counselors on a team. The fourth level of trainees are those who are sufficiently experienced and trained to function as senior counselors or senior co-counselors, for other less experienced or more junior members of a team to observe or co-counsel with. Each team is supervised by a senior staff person.

3. *The Professional Training Model*

In this model, which is patterned after the one often used in professional training programs and graduate schools, the trainee or lay counselor attends classes and receives didactic instruction, sees counselees in role-play situations or in real life, and often audiotapes or even videotapes the counseling sessions. Such counseling sessions are either observed by a supervising professional directly, or else the trainee or lay counselor and supervisor will listen to audiotapes or view videotapes of the role-play or real-life counseling sessions.

4. *The Implicit Trust Model*

In this model the supervisor never directly observes the lay counselor. Rather, the lay counselor verbally reports the counseling session to the supervisor. Unfortunately, such verbal self-reports can be unreliable and possibly misleading, even if unintentionally so.

Which practice model of supervision is used with lay counselors depends on the model for a lay counseling ministry already chosen. If an *informal, spontaneous* model of lay caring and counseling is being practiced, then usually the *minimal intervention model of supervision* (i.e., essentially with no direct supervision) will be predominant, with occasional use of the *implicit trust mode of supervision* (i.e., with some supervision based only on verbal reports provided by the lay counselor).

If an *informal, organized* model of lay caring and counseling is being practiced, then regular, ongoing supervision of the lay counselors will be provided. However, the actual practice model(s) of supervision used in this context may vary from church to church. A common model of supervision used is still the *implicit trust model* based only on verbal reports of the lay counselors. The *vertical supervision model,* or a variation of it, is also sometimes used in the context of co-counseling. An example of this is when an experienced pastor visits a parishioner together with a lay counselor (or a Stephen's minister), with the pastor and the lay counselor providing pastoral care and counseling (i.e., co-counseling) to the parishioner. The experienced pastor will therefore have an opportunity to observe the lay counselor in action in such a co-counseling context, and then provide feedback and discussion later on in a supervision session with the lay counselor. The *professional training model of supervision,* involving the audiotaping or videotaping of an actual lay counseling session (or direct observation of such a session through a one-way mirror), is usually not appropriate for an *informal, organized* model of lay caring and counseling because most of the lay counseling takes place in informal settings like homes, hospitals, and restaurants, where taping is not convenient or appropriate. However, I recommend that supervision include *some observation* of the lay counselor in action, even in the *informal, organized* model of lay caring and counseling, and co-counseling is a good way of doing this.

If a *formal, organized* model of lay counseling is adopted and a lay counseling center is set up, then it is more common to see the *professional training model of supervision* being used, as well as the *vertical supervision model* or variations of it (but with co-counseling as its main characteristic). However, there are formal and organized lay counseling centers in local churches which unfortunately still use only the *implicit trust model of supervision* and only occasionally co-counseling or the *vertical supervision* model. It is my recommendation that if the *formal, organized* model of lay counseling is being practiced, then both the *professional training model of supervision* and *the vertical supervision model* be used in the supervision of lay counselors, and not only the *implicit trust model* of supervision.

Conceptual Models of Supervision: Theoretical or Developmental

Worthington, in his article, also points out that clinical supervision can be conceptualized in two major ways: theoretical or developmental. The *theoretical model* of conceptualizing supervision is based on the counseling theory or therapeutic orientation of the supervisor. In other words, the supervisor in this model has a clear counseling theory or orientation that he or she practices within and conducts the supervision according to his or her counseling theory or therapeutic orientation. For example, if the supervisor is a cognitive therapist who believes that dysfunctional and irrational thinking underlies many emotional and psychological problems (e.g., anxiety and some types of depression), he or she will pay particular attention to such thinking in both the supervisee and the counselees and will examine how to restructure or change such thinking. Such a supervisor will also focus more on skills training and helping the supervisee learn specific cognitive therapy techniques (following cognitive or cognitive-behavior therapists like Aaron Beck, Albert Ellis, and Donald Meichenbaum) and will do less on process issues or dynamics involving the feelings of the supervisee and the reciprocal feelings of the supervisee and the counselee in the context of the counseling relationship.

On the other hand, if the supervisor is a psychodynamic or psychoanalytically oriented therapist who believes that unconscious processes and conflicts, often originating from early childhood experiences, are the root causes of many emotional and psychological problems, then he or she will pay more attention to issues like transference (when the counselee unconsciously transfers his or her feelings and attitudes connected to a significant other or parental figure in the past onto the counselor) and countertransference (when the counselor unconsciously transfers his or her feelings and attitudes connected to a significant other or parental figure in the past onto the counselee), which are more process or psychodynamic issues. Such a supervisor will also focus more on teaching therapeutic skills like intensive listening, interpretation of unconscious conflicts and defenses, and dream analysis, consistent with the psychodynamic or the psychoanalytically oriented approach to therapy which has its roots in Sigmund Freud.

The *developmental model* of conceptualizing supervision cuts across theoretical orientations of supervisors and is based more on the developmental level and needs of the supervisee. Such a model assumes that the supervisee (or lay counselor) goes through a predictable series of stages of counselor development in the process of supervision, regardless of the counseling theory or therapeutic orientation of the supervisor.

There are many versions or views regarding the actual stages of counselor development. Worthington has pointed out, however, that some of the most well-known ones are based on the foundational work of Hogan, who in 1964 proposed four stages of counselor development.[9] Worthington describes Hogan's stages as follows: "The beginning counselor is thought to be insecure and uninsightful; second stage counselors struggle with dependency-autonomy issues; third stage counselors with self-confidence and motivation; fourth stage counselors with personal autonomy and self-assurance."[10] This model has been expanded by Stoltenberg[11] and Loganbill, Hardy, and Delworth,[12] and most recently refined and updated in a textbook on a developmental approach to supervision by Stoltenberg and Delworth.[13] For stage one counselors, useful supervisory methods include the use of teaching interpretation, support and awareness training, as the trainees seek to imitate the supervisor's style and skills. For stage two counselors who struggle with being overconfident and overwhelmed, helpful supervisory methods include further support and exemplification, as well as ambivalence-clarification. For stage three counselors, supervision now includes sharing and exemplification, with professional and personal confrontation in a more collegial way. Finally, stage four counselors are actually considered to be master therapists or counselors, and supervision at this stage is very collegial.

Research findings have tended to support these theories of counselor development,[14] although alternative explanations (e.g., those used in learning theory) for such findings have been proposed by Holloway, who is more critical of the underlying assumptions and principles of developmental models of supervision.[15]

Worthington has noted that the level of development of most lay counselors is at the early stage of counseling in which the counselor's self-preoccupation is a predominant characteristic. He described this level or stage as follows: "The counselor learns active listening skills and seeks to follow the content and emotion of the client. Because the counselor has doubts about his or her counseling ability, the self-awareness of the counselor intrudes on many of the advanced conceptualization and intervention skills of the counselor. The primary tasks of the paraprofessional counselor, then, would be to learn to apply basic counseling skills without being inhibited by excessive self-focus. Rudimentary conceptualization and intervention skills are used but are rarely the primary focus of the beginning or paraprofessional level counselor."[16] He also expressed the need for supervisors to develop ways of helping lay counselors manage their anxiety, since increased supervision of lay counselors may lead them to become more self-conscious about their performance in lay counseling. For lay counselors who continue doing the ministry of lay counseling for several years, however, the later stages of counselor development and counseling will be more relevant, and they should be addressed in the supervision of more experienced or advanced lay counselors.

Good supervision will, therefore, involve the use of *both theoretical and developmental* models of supervision by the supervisor, but with some flexibility and openness in the use of theoretical models (therapeutic orientations or counseling theories) so that rigidity or formula-driven counseling is kept to a minimum. However, the need to teach *specific* counseling skills or competencies to trainees or supervisees has been recently emphasized in the field of professional training and supervision in psychotherapy, where the use of competency-based models of training and supervision has been advocated.[17] More specific criteria and rating scales are required in such models for determining or assessing the level of competency or skillfulness of the therapist or trainee in terms of his or her interventions.[18] The use of specific treatment manuals for training and supervision in particular types of psychotherapy or counseling is also advocated, for example, cognitive therapy,[19] interpersonal therapy,[20] psychodynamic therapy,[21] experiential therapy,[22] and behavior therapy.[23] The text on therapy supervision edited by

Hess also contains helpful chapters on supervision from different theoretical perspectives.[24]

In the context of *lay Christian counseling*, a number of helpful manual-like books for training in specific counseling skills and methods are now available, for example, cognitive-behaviorally oriented books by authors like Backus, Worthington, and Wright, and books on basic listening and caring skills by authors like Baldwin and Walters.[25] If such approaches to lay Christian counseling are used in the training of lay counselors, then their supervision should continue to focus on the refinement of the skills covered in these books.

The *development model* of supervision should, however, also be applied in the supervision of lay Christian counselors. It is helpful to know the stages of counselor development that most counselors go through in their training and supervision, with particular needs and issues which are important to address at different stages or levels of counselor development. The text by Stoltenberg and Delworth is a helpful one to consult for this purpose. They cover not only the stages of counselor development for the *supervisee* (level one: the beginning of the journey, level two: trial and tribulation, and level three: challenge and growth), but also apply the developmental approach to *supervisors* and their development in supervisory skills.[26]

Guest and Beutler have recently suggested in the professional training literature that supervisors should adjust the way they conduct supervision according to the changing needs of trainees over time. The first therapy or counseling training experience should focus on nonspecific technical skills, with the supervisor being supportive and highly credible. The next step in the professional training experience should address the conceptual difference of various theoretical models for understanding psychological and emotional disorders and change, as trainees grow in confidence in their skills of communication. Specific technical skills may be taught at this stage, with the supervisor functioning more in the role of teacher and authority. The third level of professional training is probably at the predoctoral intern level, and supervision may focus on issues of transference and countertransference as well as the integration of communication and technical skills learned at earlier levels. The supervisor's role at this third level may be one of case review consultant. Finally, at the posttraining or postdoctoral level, the supervisor's role should more appropriately be that of a peer or colleague, and the focus should be on refining technical skills and learning new developments in the field.[27] These helpful guidelines can be adapted and modified for use in the supervision of lay counselors.

The "Ideal" Supervisor: Clinical, Research, and Biblical Perspectives

In another helpful publication in the professional training literature Carifio and Hess reviewed recent research and theory directly bearing on behaviors or characteristics that describe the "ideal" or good supervisor. They summarized their findings thus:

> Published literature suggests that high-functioning supervisors perform with high levels of empathy, respect, genuineness, flexibility, concern, investment, and openness. Good supervisors also appear to be knowledgeable, experienced, and concrete in their presentation. They use appropriate teaching, goal-setting, and feedback techniques during their supervisory interactions. Last, good supervisors appear to be supportive and noncritical individuals who respect their supervisees and do not attempt to turn the supervisory experience into psychotherapy. Although there seems to be no one way of conducting supervision, research in this area has been suggestive of several qualities that can help supervisors to practice in a variety of settings.[28]

With regard to teaching techniques that a good supervisor can use to communicate information and knowledge to the supervisee, Brannon has provided helpful descriptions of *brainstorming, role play, modeling behavior (by the supervisor in order to demonstrate particular counseling skills), and guided reflection*.[29] Freeman has noted that for a supervisor to provide good feedback to the supervisee, the feedback should be *systematic* (objective, accurate, consistent, and reliable), *timely, clearly understood,* and *reciprocal* (with openness for further discussion and interaction with the supervisee).[30]

Finally, Rosenblatt and Mayer have found that supervisees particularly object to the following four supervisory styles which good supervisors will try to avoid: *constrictive* (rigidly limiting the supervisee's use of certain techniques in therapy or counseling), *amorphous* (providing unclear guidance or insufficient direction), *unsupportive* (being cold, distanced, uncaring, or even hostile), and *therapeutic* (focusing on the supervisee as a patient or counselee and his or her personality structure and therefore turning supervisory sessions into therapy sessions for the supervisee). The "therapeutic" style of supervisors was found to be the most objectionable one to supervisees.[31]

From a biblical, Christian perspective, I believe that the "ideal" or good supervisor must also be a spiritually mature person who will focus on the spirituality of the supervisee as well as the counselees he or she is seeing. Explicit use of spiritual resources like prayer and the Scriptures, and discussion of spiritual issues will be encouraged in both supervision and counseling sessions, as far as possible and where appropriate and ethical, in dependence on the Holy Spirit. This will usually be the case in the context of lay Christian counseling, especially within a local church context, because many, if not most, of the counselees will probably be Christians who want a Christ-centered, biblically based counseling approach to be used by the lay counselors, with open discussion of spiritual issues and explicit use of spiritual resources made available. I have called such an approach "explicit integration" in psychotherapy or counseling and provided guidelines elsewhere for how it can be practiced even by professional Christian counselors or therapists in a clinically sensitive, ethically responsible, and professionally competent way.[32]

An ultimate goal of all Christian therapy or counseling, including lay Christian counseling, should therefore be to help facilitate the spiritual growth and development of the counselee as far as possible. Similarly, an ultimate goal of all Christian supervision should be the facilitation of the spiritual growth of the supervisee (as well as of the supervisor). While Christian counseling is *not* completely synonymous with Christian discipleship training, good Christian counseling will involve some spiritual direction and what Gary Collins has called "discipleship counseling." Again, in similar fashion, while Christian supervision is *not* completely identical with Christian discipleship training, good Christian supervision will include some spiritual direction and discipleship training as a crucial component, especially in the context of lay Christian counseling. Similar emphases on the need to focus on such biblical integration issues and spirituality in supervision have been made recently by Lipsker[33] in the context of professional graduate school training of Christian therapists, and Worthington in the context of training lay Christian counselors.[34]

I have previously written on *intrapersonal integration* (i.e., our own appropriation of faith and our personal integration of psychological and spiritual experience as Christians) and emphasized that it should be viewed as the most fundamental and foundational category of integration, without which true, biblical integration of psychology and Christianity cannot be substantially achieved in the other categories of integration (i.e., conceptual-theoretical, research, and professional or clinical). I have also asserted that the *spirituality* of the person doing integration is a key dimension of intrapersonal integration, and I have described several dimensions of true Christian spirituality or greater Christlikeness, which can be helpful for facilitating the development of such spirituality in the supervisee or lay counselor, the counselee, as well as the supervisor, as follows:

> The term spirituality is often used to refer to the disposition or internal condition of people when in such a state as prepares them to recognize and fully appreciate spiritual realities, and such spirituality is ultimately the result of the inworking of the Holy Spirit (1 Cor. 2:14, 15; 3:1, 16). . . . Spirituality, therefore, has many aspects and dimensions to its true, deep meaning.
>
> First, spirituality means *a deep thirst or hunger for God* (Ps. 42:1; Matt. 5:6), what A. W. Tozer has called, "The pursuit of God." . . . Such a sincere and Holy Spirit-inspired desire to know God will lead to a growing knowledge of God personally. . . .
>
> Second, spirituality means a *love for God* based on intimate knowledge of God, that leads naturally to *worship and obedience* (Matt. 22:37, 38; John 14:21, 23; cf. Rev. 2:1–7). . . .
>
> Third, spirituality means *being filled with the Holy Spirit and yielding to God's deepening work of grace in our lives and not to the flesh* (Eph. 5:18; Gal. 5:16; Rom. 6:12–13). This will require the consistent use of the following spiritual disciplines of the Christian life as explicated by Foster (1978): the *inward disciplines* of meditation, prayer, fasting, and study; the *outward disciplines* of simplicity, solitude, submission, and service; and the *corporate disciplines* of confession, worship, guidance, and celebration. These disciplines involve *both individual and group life*. . . .
>
> Fourth, spirituality means *acknowledging and using the gifts of the Spirit* for God's purposes and glory (Eph. 4; 1 Cor. 12; Rom.

12; 1 Peter 4) and *manifesting the fruit of the Spirit* (Gal. 5:22–23), which ultimately means *being more Christlike* (Rom. 8:29). . . .

Fifth, spirituality means *developing biblical thinking and a world view that is consistent with God's perspective as revealed in Scriptures* (cf. Rom. 12:2; Phil. 4:8; Col. 3:16a; 2 Tim. 3:16–17). Such thinking will lead, amongst other things, to a balanced ministry to a whole person, to being involved in "Kingdom Business" (Matt. 6:33) in all its breadth and depth. . . .

Sixth, spirituality means *being involved in spiritual warfare requiring the use of supernatural power and resources from God* (cf. 1 Cor. 4:20; Eph. 6:10–18), including the use of prayer and the Scriptures.

Finally, spirituality has *"mystical" aspects,* including what St. John of the Cross described as *"the dark night of the soul"* (cf. Isa. 50:10).[35]

Both counselor and supervisor should keep in mind such dimensions of true, Christian spirituality as ultimate goals for themselves and their counselees. They should encourage the use of the spiritual disciplines (as described by Foster) in a gentle, gracious, and nonlegalistic way. The lay counselor needs to model such spirituality for the counselee, just as the supervisor should model it for the supervisee, in dependence on God's grace and the inworking of the Holy Spirit.

Other Issues in the Supervision of Lay Christian Counseling

Worthington has pointed out a number of other issues that need to be addressed in supervising lay Christian counselors. First is the issue of deciding *who* the supervisor of the lay counselors should be. Will the supervisor be an experienced pastor, elder, lay counselor, or professional counselor? And how much authority and autonomy will the supervisor have in the context of church leadership and authority structures? Some authors like Lukens have proposed that the supervisor of lay Christian counselors should be a licensed mental health professional who is a Christian as well.[36]

While I believe that it would be ideal or preferable for the supervisor to be a professional counselor or licensed mental health professional, I do not believe that this is essential or realistic in every context of lay counseling ministry. My recommendation is that the supervisor of the lay counselors should be at least an experienced or better trained pastor or lay leader/counselor, who can then consult with a Christian professional counselor or licensed mental health professional.

A second issue has to do with the need for supervisors of lay Christian counselors to focus on the unique strengths of *lay* or *friendship* counseling, and therefore to stress what friends do (and don't do) well, including providing daily and multisituational support, especially during times of crisis for the counselees or clients. Lay counselors also need a continual reminder of their limits, and therefore of the need for making referrals to professionals where appropriate and necessary.

A third issue involves the need for the supervisor to help lay Christian counselors avoid two common abuses of lay counseling. Worthington has called these abuses "formula-driven counseling," in which the lay counselor is trained in and uses only a limited set of counseling skills in a rigid way with little sensitivity to the needs and struggles of the counselee; and "Holy Spirit-driven counseling," in which the lay counselor believes the Holy Spirit will provide all the answers and therefore orderly preparation and forethought are not necessary. The supervisor should teach and model a balanced approach to lay Christian counseling, using a broader range of counseling skills and methods, but relying on the Holy Spirit for his guidance and empowering as well.

Worthington also delineated five other issues in the supervision of ongoing lay Christian counseling. They include economic and legal issues (e.g., not charging fees for lay counseling and being prepared for possible lawsuits), the need for continuing education of lay counselors (including the provision of reference materials for them), maintaining or protecting the confidentiality of client information, evaluation of lay counseling (including clearer identification of the goals of the lay counselor for each client or counselee), and the utilization of prayer during supervision, which should also be viewed as an opportunity for the supervisor to disciple the lay counselor.[37]

In a 1986 survey of fifteen church-based lay counseling ministries conducted by the Center for Church Renewal of Plano, Texas, six out of the fourteen responding to questions concerning the supervision of lay counselors described their supervision as informal, and eight out of the fourteen as formal. However, whether supervision was formal or informal, only three out of fourteen said that staff actually directly *observed* the lay counselors at work, although seven out of the fifteen churches did offer some kind of co-counseling.[38] Lay Christian counseling therefore is in need of more regular and systematic supervision, as well as better and more effective methods and models of supervision, including more observation of actual counseling done by lay counselors. Such observation can be conducted directly through co-counseling or a one-way mirror, or indirectly through audiotapes or videotapes of counseling sessions, where appropriate. The methods and models of good supervision provided in this chapter will hopefully be helpful in developing better and more regular supervision of lay Christian counselors, leading to more effective ministry.

It may be helpful to examine a hypothetical verbatim example of how some of the principles for good supervision can be applied in a supervision session involving a one-on-one format with a lay counselor.

One-on-One Supervision: A Verbatim Example

Supervisor (S):   Hi, Susan, how're you doing?

Lay Counselor (C):   Hi, John. I'm doing okay—a little tired this week, but I'm fine otherwise.

S: Yeah, I understand you have been busy this week with two counselees seeing you.

C: That's right. It's the first time since I began as a lay counselor that I've had more than one counselee in any one week! It's great to be able to be used by the Lord to help others who are hurting, but it's hard work!

S: It sure can be! Before we discuss the two counselees and their needs, shall we begin with prayer?

C: Sure!

S: Would you like to start, and I'll close in prayer? Then we'll begin our discussion and supervision time.

C: Yes. Dear Lord, thank you for this time with John and for all his help and guidance as I continue to serve you in our lay counseling service here at our church. I pray that your

Holy Spirit will grant us wisdom, discernment, and compassion in our work with my two clients. I also ask for your loving and healing touch upon their lives, so that they'll grow spiritually and be made more whole by you. Bless us now I pray, in Jesus' name. Amen.

S: Amen. So, Lord, as Susan has prayed, do guide us both by your Spirit in knowing how to best aid her in helping these two persons you have given her the opportunity and responsibility of caring for and counseling with. Lead us and bless this supervision time together, to the end that we too may learn from you and from each other and therefore grow, and may the two counselees be further helped and blessed by you as well. In Christ's name we pray. Amen.

C: Amen. Well, it's been an interesting week! Shall I begin with the first counselee, Yvonne?

S: Sure, go ahead.

C: As you already know, Yvonne is a single woman, age thirty-five, whom I have seen now for two sessions. She is struggling with loneliness and depression, mainly over being single when most of her friends are already married. She is a seriously committed Christian who loves the Lord, but finds it hard to cope with what she calls "being passed by." In the session this past week, she shared a lot more of her deep feelings of loneliness and cried several times. As you suggested, I audiotaped this session with her permission, and I understand you've had a chance to listen to parts of it since I gave it to you a couple of days ago.

S: Um hmm. I did have a chance to listen to some of the tape, but we could spend some of our time today listening to particular segments of it that you or I may be especially interested in. Before we do that or discuss the session further, could you please tell me how you felt about the session yourself?

C: Yeah. It was a somewhat difficult session because she was sharing a lot of her pain, and I felt for her. I remembered, however, what I had learned from our lay counseling training course a few months ago about the need to be

empathic and understanding, and not to be too
sympathetic or feel so sorry for her that I lose my
objectivity in trying to help her. I used the basic listening
skills and provided summary reflections of her feelings
and thoughts from time to time to convey warmth and
empathy and Christian love. I believe I managed to
maintain some kind of balance between feeling with her
and for her without losing my objectivity, although it was
a bit of a struggle with her crying so often.

S: It sure was an emotional session for her and for you too,
but I feel you did manage to maintain a healthy
objectivity. Your paraphrases and summary reflections in
the first part of the session were actually right on, and the
counselee opened up even more as a result, as the session
progressed. It's hard to "contain" a counselee's pain, and
I'm sure you were tempted to rush in to "fix it" quick, but
I'm glad you didn't. You probably remembered too the
need to explore and understand or empathize with
feelings in good counseling *before* taking any steps of
action or intervention with the counselee.

C: Yes, I did, and in that sense I felt good about what I did.

S: Tell me, what else did you do after exploring and trying to
understand and empathize with Yvonne's feelings?

C: Well, later on in the session, following Larry Crabb's
model, I asked her what she's been doing in order to
identify possible problem behaviors (after exploring and
identifying her problem feelings of loneliness,
depression, and some anger and resentment). She
mentioned staying home a lot and not attending church
fellowship meetings as often recently because most of the
people in her fellowship are married couples. She's also
been eating more junk food, and she feels rotten
afterward, although eating food soothes her temporarily
from the pain of loneliness and depression. I then asked
her what thoughts tend to go through her mind when she's
feeling this way, in order to identify possible problem
thinking. She was able to note that she would often say the
following things to herself when she is alone and feeling
lonely and depressed: "I'm not attractive enough for the
guys to notice me, and I might as well resign myself to a

life of singleness. But I can't take that! It's terrible to be a "spinster" and not have a husband and kids! I need someone to hold me and love me and take care of me. O God, why have you deprived me of this need? I feel so lonely and depressed, sometimes I wish I were dead! How long more will I have to experience this pain of being ignored by men and passed by when all my other friends are getting married or are already married. And I am thirty-five! There's no more hope for me but I can't stand being alone!" She will then cry for a while and beg God in prayer to send her a mate soon.

S: Sounds like Crabb's model helped you to identify some problem behaviors and problem thinking that are associated with her struggles and emotional pain. Good job! You asked some very good questions. What else did you explore regarding her possible problem thinking?

C: I remembered the need to further check out the possibility of suicidal thinking and suicidal risk, since she is depressed. In our first session she already denied any suicidal intentions, but I felt I needed to pursue this a bit more, so in our last session, I asked her whether she ever felt so down that she wanted to end it all. Her reply was that she sometimes wished she were dead but she would never end her own life since she believes suicide is sinful and not an option for a Christian. I pushed a bit more and asked if she ever thought of how to end it all even if she did not feel it was the right thing to do. She said only occasionally she would think of taking some pills, but she did not know what to take and how many, and then would block that thought out of her mind. She is not currently taking any medications and did say she tried to avoid pills as much as possible, even aspirin for a headache!

S: So you did check further for suicidal thoughts and suicidal risk. From Yvonne's answers, what is your opinion regarding the suicidal risk for her?

C: I feel there is some risk since she is feeling quite depressed and hopeless about being single, but I don't think the risk is very high at present because she does not have a definite plan, and she has strong Christian beliefs against taking her own life. Also, despite the social isolation she is putting upon herself, she did note that a couple of people from her fellowship do call her and go out sometimes with her for dinner or to a movie, and she feels they do support her with their understanding and prayers. So Yvonne is not completely isolated. Also, she has been seeing me weekly for counseling and further support, and she has been able to continue working full-time as a receptionist.

S: Well, you certainly have covered the bases well here, and I really want to commend you for doing a thorough job in determining the suicidal risk for Yvonne. And I'm glad that you are aware of the need to keep monitoring this, since it can change over time—especially if she isolates herself even more and feels more severely depressed and hopeless. She may then need a referral to a professional therapist or even psychiatrist if antidepressant medication becomes necessary.

C: Yes, I'm planning to keep on monitoring the suicidal risk from time to time as we counsel together. I am also aware of the possibility of the need to refer her to a professional therapist or even psychiatrist, if her depression worsens.

S: You also did a good job in helping her to identify her problem thinking. What else happened after that?

C: Yvonne actually was a bit surprised that she was saying all these negative thoughts to herself, but she feels them very deeply when she is depressed and lonely. I took the opportunity to help her see how our thinking can affect our feelings, and I gave her a couple of other examples. She responded quite positively to this. So I decided to assign an A-B-C diary to help her record the activating event (A) triggering off negative thinking or misbeliefs or irrational beliefs (B), leading to particular emotional or behavioral consequences (C), following Albert Ellis and Aaron Beck, which I recalled from the training classes we had. She understood this homework assignment and readily accepted it. I also assigned Backus and Chapian's book *Telling Yourself the Truth* for homework reading as "bibliotherapy," and I loaned her my copy. In retrospect, I feel it might have been better just to assign the A-B-C diary first and discuss it at our next session before assigning Backus and Chapian. I therefore wonder if I overloaded her with homework!

S: That's a good question, and it raises the issue of good timing and pacing in counseling and helping others. I don't necessarily think that you overloaded her, but it would probably have been better to wait till the next session before assigning Backus and Chapian, so you can see further examples of her negative thinking or misbeliefs from her A-B-C diary before intervening further with cognitive restructuring or changing the misbeliefs. Also, it is important when assigning homework readings as bibliotherapy to be more specific about what chapters you would like her to read during the next week, especially since Yvonne is depressed, which may mean she may not be motivated enough to read too much. You want to give her homework assignments that are clear and easy to accomplish, at least initially.

C: Thanks for reminding me of that! I guess I need to be more sensitive to how much she can do at this time, since she is depressed and not as motivated or energetic.

S: Yes, that's right. But overall, you've done a really good job at helping her in this last session. Before we listen to parts of the audiotape, tell me how you ended the session.

C: After assigning the homework, I asked her if she would like us to close in prayer, and she said, "Definitely." So I asked her to pray first, and then I closed in prayer, asking for the Lord's help and healing for her. From her prayer, which we can listen to on the tape, I sensed again a deep pain and longing for God's help, as well as a genuine faith in him. There are definitely some misbeliefs, however, concerning having to have a husband in order for her life to be happy, etc., which we'll have to deal with in future sessions.

S: Good. Okay, let's listen to parts of the tape now, and then afterward you can tell me about the new counselee who came in to see you for the first time last week.

This hypothetical verbatim example of a supervision session with a lay counselor illustrates how a number of principles and guidelines for good supervision can be applied. They include: giving support and encouragement to the lay counselor by a supervisor who is warm, understanding, not harshly critical, and spiritually mature; asking for specific details and using an audiotape (where appropriate) so that the supervisor can provide specific, clear, and helpful feedback to the lay counselor to facilitate effective counseling; teaching and reviewing skills (e.g., how to give homework, assessing suicidal risk and need for referral, briefly reviewing Crabb's model and cognitive restructuring of misbeliefs, etc.); focusing a bit on how the lay counselor is feeling (i.e., process or dynamic issues); and using prayer in the supervision session as well as discussing spiritual issues openly (e.g., Yvonne's use of prayer and her misbeliefs about what she needs for a fulfilling life, etc.).

In a dyadic or group supervision context, the same principles and guidelines for good supervision can be applied, except that more time is needed, and other lay counselors should be given opportunities to present their counselees, as well as to provide their feedback and suggestions to the lay counselor whose counselee is being discussed. The confidentiality of the counselee should, however, be safeguarded, and this can be done in a number of ways (e.g., using first names only, getting permission from the counselee to discuss his or her problems in group supervision with the assurance that nothing will be shared *outside* of the supervision group, etc.). Confidentiality issues will be discussed in chapter 11, which covers potential pitfalls or legal and ethical issues in lay Christian counseling.

NOTES

[1]See C. Loganbill, E. Hardy, and U. Delworth, "Supervision: A Conceptual Model," *The Counseling Psychologist* 10, no. 1 (1982): 3–42, p. 14.

[2]See M. O'L. Wiley, "Developmental Counseling Supervision: Person-Environment Congruency, Satisfaction, and Learning." Paper presented at the Annual Convention of the American Psychological Convention, August 1982, in Washington, D.C.

[3]For an example of a predoctoral internship training program in a Christian context that is approved or accredited (provisional) by the American Psychological Association, see S. Y. Tan, "Internship Training and Supervision in The Psychological Center at Fuller Theological Seminary." Invited paper presented at the International Congress on

Christian Counseling, Clinical Supervision Track, November 11, 1988, in Atlanta, Georgia.

[4]For some helpful books on clinical supervision see: R. Ekstein and R. Wallerstein, *The Teaching and Learning of Psychotherapy*, 2d ed. (New York: International Universities Press, 1972); G. M. Hart, *The Process of Clinical Supervision* (Baltimore: University Park Press, 1982); A. K. Hess, ed., *Psychotherapy Supervision: Theory, Research, and Practice* (New York: Wiley, 1980); F. E. Kaslow, ed., *Supervision, Consultation, and Staff Training in the Helping Professions* (San Francisco: Jossey-Bass, 1977); A. Robbins, *Between Therapists: The Processing of Transference/Countertransference Material* (New York: Human Sciences Press, 1988); C. D. Stoltenberg and U. Delworth, *Supervising Counselors and Therapists: A Developmental Approach* (San Francisco: Jossey-Bass, 1987). For a recent book on clinical supervision written from the special perspective of pastoral counseling, see B. K. Estadt, Jr.; J. Compton; and M. C. Blanchette, *The Art of Clinical Supervision: A Pastoral Counseling Perspective* (New York: Paulist, 1987). A number of helpful journals on clinical supervision are also available, including *Counselor Education and Supervision* and *The Clinical Supervisor*, as well as a specifically Christian ministry oriented one called the *Journal of Supervision and Training in Ministry*.

[5]See Special Issues on "Supervision in Counseling I," *The Counseling Psychologist* 10, no. 1 (1982): 1–96; and "Supervision in Counseling II," *The Counseling Psychologist* 1, no. 1 (1983): 1–112; and Special Series on "Advances in Psychotherapy Supervision," *Professional Psychology: Research and Practice* 18 (1987): 187–259.

[6]Series on "Training to Competency in Psychotherapy," *Journal of Consulting and Clinical Psychology* 56 (1988): 651–709.

[7]See R. K. Russell, A. M. Crimmings, and R. W. Lent, "Counselor Training and Supervision: Theory and Research," in S. D. Brown and R. W. Lent, eds., *Handbook of Counseling Psychology* (New York: Wiley, 1984).

[8]See E. L. Worthington, Jr., "Issues in Supervision of Lay Christian Counseling," *Journal of Psychology and Christianity* 6, no. 2 (1987): 70–77.

[9]See R. A. Hogan, "Issues and Approaches to Supervision," *Psychotherapy: Theory, Research, and Practice* 1 (1964): 139–41.

[10]Worthington, "Issues in Supervision of Lay Christian Counseling," 72.

[11]See C. Stoltenberg, "Approaching Supervision from a Developmental Perspective: The Counselor Complexity Model," *Journal of Counseling Psychology* 28 (1981): 59–65.

[12]See C. Loganbill, E. Hardy, and U. Delworth, "Supervision: A Conceptual Model," *The Counseling Psychologist* 10, no. 1 (1982): 3–42.

[13]Stoltenberg and Delworth, *Supervising Counselors and Therapists.*

[14]See E. L. Worthington, Jr., "Changes in Supervision as Counselors and Supervisors Gain Experience: A Review," *Professional Psychology; Research and Practice* 18 (1987): 189–208.

[15]See E. L. Holloway, "Developmental Models of Supervision: Is It Development?" *Professional Psychology: Research and Practice* 18 (1987): 209–16.

[16]Worthington, "Issues in Supervision of Lay Christian Counseling," 72.

[17]See series on "Training to Competency in Psychotherapy," 651–709.

[18]See B. F. Shaw and K. S. Dobson, "Competency Judgments in the Training and Evaluation of Psychotherapists," *Journal of Consulting and Clinical Psychology* 56 (1988): 666–720.

[19]See K. S. Dobson and B. F. Shaw, "The Use of Treatment Manuals in Cognitive Therapy: Experience and Issues," *Journal of Consulting and Clinical Psychology* 56 (1988): 673–80.

[20]See B. J. Rounsaville, S. O'Malley, S. Foley, and M. M. Weissman, "Role of Manual-Guided Training in the Conduct and Efficacy of Interpersonal Psychotherapy for Depression," *Journal of Consulting and Clinical Psychology* 56 (1988): 681–88.

[21]See H. H. Strupp, S. F. Butler, and C. L. Rosser, "Training in Psychodynamic Therapy," *Journal of Consulting and Clinical Psychology* 56 (1988): 689–95.

[22]See L. S. Greenberg and R. L. Goldman, "Training in Experiential Therapy," *Journal of Consulting and Clinical Psychology* 56 (1988): 696–702.

[23]See R. R. Bootzin and J. S. Ruggill, "Training Issues in Behavior Therapy," *Journal of Consulting and Clinical Psychology* 56 (1988): 703–9.

[24]See Hess, *Psychotherapy Supervision.*

[25]See chap. 4, n. 46.

[26]See Stoltenberg and Delworth, *Supervising Counselors and Therapists.*

[27]See P. D. Guest and L. E. Beutler, "Impact of Psychotherapy Supervision on Therapist Orientation and Values," *Journal of Consulting and Clinical Psychology* 56 (1988): 653–58.

[28]See M. S. Carifio and A. K. Hess, "Who Is the Ideal Supervisor?" *Professional Psychology: Research and Practice* 18 (1987): 244–50, p. 244.

29See D. Brannon, "Adult Learning Principles and Methods for Enhancing the Training Role of Supervisors," *The Clinical Supervisor* 3 (1985): 27–41.

30See E. Freeman, "The Importance of Feedback in Clinical Supervision: Implications for Direct Practice," *The Clinical Supervisor* 3 (1985): 5–26.

31See A. Rosenblatt and J. Mayer, "Objectionable Supervising Styles: Students' Views," *Social Work* 18 (1975): 184–89.

32See S. Y. Tan, "Explicit Integration in Psychotherapy." Invited paper presented at the International Congress on Christian Counseling, Counseling and Spirituality Track, November 10, 1988, in Atlanta, Georgia.

33See L. E. Lipsker, "Integration in Graduate Student-Therapist Supervision." Paper presented at the International Congress on Christian Counseling, Clinical Supervision Track, November 11, 1988, in Atlanta, Georgia. See also n. 3.

34Worthington, "Issues in Supervision of Lay Christian Counseling."

35See S. Y. Tan, "Intrapersonal Integration: The Servant's Spirituality," *Journal of Psychology and Christianity* 6, no. 1 (1987): 36–37. Also see R. Foster, *Celebration of Discipline* (New York: Harper & Row, 1978; rev. ed., 1988); D. Willard, *The Spirit of the Disciplines* (New York: Harper & Row, 1988); and L. O. Richards, *A Practical Theology of Spirituality* (Grand Rapids: Zondervan, 1987).

36See H. C. Lukens, Jr., "Lay Counselor Training Revisited: Reflections of a Trainer," *Journal of Psychology and Christianity* 6, no. 2 (1987): 10–13.

37Worthington, "Issues in Supervision of Lay Christian Counseling."

38See "Lay Counseling Survey," available from Floyd Elliott, Director of Counseling and Family Renewal, Center for Church Renewal, 200 Chisholm Place, Suite 228, Plano, TX 75075.

9

Evaluation of Lay Counselors

How do we know that a lay Christian counselor training program has been effective in improving the counseling skills (and personal growth) of the lay counselors? And how can we tell that the lay counselors who have been trained are now actually doing effective counseling with people who need help, producing positive therapeutic effects? These are the two major questions that researchers attempt to answer in some way in the evaluation of lay Christian counselors. In other words, how effective is a training program for lay *Christian* counselors, and how effective is lay Christian counseling itself?

Unfortunately, little evaluation research has been conducted to date to answer such questions. The whole field of Christian counseling, whether professional or lay, has been far behind in doing solid research to determine the effectiveness of training programs as well as different forms of Christian counseling.

Dr. Allen Bergin, a noted researcher in evaluating psychotherapy effectiveness, briefly reviewed Roland Fleck and John Carter's book *Psychology and Christianity: Integrative Readings* several years ago. His remarks are by and large still applicable to the whole field of Christian counseling:

Empirical data are minimal, though research studies are frequently proposed. Indeed, we might say that the entire approach is at the proposal stage—possibly promising but largely untried and untested in ordinary professional terms. What is intriguing is that bright, well-trained people are working at it.[1]

He quoted the following challenges from the book of readings which should also be heeded in the context of lay Christian counseling:

> Outcome studies in "Christian psychotherapy" also are important—if we are claiming some sort of superiority for "Christian counseling" it's about time we stopped to see if claims are backed up by solid data. . . .
>
> We must not allow ourselves to be second-rate professionals. . . . For too long Christians have copped out on rigorous study and research by claiming all the truth they need to know is contained in the Bible. . . .
>
> We are unlikely to arrive at one biblical approach to counseling. . . . The universities do not encourage research into religious experience—variables such as Christian maturity, faith in God, or counseling effectiveness are very hard to investigate empirically. . . . These obstacles have dissuaded many from entering psychological research, but this work must be done if we are to counsel, train, prevent, and theorize effectively.[2]

The needed research involving the evaluation of lay Christian counselors can be done not only by Christian mental health professional researchers but also by pastors, church leaders, and other parachurch or missionary organizations involved in the training and use of lay Christian counselors. The level of methodological sophistication in the evaluation research done will, of course, vary from setting to setting, depending on the experience and research training of those conducting the evaluation research. However, I believe that some evaluation of lay Christian counselors should be conducted by all leaders who are involved in the training and use of lay counselors in ministry to hurting people.

Such evaluation research is probably best conducted in collaboration or consultation with Christian mental health professionals who are well-versed and experienced in research. However, I am aware that in some settings professional researchers may not be available for consultation or collaboration, and hence the evaluation of lay Christian counselors may have to be done by the leader (e.g., a pastor or church elder or deacon) responsible for the lay counseling ministry. This chapter will therefore review and describe the major evaluation approaches and measures or tools available for conducting such research, whether it is done by professional researchers, or church leaders and others involved in the ministry of lay Christian counseling who are not academicians or professional researchers. It will also provide some future directions for the evaluation of lay counselors in general, as well as lay *Christian* counselors in particular. The relevant research literature covering evaluation studies on the effectiveness of lay Christian counselor training programs and lay Christian counseling per se has already been reviewed in chapter 4. This chapter will focus on the methods and measures used in such research so that more people involved in lay Christian counseling will know how to go about evaluating lay Christian counselors, and will hopefully actually end up *doing* such evaluation.

Evaluation of Training Programs for Lay Christian Counselors

Before I begin to describe how to go about evaluating training programs for lay Christian counselors, I would like to point out that much evaluation research remains to be done even in *professional* clinical training programs. Several years ago, the American Psychological Association Task Force on the Evaluation of Education, Training, and Service in Psychology stated the following alarming finding: "There is no evidence that any specific educational or training program or experience is related to professional competence."[3] The Task Force, therefore, concluded in 1982 that it is "important, perhaps imperative, that psychology begin to assemble a body of persuasive evidence bearing on the value of specific educational and training requirements."[4] Since then, several helpful publications have appeared pertaining to evaluation and accountability in professional clinical training, and to standards and evaluation in the education and training of professional psychologists.[5] These publications or books can be consulted with benefit if one is interested in a sophisticated approach to evaluating lay counselors, although some modification or adaptation of the evaluation methods or measures used will be needed, and several of the issues and measures discussed will not be relevant to the more narrowly focused evaluation of lay counselors.

Several good books having an academic, technical perspective are available. They cover more comprehensively general research methods applicable to clinical and educational settings.[6]

Returning to the more specific topic of evaluating lay Christian counselor training programs, I would like to point out that the major focus of evaluation should be on the *counseling knowledge and skills* acquired by the lay counselors through a particular training program. A secondary focus of evaluation could be on the *personal growth* of the lay counselors, including their *spiritual growth*. More comprehensive analyses of the long-term effects of professional training on counselor behavior and growth have been reported in the recent secular research literature.[7] For example, Thompson evaluated changes in counselor behavior in three main areas: actual verbal response mode as measured by the Hill Counselor Verbal Response Category System,[8] personal growth as measured by the Personal Orientation Inventory (POI),[9] and general counseling effectiveness as rated by Master's level therapists or counselors. Following a similar methodology or approach, several measures can be used to evaluate both the *counseling knowledge and skills* acquired by lay Christian counselors through a specific training program, and their *personal and spiritual growth*.

1. Measures for Evaluation of Counseling Knowledge and Skills

There are several approaches to evaluating the counseling knowledge and skills gained by lay counselors. One approach is to use *self-report measures,* which are usually questionnaires or rating scales filled in by the lay counselors themselves. Another approach is to use *written responses by the lay counselors to counseling situations* presented to them in written form (or even in audiotaped or videotaped form). A third approach is to use *ratings by others (usually trained raters) of the lay counselors' behaviors and skills in a counseling session,* whether simulated (i.e., role play) or actual, and usually audiotaped or videotaped. A fourth approach is to have *peer ratings provided by other lay counselors of a particular lay counselor's skills and effectiveness.* Some examples of specific measures that can be used in the various approaches will now be described.

a. *Self-report measures.* An obvious self-report measure to assess the actual counseling knowledge gained by lay counselors is the use of a *quiz or multiple-choice exam/test* covering specific content areas of the training program provided, to be taken by the lay counselors after the completion of the training program.

Another self-report measure to assess not only subjective ratings by the lay counselors of how much they think they know about counseling or Christian counseling but also their subjective ratings of how competent or skillful they feel they are in counseling is the *Counselor Training Program Questionnaire* (CTPQ) which I developed as a simple self-report measure for evaluating lay counselor training programs.[10] There are two versions of this questionnaire. The *pretraining questionnaire* is to be given to lay counselors just before the start of a training program. It contains basic questions about name, age, sex, occupation, education, previous courses in counseling/psychology, and six main items, using 0–100 subjective rating scales, as shown on the next page.

The *posttraining questionnaire* is to be given to lay counselors just *after* the training program has been completed. It contains the same six main items, but it also includes questions about the number of training sessions attended, positive or negative features of the training program, and suggestions for its improvement, if any. The CTPQ therefore consists of six major items assessing a lay counselor's subjective ratings of his or her *knowledge of counseling, knowledge of Christian counseling, competence* (or skillfulness) *in counseling, confidence* (or certainty) *in competence in counseling, competence* (or skillfulness) *in Christian counseling,* and *confidence* (or certainty) *in competence in Christian counseling.* These same six items are completed by lay counselors just before and just after the training program so that pretraining and posttraining scores can be compared and any significant changes noted. An effective training program should result in significant improvements (i.e., higher scores) on at least four of the six items (i.e., questions 1, 2, 3, and 5), if not on all six items.

b. *Written responses to counseling situations/scenarios.* An example of a measure involving written responses by counselors to counseling situations or scenarios presented to them in written form is the *Helping Relationship Inventory.*[11] This measure was developed to classify or categorize the response-style preferences of the person (lay counselor) answering the inventory by having him or her rank, according to what he or she would most likely say in a particular counseling situation, the

1.   How much do you know about *counseling*?

0	10	20	30	40	50	60	70	80	90	100

Nothing   Some   A Lot
at all

2.   How much do you know about *Christian counseling*?

0	10	20	30	40	50	60	70	80	90	100

Nothing   Some   A Lot
at all

3.   How competent do you think you are in *counseling*?

0	10	20	30	40	50	60	70	80	90	100

Not competent   Moderately   Very
at all   competent   competent

4.   How confident or certain are you of your competence
      in *counseling*?

0	10	20	30	40	50	60	70	80	90	100

Not confident   Moderately   Very
at all   confident   confident

5.   How competent do you think you are in *Christian
      counseling*?

0	10	20	30	40	50	60	70	80	90	100

Not competent   Moderately   Very
at all   competent   competent

6.   How confident or certain are you of your competence
      in *Christian counseling*?

0	10	20	30	40	50	60	70	80	90	100

Not confident   Moderately   Very
at all   confident   confident

five different responses that are listed after each of twenty-five such scenarios involving short client or counselee statements. It has five subscale scores corresponding to the five response styles: Understanding, Probing, Interpretive, Supportive, and Evaluative. It is usually expected that good training programs would lead to a significant increase in preference for Understanding responses by the lay counselors. This inventory is to be given to the lay counselors just before and just after the training program.

c. *Ratings by others (trained raters) of the lay counselor's behavior and skills in a counseling session.* A common method of utilizing this approach is to have a lay counselor role play a counseling session just before and just after the training program. However, a real life counseling situation with an actual client or counselee would also be appropriate and actually preferable. The counseling session, whether simulated or real life, is usually audiotaped or videotaped, with permission obtained, of course, from the client or counselee if it is a real life situation. The lay counselor's behavior and counseling skills during such a session can then be rated by two or more trained raters (so that interrater reliability or agreement can be determined), using appropriate rating scales. One of the most commonly used rating scales is the one developed by Dr. Robert Carkhuff called *A Scale for the Measurement of Empathic Understanding, Respect, and Genuineness.*[12] It consists of three 5-point subscales or dimensions developed to measure core counseling skills of empathy, respect, and genuineness by trained raters. Usually 8–10 minute segments of the audiotape or videotape are rated independently by two or more trained raters who have had previous training and experience in using the Carkhuff Scale. The lay counselors are rated before and after the training program, so that changes on these three dimensions of core counseling skills can be noted. In a simulated or role play counseling session, either the same person playing the role of the client or counselee or a different person can be used after the training program, but the presenting problem after the training program should be different from the one used before the training program.

In a study reported by Jernigan, Tan, and Gorsuch,[13] the following instructions were given to the lay counselor trainee before videotaping a role play counseling session: "You are a counselor here at the church counseling center. The person whom I will introduce to you has come to the center for help with a personal problem. Do whatever you think may be helpful for this person." The problem presented before the training program involved depression, whereas the one presented after the training program involved fear of failure.

While the Carkhuff Scale has been widely used and is still an important one for measuring empathy, respect, and genuineness, it should be pointed out that the necessary core counseling skills for producing therapeutic change in counselees have been challenged somewhat, although there is still considerable support for the positive effect these core conditions have on clients.[14] Furthermore, the Carkhuff Scale does not measure other more specific counseling skills—like cognitive-behavioral intervention or problem-solving skills—often taught in lay Christian counselor training programs.

Other rating scales or checklists for assessing a lay counselor's competence or skillfulness in more specific counseling skills are therefore needed in order to evaluate more comprehensively the effectiveness of a particular training program which may teach such skills like problem-solving and cognitive-behavioral interventions in addition to basic listening skills. A good source of helpful checklists of more specific counseling and cognitive-behavioral skills which can be adapted for use as rating scales is Cormier and Cormier's book *Interviewing Strategies for Helpers: Fundamental Skills and Cognitive-Behavioral Interventions* (2d ed.), already cited in earlier chapters. There is also a Cognitive Therapy Scale[15] developed specifically to assess cognitive therapy skills of counselors and therapists trained in Dr. Aaron Beck's approach to counseling and therapy. More specific rating scales for evaluating *Christian counseling skills,* including the appropriate use of prayer and the Scriptures, are also needed.

Audiotapes or videotapes of several counseling sessions (rather than just a single session) would be preferable so that ratings of different counseling skills can be better assessed.

d. *Peer ratings of a lay counselor's skills and effectiveness.* In this approach, other lay counselors provide peer ratings, usually using a rating scale or questionnaire of the skills and effectiveness of a particular lay counselor in question, based on their knowledge and observation of this lay counselor in training and supervision sessions. An example of a measure that can be used for this purpose is the one developed by Boan and Owens,[16] who found that the mean scores of such peer ratings of lay counselor skill are related to client satisfaction.

Their revised paraprofessional evaluation form (summer 1983) for use as peer ratings of lay counselor skill contains the following instructions: "Please rate your paraprofessional peers on the following items using a scale of 1 to 10. One (1) will indicate a very low score, an almost absence of that quality. Ten (10) will indicate perfection *for a paraprofessional*. A score of 5 indicates the minimally acceptable level, an indication this is not actually a problem, but some improvement is needed. Please try to rate all items, but leave blank any you have not been able to observe. Remember, your impressions count. All ratings are confidential." The name of the lay counselor or person to be rated is then filled in, with peer ratings by another lay counselor provided in three major areas, each with five items and thus with a total of fifteen items to be rated on the 1–10 point scale.

The first area is the *use of supervision* with the following items: (1) open to feedback from others; (2) uses time effectively; (3) communicates needs clearly; (4) appears able to understand the nature of the problem; (5) puts feedback to good use.

The second area is *counseling skills* with the following items: (6) demonstrates empathic ability; (7) shows nonjudgmental acceptance; (8) able to be appropriately confrontive; (9) communicates precisely and concretely; (10) able to develop rapport with clients.

The third and final area is *personal qualities* with the following items: (11) able to not be defensive; (12) approach to program consistent with training; (13) evokes confidence from others; (14) open to learning; (15) applies faith in a comfortable and appropriate manner.

2. Measures for Evaluation of Personal and Spiritual Growth

Another focus of training programs for lay Christian counselors (in addition to training them in counseling knowledge and skills from a biblical, Christian perspective) should be to help facilitate the personal and spiritual growth of the lay counselors. Some of the training curriculum may be devoted to topics like "Personal Growth of the Counselor," "Growing in Self-Awareness," and "Managing Stress and Preventing Burnout." There are several measures which can be used to evaluate whether lay counselors have grown personally and spiritually after undergoing a training program in lay Christian counseling.

A widely used psychological measure of personal growth is the *Personal Orientation Inventory* (POI) developed by Shostrom to assess self-actualization as defined by Abraham Maslow. A self-actualizing human being is "a person who is more fully functioning and lives a more enriched life than does the average person."[17] The POI consists of 150 forced choice questions or items and takes about 30 minutes to complete. The items are scored twice, first for two basic scales of personal orientation, i.e., inner directedness and time competence. The second scoring yields 10 subscales which measure the following components of self-actualizing: self-actualized value, existentiality, feeling reactivity, spontaneity, self-regard, self-acceptance, nature of man (constructive), synergy, acceptance of aggression, and capacity for intimate contact. While this measure has been widely used in both secular and Christian contexts for evaluating the personal growth of counselors as they go through a counselor training program, some serious questions need to be raised with regard to the relevance or appropriateness of some of the subscales on the POI for Christians. For example, one such subscale that several Christian subjects have had trouble responding to is the nature of man subscale. In an unpublished preliminary study evaluating the effectiveness of growth facilitator training for cross-cultural ministry with a small group of subjects, Schaefer, Dodds, and Tan commented:

> Many participants expressed difficulty with some of the items comprising the nature of man subscale on the POI. Their expressed conflict concerned whether to respond to the items based on their religious belief that persons are corrupted by sin or by their desire to accept persons and view them positively. . . . The conflict regarding this subscale is suggestive of the problems incurred using a secular instrument to evaluate an explicitly Christian program.[18]

Nevertheless, the POI and other secular instruments for measuring personal growth or change can still be used with some benefit as well as caution in the evaluation of training programs for lay Christian counselors. Other examples of secular measures which have been used or which have potential usefulness include the 16PF, the Myers-Briggs Temperament Type Indicator, and the Taylor-Johnson Temperament Analysis.

There is, however, an obvious need for more explicitly Christian measures of spiritual growth as part of the personal growth of the lay Christian counselor. I therefore recommend that some attempt be made to evaluate the spiritual growth of the lay Christian counselor as part of the evaluation of a training program's effectiveness in impacting personal development or growth.

Several measures are now available for assessing spirituality and spiritual growth, and they have been described in chapter 6. Among such measures, I would recommend the following as being of potential usefulness for assessing the spirituality and spiritual growth of the lay Christian counselor: the *Spiritual Well-Being Scale* developed by Ellison and Paloutzian, the *Character Assessment Scale* developed by Schmidt, the *Wagner-Revised Houts Questionnaire* for discovering spiritual gifts, revised by Wagner, and the *Spiritual Leadership Qualities Inventory* developed by Wichern.[19] In addition to these instruments, a more recently developed and somewhat promising measure of optimal religious functioning and Christian religious maturity that should also be noted is the *Religious Status Interview* (RSI) developed by my colleague Dr. H. Newton Malony of the Graduate School of Psychology at Fuller Theological Seminary. Now available is a self-report version of the RSI called the Religious Status Inventory, with 160 items to be rated on a 5-point scale.[20] It has scores on eight major subscales: awareness of God, acceptance of God's grace and steadfast love, being repentant and responsible, knowing God's leadership and direction, involvement in organized religion, experiencing fellowship, being ethical, and affirming openness in faith.

Another measure I would like to mention is the *Spiritual Growth Survey* developed by Smith in an unpublished dissertation submitted to the School of World Mission, Fuller Theological Seminary.[21] It consists of sixty items designed to measure spiritual growth in individuals or groups. It provides scores on the following twelve dimensions: worship, personal devotions, giving, lay ministry, Bible knowledge, missions, fellowship, witnessing, attitude toward religion, distinctive lifestyle, service, and social justice.

Finally, the *Age Universal Religious Orientation Scale (I-E Scale)* developed by Gorsuch and Venable as an adaptation of the Religious Orientation Scale originally put together by Allport and Ross, should also be noted.[22] It consists of twenty statements to be rated on a 5-point scale, and provides a ratio of an individual's intrinsic versus extrinsic religious orientation, with intrinsic orientation or motivation being preferable.

There are, therefore, several scales or measures which are now available for assessing different dimensions of spirituality or spiritual growth. At least one or two of them (e.g., the Spiritual Well-Being Scale or the I-E Scale, but not both of them since they are highly correlated with each other, and the Religious Status Inventory) should be used to evaluate the personal and spiritual growth of lay Christian counselors undergoing a training program in lay Christian counseling. It should be noted, however, that measures of spirituality or spiritual growth (e.g., the I-E Scale, the Spiritual Well-Being Scale, or the Spiritual Growth Survey) in Christian lay counselors did not improve significantly after a training program, mainly because the lay counselors or trainees already scored high on these measures before the training programs began.[23] Lay Christian counseling trainees are often specially selected, and spiritual maturity and well-being are usually a significant part of the selection criteria used. Nevertheless, it may still be helpful to use measures of spirituality in future evaluation research in this area since further studies are needed before more definitive conclusions can be made.

In concluding this section on the evaluation of training programs, I would like to suggest that the minimal requirement for evaluation research be the following evaluation package: Counselor Training Program Questionnaire (CTPQ), Helping Relationship Inventory (HRI), and the Spiritual Well-Being Scale (or alternatively, the I-E Scale). These measures are relatively easy to administer and usually will not take more than an hour to complete, although they do have limitations since they are all paper-and-pencil self-report measures. They should be given just before and just after a training program. It would be preferable, however, if the following measures are also used: Religious Status Inventory (or RSI), POI or some other psychological measure such as the 16PF, and audiotapes or videotapes of simulated or real-life counseling sessions to be rated by trained raters using the Carkhuff Scale and/or other more specific rating scales of lay counselor behavior and skills. In place of the RSI, several other measures of spiritual maturity or spiritual growth described earlier can be used as alternatives. Peer ratings of lay counselor skills can also be helpful.

I have, of course, not listed or described exhaustively all possible measures that can be used in this area of evaluation research, but I do hope that the measures and approaches I have mentioned and suggested will help those responsible for conducting lay Christian counselor training programs to do more systematic and consistent evaluations of such programs.

A Note on Research Design for Evaluation of Training Programs

In conducting evaluation research in this area, it is important not only to choose the best measures for evaluation but also to use the most appropriate research design for the evaluation study. An example of a somewhat ideal research design (which will probably cost more time, energy, and money as well as require the expertise of well-trained researchers) is one in which a large enough number of lay counselor trainees (for example, a total of thirty) is selected and then randomly assigned to two groups (with fifteen in each group). One group will receive the lay counselor training program (usually lasting three to six months), and the other group will either be a "waiting-list" control group who will receive no training (or anything else) but just wait until the training program is over for the first group, or else be a comparison group who will receive some other kind of training unrelated to counseling skills, for example, training in Bible study skills at the same time that the first group is receiving counseling training. (If enough trainees can be recruited for such a study, it would be even more ideal to use all three groups, i.e., a training group, a "wait-list" group, and a comparison/control group).

Appropriate evaluation measures (e.g., CTPQ, HRI, Spiritual Well-Being Scale, RSI, POI or 16PF, videotape ratings of lay counselor behavior and skills during a simulated or real-life counseling session, and possibly peer ratings of lay counselor skill) will be given to all lay counselor trainees or subjects just before and just after the training program. This example of a somewhat ideal research design will allow us to answer two basic questions: *Did the lay counselor trainees who received the training program improve significantly on the different evaluation measures,* comparing their posttraining scores on such measures to their pretraining scores? Secondly, and more importantly, *did they improve significantly more than the other group of trainees* who either waited or served as a comparison group who received some other kind of training? If some other kind of training is provided to the second group as a comparison group, it is important to specify what kind of training. It should *not* include counseling skills training, but even training in Bible study skills may lead to personal and spiritual growth, so the two groups may *not* differ significantly on measures of personal and spiritual growth. However, if the training program is to be judged as effective, they should differ significantly on measures of counseling knowledge and skills, with the group who received the training program doing better.

I realize that what I have just described is one example of a somewhat ideal research design. Many local churches and parachurch or missionary organizations that run lay counselor training programs will not have the time, energy, money, or expertise to conduct such an elaborate study. Hopefully, several academic or professional researchers will take up the challenge to conduct evaluation studies similar to the one I have just described. For the majority of others conducting lay counselor training programs, it will be good enough if they attempt to do some evaluation of their programs, using at least something like the minimal evaluation package I have suggested, and administering it before and after a particular training program.

Evaluation of Outcome of Lay Christian Counseling

The acid test of the effectiveness of any lay Christian counselor training program, however, must eventually involve evaluating the effectiveness of the lay counseling provided by the trained lay counselors in terms of therapeutic outcome.

A large body of literature now exists on the evaluation of psychotherapy outcome in the field of professional counseling and psychotherapy. It includes key books edited by Garfield and

Bergin; Lambert, Christensen and DeJulio; Williams and Spitzer; Harvey and Parks; and Waskow and Parloff.[24]

Special issues on psychotherapy research also appeared a few years ago in two important professional journals published by the American Psychological Association—the February 1986 issues of the *American Psychologist* and the *Journal of Consulting and Clinical Psychology*.[25] These significant books and publications provide guidelines and methods for conducting evaluation studies of psychotherapy or counseling outcomes. These guidelines can also be applied to the evaluation of the outcomes of lay Christian counseling, with some adaptation or modification where necessary. Evaluation research on the effectiveness of lay Christian counseling is unfortunately at the present time even more scarce than the already limited research that has been done evaluating lay counselor training programs. The few studies that have been completed in both these areas of evaluation of lay Christian counselors have been reviewed in chapter 4. As in the previous section of this chapter, I will first review and describe the various approaches and measures which can be used to evaluate the therapeutic outcomes of lay Christian counseling and then suggest a basic or minimal evaluation package of measures (and variations of it) for use in various lay Christian counseling settings. I will end the present section of this chapter with some comments on research design for conducting such outcome evaluation studies, and on several other issues relevant to the evaluation of lay counselors.

Measures for Outcome Evaluation

Lambert, Shapiro, and Bergin have recently written a very helpful review chapter on the effectiveness of psychotherapy and the evaluation of therapeutic outcomes. In order to overcome systematic bias and invalid conclusions as well as to provide a more comprehensive assessment of therapeutic change or effects, they recommend the use of multiple outcome measures from a variety of viewpoints, under the following five categories indicating their source: (1) Patient (Counselee/Client) Self-Report; (2) Trained Outside Observer/Expert Observer Ratings; (3) Relevant Other Ratings; (4) Therapist (Counselor) Ratings; and (5) Institutional Ratings.[26] Examples of helpful measures in each of these categories will now be briefly listed. Lambert, Shapiro, and Bergin's chapter should be consulted for further details and information.

1. Patient/Client Self-Report

Five main types of measures were listed under this category:

a. *Posttherapy (postcounseling) questionnaires/satisfaction measures* evaluating client-felt improvement, including both global estimates of therapy or counseling-induced improvement, and improvements on specific targets, as well as overall client satisfaction with the counseling or therapy provided;

b. *Symptom checklists,* whether single symptoms/single trait such as the Beck Depression Inventory or the State-Trait Anxiety Inventory, or multiple symptom checklists like the Hopkins Symptom Checklist or its revision called the Symptom Checklist-90R (SCL-90R);

c. *Self-monitoring* procedures requiring the client to record his or her own thoughts, feelings, and specific behaviors, examples of which include measures of self-talk like the Self-Statement Inventory, the Automatic Thoughts Questionnaire, and the Irrational Beliefs Test;

d. *Personality tests,* including the Minnesota Multiphasic Personality Inventory or MMPI (which unfortunately has serious limitations and appears to be too cumbersome and possibly insensitive for it to be used as a measure of therapeutic change), and the Millon Clinical Multi-Axial Inventory or MCMI; and

e. *Measures of self-regulation/self-esteem,* including the Tennessee Self-Concept Scale, Personal Attribute Inventory, Rosenberg Self-Esteem Scale, and the recent Self-Control Schedule, as well as self-monitoring devices like timing devices, mechanical counters, and self-monitoring cards.

2. Expert and Trained Observers

Two main types of expert or trained observer ratings or judgments, using a person or persons external to the therapy as the judge(s), were listed under this category:

a. *Standardized interviews and expert ratings,* including the Social Adjustment Scale, the Denver Community Mental Health Questionnaire, the Global Adjustment Scale, and the Hamilton Rating Scale for Depression;

b. *Behavioral counts,* which include a variety of observational rating forms for particular behaviors and their frequencies, durations, etc., that can be completed by nonprofessional observers. Role Play Tests are one example.

3. Evaluation by Relevant Others

Relevant others can include parents, spouse, siblings, friends, teachers, employer, and other relatives or third parties who are related to the client and can therefore provide outside data to corroborate or verify self-report data on particular behaviors or symptoms. Two main types of measures were mentioned in this category: (a) *Measures of Social Adjustment* like the Katz Adjustment Scale-Relatives Form (KAS-R) and the Personal Adjustment and Role Skills-III (PARS-III); (b) *Measures of Sexual Behavior and Marital Satisfaction* such as the Locke-Wallace Marital Adjustment Test and the Sexual Interactional Inventory.

4. Evaluation by the Therapist/Counselor

The counselor can provide ratings of client improvement using measures like target complaints (which require the counselor to list three major target problems the client wants help for and then rate their severity at the beginning and at the termination of counseling—the counselee can also do the same, in which case target complaints become a client self-report measure), Goal Attainment Scaling, Problem-Oriented Record, and the Davis Goal Scaling Form.

5. Assessment Through Institutional Means

This method involves the use of data obtained through records kept mainly for the internal use of agencies or organizations like schools, law enforcement agencies, employment offices, hospitals, churches, community organizations, etc. Examples of such data or measures are recidivism or relapse rates (like rearrest records), hospital readmission rates, and medical utilization records. There are obvious limitations, however, with such measures or data, but they can also be helpful.

It is difficult, however, to use all five of the major categories of outcome measures just mentioned in the evaluation of psychotherapy or counseling effectiveness, especially in a community setting like a church counseling service or a community mental health center, whose top priority is not research but providing counseling services. Nevertheless, some attempt at evaluation of counseling effectiveness can still be made. Dr. Robert Manthei has described a comprehensive, effective, and simple means of evaluating therapeutic outcome at a community mental health center that can be applied in any treatment or counseling setting by using the following measures: (1) *number of counseling sessions attended* by clients; (2) *type of termination* (mutual counselor and client decision versus unilateral client decision); (3) *three main target complaints* rated by clients as well as counselors; (4) *the 18-item General Well-Being Schedule* as a measure of clients' general psychological well-being during the past month; and (5) *the Current Adjustment Rating Scale* as a measure of counselors' ratings of their clients' general well-being before and after therapy or counseling.[27] This helpful package of measures can be adapted and modified for use in a local church lay counseling center functioning within a formal, organized model of lay counseling ministry. I will now describe such a modified package, including a number of measures of spirituality or spiritual well-being, as well as a couple of postcounseling questionnaires or surveys.

Suggested Measures for Evaluating the Counseling Effectiveness of Lay Christian Counselors

In addition to documenting the number of counseling sessions attended by clients and the type of termination experienced, the following measures are recommended for use in the evaluation of the counseling effectiveness of lay Christian counselors providing counseling to adult clients, particularly in the context of a formal church lay counseling center:

1. Target Complaints

Three target complaints should be obtained from each client at the beginning of counseling by asking, "What kinds of problems or difficulties are you seeking counseling for? What else? . . . What else?" Clients should then be asked to describe the situations in which each problem or difficulty occurred, and to rate how much the problem or complaint is bothering them, using a thirteen-point box scale with five descriptors (starting with "not at all" at the bottom box, to "a little" at the fourth box, to "pretty much" at the seventh box, to "very much" at the tenth box, and ending with "couldn't be worse" at the thirteenth or top box). Clients are asked to check the appropriate box for each target complaint or problem,[28] at the beginning and at termination of counseling. The same three target complaints noted at the beginning of counseling should be rated at the end of counseling.

2. Symptom Checklist-90R (SCL-90R)

This is a revision of the longer Hopkins Symptom Checklist, with ninety items divided into nine symptom dimensions and three global indices of distress. It is most useful as a global measure of psychological distress or psychopathology.[29] Clients should be asked to complete this inventory at the beginning and at the end of counseling. An alternative measure to the SCL-90R is the 18-item General Well-Being Schedule used by Manthei.[30]

3. Counselor's Global Rating of Client's Psychological Adjustment

At the beginning and termination of counseling, the counselor should make a global rating of the client's psychological adjustment, using a ten-point scale (ranging from 1, most extreme maladjustment, to ten, optimal adjustment).[31] An alternative to this global ten-point scale is the current Adjustment Rating Scale used by Manthei, consisting of fourteen items to be rated on nine scales by the counselor to evaluate the client's current functioning, satisfactions, and social stimulus value.[32]

4. Measures of Spirituality

The Spiritual Well-Being Scale as well as the Religious Status Inventory already described earlier are recommended as measures of spiritual well-being and spiritual maturity respectively. They should be completed by the client at the beginning and at termination of counseling.

5. Postcounseling Questionnaires/Surveys

Two versions of a postcounseling questionnaire, one to be filled in by the client and the other by the counselor, are recommended. They are adapted from the posttherapy questionnaires used by J. Craig Yagel in a doctoral dissertation submitted to the Graduate School of Psychology at Fuller Theological Seminary in 1984.[33] The questionnaires contain items on overall success, overall satisfaction, and overall amount of improvement due to the counseling provided, to be rated on a six-point scale (ranging from 1, extremely poor, to 6, superb). They also include symptom change, personal change, recommending counseling to a close friend with emotional problems, present functioning, current problem-solving ability, and need for further counseling. Five additional items adapted from Lazarus were included in the client form of the questionnaire to evaluate the client's perception of how helpful, competent, sincere, likable, and interested the counselor was,[34] reflecting the *credibility* of the counselor and the counseling provided.

The counselor form of the questionnaire also contains two additional items at the end, on the degree of personal integration or psychological health of the client and on the life adjustment or social/vocational functioning of the client, rated for the beginning as well as the end of counseling. Both forms of the postcounseling questionnaires are reprinted in appendices A and B.

An alternative to these questionnaires is a postcounseling follow-up survey or questionnaire developed by the Family Service Association called the *FSA Questionnaire* (Form No. 26, Revised).[35] This measure was used by Richard Walters to survey client satisfaction as well as client change six months after termination of counseling in a lay counseling program at the First Presbyterian Church in Boulder, Colorado (the results of the survey have been described in chapter 4). Walters also found that out of seventeen lay counseling programs surveyed in early 1985, only two were asking clients to evaluate their programs, both at termination of the lay counseling provided. Follow-up evaluations can also be conducted by using the measures already described earlier and readministering them several months after the termination of counseling. Using only a follow-up survey or questionnaire a few months after the end of counseling without any pre- and postcounseling measures like the ones just described, however, can lead to biased reports, probably in too positive a direction.

I therefore recommend the use of *target complaints* (rated by the client), *the SCL-90R*, the *10-point scale global rating of the client's adjustment* (rated by the counselor), the *Spiritual Well-Being Scale*, the *RSI*, and the *postcounseling questionnaires* (both client and counselor forms) in the evaluation of the effectiveness of lay Christian counselors. However, in most local church or parachurch contexts in which lay counseling occurs, this suggested package may still be too ambitious. If so, then I would suggest *at the very least,* the use of *target complaints,* the *10-point global rating of client adjustment, the Spiritual Well-Being Scale,* and the *postcounseling questionnaires* (or alternatively, the FSA Questionnaire at termination and/or follow-up). The use of this suggested minimal package of evaluation measures will help to expand the data base supporting or refuting the effectiveness of lay Christian counseling ministries, as well as facilitate comparisons of outcomes across different facilities and contexts.

Using a standard package of evaluation measures, however, has a number of obvious drawbacks. First, the package I have suggested may not be specific enough to evaluate effects of other types of counseling like marriage or family counseling, in which case other more relevant measures of marital or family functioning should be used.[36] Second, if specific types of client problems are being seen in the lay counseling center or service, then more specific measures of those problems (e.g., depression, or anxiety) should also be used.[37] Finally, the measures I have suggested apply mostly to adult clients. Other measures are needed to evaluate the effectiveness of counseling with younger clients or children.[38]

A Note on Research Design for Evaluation of the Effectiveness of Lay Christian Counseling

Dr. Gary Collins has commented, "I know of no competent research study that investigates the effectiveness of lay counseling among Christians."[39] This comment is still largely true. The evaluation of counseling effectiveness is a very complex endeavor, fraught with methodological issues and difficulties, and therefore controversial. Nevertheless, I would like to make several suggestions for better or more competent evaluation research to be conducted on the effectiveness of lay Christian counseling.

First, appropriate and good measures of outcome, such as the ones I have described (including measures of spiritual maturity and spiritual well-being) should be used. These measures should be administered at least at pre- and postcounseling, and, if possible, at follow-up a few months or more after the termination of counseling.

Second, as far as possible, in a somewhat ideal research design, clients should be randomly assigned to at least two groups—a group which receives the lay counseling, and a control group which receives nothing but waits (waiting-list, "no-treatment" control group). This approach attempts to answer the question of whether lay counseling is more effective than no counseling. An alternative approach, called the comparative design,[40] involves randomly assigning clients to two types of lay counseling (e.g., nouthetic counseling as developed by Jay Adams versus biblical counseling as developed by Lawrence Crabb), and comparing the relative effectiveness of the two types of lay counseling without the use of formal control groups, an approach which may be more realistic and ethical to employ in local church lay counseling centers. While random assignment of clients is ideal, it is often not practical or ethical to place some clients on a waiting list randomly. However, some local church lay counseling centers have a natural waiting list of clients because of the high demand for lay counseling, and this group can then be used as the waiting list control group, although no random assignment of clients has been done. Statistical procedures can then be employed to determine the comparability of the group of clients receiving lay counseling and the waiting-list control group of clients on a number of measures at precounseling. If the two groups do not differ significantly on these measures before counseling or at the start of counseling, then some comparability of the two groups at the beginning of the evaluation study can be assumed.

Third, lay counselors should be given a clearly described manual or protocol to follow, especially if a comparative design is used. For example, those providing nouthetic counseling should be following closely Jay Adams' approach and methods, and those providing biblical counseling should be following closely Lawrence Crabb's approach and methods. Counseling sessions should be audiotaped or videotaped so that ratings by other objective judges or raters can subsequently be made regarding the extent to which the lay counselors followed the counseling protocol or guidelines to be used in a particular evaluation study.

Finally, evaluation studies should eventually go beyond

global studies comparing lay counseling to no counseling, or one type of lay counseling to another type of lay counseling. More specific questions need to be answered, including those having to do with mechanisms of change and particular components or factors of the lay counseling provided that may be more responsible for the outcomes or effects obtained. Different research designs can be employed to answer some of these specific questions, but as Dr. Alan Kazdin, a well-known researcher in this field, has pointed out, the questions that can be addressed by research are astronomical! He made the following comment in reviewing the methodology of psychotherapy outcome research:

> Many basic issues about assessment and design that dictate how to address outcome questions appropriately are also far from resolved. Hence there is no singularly or universally agreed-upon assessment battery or design strategy that could, in any definitive fashion, put to rest particular questions about therapy.[41]

No definitive or perfect evaluation study on the outcome of lay counseling is therefore possible, but I do hope that the suggestions I have made will help increase the number of "competent" evaluation or outcome studies in the area of lay Christian counseling.

Adequate attention should also be paid to the ethical issues involved in conducting evaluation research on the effectiveness of psychotherapy or counseling, including lay counseling. Space does not permit a detailed discussion of such important ethical issues (e.g., informed consent, confidentiality of records, appropriateness of using control groups and random assignment of clients, etc.), many of which have been delineated in a helpful article by Stanley Imber and his colleagues.[42] Such ethical considerations should be addressed *before* starting any evaluation study to ensure that all research is conducted in an ethical manner.

Concluding Comments

There are several other issues pertaining to the evaluation of the effectiveness of lay Christian counseling which I would like to mention briefly as I conclude this chapter. First, I have not described the various approaches and methods for investigating the *process* of therapy or counseling.[43] This is an important area of research, and further studies evaluating the process or actual dimensions and factors of lay Christian counseling that contribute significantly to good outcomes or effects are therefore needed. Second, the criteria for evaluating the effectiveness of lay Christian counseling should also be widened to include not only measures of client change and client satisfaction, but also the durability and clinical significance (not just statistical significance) of such change, and cost-benefit analyses pertaining to the *efficiency,* and not just the efficacy or effectiveness, of the counseling provided.[44] *Program evaluation* of the effects of the total lay counseling ministry on others in addition to the clients served (for example, on the pastoral staff, church board, congregation, and church life and ministry, as well as the lay counselors themselves) should also be conducted. Third, funding to financially support better or more competent evaluation studies in the area of lay Christian counseling will be needed. Organizations like the Christian Association for Psychological Studies International, the California Peer Counseling Association, and the National Peer Helpers Association[45] can also be involved in encouraging more evaluation research on lay or peer counseling, and possibly making funds available to support such research. Fourth, more studies are needed which attempt to evaluate *both* the effectiveness of training programs for lay Christian counselors as well as the effectiveness of the lay counseling provided by such trained lay Christian counselors. Such studies, while more elaborate and complex, will help to determine what specific lay counselor skills or competencies are related to good outcomes, and how well lay Christian counselors can be trained in such skills. A related need is to further determine what selection criteria or measures for lay counselors are significant predictors of good lay counselor training effects, as well as effective lay counseling.

Finally, I should point out that what I have suggested in this chapter for the evaluation of the effectiveness of lay Christian counseling is most applicable and relevant to the *formal, organized model* of lay counseling ministry (e.g., in the context of a lay counseling center or service), although some of the measures I have described can also be used with some modification in the context of an *informal, organized model* of lay counseling ministry. The suggestions I have made regarding the evaluation of *training programs* for lay Christian counselors can, however, be applied to *both* the *formal, organized* and *informal, organized* models of lay counseling ministry.

Let me conclude this chapter with the following comments; made over a decade ago by Dr. Joseph Durlak after reviewing the literature on the comparative effectiveness of paraprofessional (lay) and professional helpers or counselors, which are still valid today:

> Data indicate that paraprofessionals can make an important contribution as helping agents, but the factors accounting for this phenomenon are not understood. . . . It would be a mistake to continue using paraprofessionals without more closely examining their skills, deficiencies, and limitations.[46]

More and better evaluation studies of the skills, deficiencies, and limitations of lay *Christian* counselors providing lay *Christian* counseling in particular, are definitely needed.

NOTES

[1]See A. E. Bergin, "Briefly Noted—Book review of J. Roland Fleck and John D. Carter, eds., *Psychology and Christianity: Integrative Readings,*" *Contemporary Psychology* 27 (1982): 657.

[2]Fleck and Carter, *Psychology and Christianity,* 41, 43, 53.

[3]American Psychological Association. *Report of the Task Force on the Evaluation of Education, Training and Service in Psychology* (Washington, D.C.: A.P.A., 1982), 2.

[4]Ibid.

[5]See, e.g., B. A. Edelstein and E. S. Berler, eds., *Evaluation and Accountability in Clinical Training* (New York: Plenum, 1987); J. E. Callan, D. R. Peterson, and G. Strickler, eds., *Quality in Professional Psychology Training: A National Conference and Self-Study* (Norman, Okla.: Transcript Press, 1986); and E. F. Bourg, R. J. Bent, J. E. Callan, N. F. Jones, J. McHolland, and G. Stricker, eds., *Standards and Evaluation in the Education and Training of Professional Psychologists; Knowledge, Attitudes, and Skills* (Norman, Okla.: Transcript Press, 1987). Also see R. G. Matarazzo and D. Patterson, "Methods of Teaching Therapeutic Skills," in S. L. Garfield and A. E. Bergin eds., *Handbook of Psychotherapy and Behavior Change,* 3d ed. (New York: Wiley, 1986), 821–43.

[6]See, e.g., P. C. Kendall and J. N. Butcher, eds., *Handbook of Research Methods in Clinical Psychology* (New York: Wiley, 1982); A. S. Bellack and M. Hersen, eds., *Research Methods in Clinical Psychology* (New York: Pergamon, 1984); A. E. Kazdin, *Research*

Design in Clinical Psychology (New York: Harper & Row, 1980); and D. H. Barlow, S. C. Hayes, and R. O. Nelson, *The Scientist-Practitioner: Research and Accountability in Clinical and Educational Settings* (New York: Pergamon, 1984).

[7]See C. E. Hill, D. Charles, and K. G. Reed, "A Longitudinal Analysis of Changes in Counseling Skills During Doctoral Training in Counseling Psychology," *Journal of Counseling Psychology* 28 (1981): 203–12; and A. P. Thompson, "Changes in Counseling Skills During Graduate and Undergraduate Study," *Journal of Counseling Psychology* 33 (1986): 65–72.

[8]C. E. Hill, "Development of a Counselor Verbal Response Category System," *Journal of Counseling Psychology* 25 (1978): 461–68; C. E. Hill, C. Greenwald, K. G. Reed, and D. Charles, *Manual for the Counselor and Client Verbal Response Category Systems* (Columbus, Ohio: Marathon Consulting & Press, 1981).

[9]E. L. Shostrom, *Personal Orientation Inventory* (San Diego, Calif.: EdITS, 1963).

[10]See S. Y. Tan, "Training Lay Christian Counselors: A Basic Program and Some Preliminary Data," *Journal of Psychology and Christianity* 6, no. 2 (1987): 57–61, and other studies using the CTPQ reviewed in chap. 4.

[11]E. J. Jones and J. W. Pfeiffer, "Helping Relationship Inventory," in E. J. Jones and J. W. Pfeiffer, eds., *The Annual Handbook for Group Facilitators* (San Diego: University Associates Publishers, 1973).

[12]See R. Carkhuff, *Helping and Human Relations: A Primer for Lay and Professional Helpers*, vols. 1, 2 (New York: Holt, Rinehart and Winston, 1969); and C. B. Truax and R. R. Carkhuff, *Toward Effective Counseling and Psychotherapy* (Chicago: Aldine, 1967).

[13]See R. Jernigan, S. Y. Tan, and R. L. Gorsuch, "The Effectiveness of a Local Church Lay Christian Counselor Training Program: A Controlled Study," paper presented at the International Congress on Christian Counseling, Lay Counseling Track, November 1988, in Atlanta, Georgia.

[14]See M. J. Lambert, S. S. DeJulio, and D. M. Stein, "Therapist Interpersonal Skills: Process, Outcome, Methodological Considerations, and Recommendations for Future Research, *Psychological Bulletin,* 85 (1978): 467–89; and M. J. Lambert, "Implications of Psychotherapy Outcome Research for Eclectic Psychotherapy," in J. C. Norcross, ed., *Handbook of Eclectic Psychotherapy* (New York: Brunner/Mazel, 1986), 436–62, p. 445.

[15]See T. M. Vallis, B. F. Shaw, and K. S. Dobson, "The Cognitive Therapy Scale: Psychometric Properties," *Journal of Consulting and Clinical Psychology* 54 (1986): 381–85. Also see B. F. Shaw and K. S. Dobson, "Competence Judgments in the Training and Evaluation of

Psychotherapists" *Journal of Consulting and Clinical Psychology* 56 (1988): 666–72; and K. S. Dobson and B. F. Shaw, "The Use of Treatment Manuals in Cognitive Therapy: Experience and Issues," *Journal of Consulting and Clinical Psychology* 56 (1988): 673–80.

[16]See D. M. Boan and T. Owens, "Peer Ratings of Lay Counselor Skill as Related to Client Satisfaction," *Journal of Psychology and Christianity* 4, no. 1 (1985): 79–81.

[17]See E. L. Shostrom, *EdITS Manual for the Personal Orientation Inventory* (San Diego: EdITS, 1974), 4. See also n. 9.

[18]See C. A. Schaefer, L. Dodds, and S. Y. Tan, "Changes in Attitudes Toward Peer Counseling and Personal Orientation Measured During Growth Facilitator Training for Cross-Cultural Ministry," unpublished manuscript, 1988, pp. 12–13.

[19]See chap. 6, n. 16.

[20]See H. N. Malony, "The Clinical Assessment of Optimal Religious Functioning," *Review of Religious Research* 30, no. 1 (1988): 3–17. The self-report version of the RSI is available from Dr. Malony, who can be contacted at the Graduate School of Psychology, Fuller Theological Seminary, 180 N. Oakland Ave., Pasadena, CA 91101.

[21]F. Smith, "Measuring Quality Church Growth," unpublished doctoral diss., School of World Mission, Fuller Theological Seminary, 1985.

[22]R. L. Gorsuch and G. D. Venable, "Development of An 'Age Universal' I-E Scale," *Journal for the Scientific Study of Religion* 22 (1983): 181–87.

[23]See n. 13 and S. Y. Tan and P. Sarff, "Comprehensive Evaluation of a Lay Counselor Training Program in a Local Church," invited paper presented at the International Congress on Christian Counseling, Lay Counseling Track, November 1988, in Atlanta, Georgia.

[24]See S. L. Garfield and A. E. Bergin, eds., *Handbook of Psychotherapy and Behavior Change*, 3d ed. (New York: Wiley, 1986); M. J. Lambert, E. R. Christensen, and S. S. DeJulio, eds., *The Assessment of Psychotherapy Outcome* (New York: Wiley, 1983); J. Williams and R. Spitzer, eds., *Psychotherapy Research: Where Are We and Where Should We Go?* (New York: Guilford, 1984); J. H. Harvey and M. M. Parks, eds., *Psychotherapy Research and Behavior Change* (*The Master Lecture Series*, vol. 1), (Washington, D.C.: American Psychological Association, 1982); and I. E. Waskow and M. B. Parloff, eds., *Psychotherapy Change Measures* (Washington, D.C.: U.S. Dept. of Health, Education, and Welfare, 1975).

[25]See *American Psychologist* 41 (1986): 111–214 (Special Issue: Psychotherapy Research), and *Journal of Consulting and Clinical Psychology* 54 (1986): 3–118 (Special Issue: Psychotherapy Research).

[26]See M. J. Lambert, D. A. Shapiro, and A. E. Bergin, "The Effectiveness of Psychotherapy," in S. L. Garfield and A. E. Bergin, eds., *Handbook of Psychotherapy and Behavior Change*, 3d ed. (New York: Wiley, 1986), 157–211.

[27]See R. J. Manthei, "Evaluating Therapy Outcome at a Community Mental Health Center," *Professional Psychology* 14 (1983): 67–77.

[28]See C. C. Battle, S. D. Imber, R. Hoehn-Saric, A. R. Stine, E. R. Nash, and J. D. Frank, "Target Complaints as Criteria for Improvement," *American Journal of Psychotherapy* 20 (1966): 184–92.

[29]See L. R. Derogatis, R. S. Lipman, R. Rickels, E. H. Uhlenhuth, and L. Covi, "The Hopkins Symptom Checklist (HSCL): A Self-Report Symptom Inventory," *Behavioral Science* 19 (1974): 1–15.

[30]See A. F. Fazio, *A Concurrent Validational Study of the NCHS General Well-Being Schedule* (U.S. Dept. of Health, Education, and Welfare, Publication No. HRA 78–1347) (Washington, D.C.: U.S. Government Printing Office, 1977).

[31]See D. S. Cartwright, R. J. Robinson, D. W. Fiske, and W. L. Kirtner, "Length of Therapy in Relation to Outcome and Change in Personal Integration," *Journal of Consulting Psychology* 25 (1961): 84–88.

[32]See J. I. Berzins, R. L. Bednar, and L. J. Severy, "The Problem of Intersource Consensus in Measuring Therapeutic Outcomes: New Data and Multivariate Perspectives," *Journal of Abnormal Psychology* 84 (1975): 10–19.

[33]See J. Craig Yagel, *The Relationship of Therapist's Personality to Psychotherapy Outcome Measured Via Target Complaints Assessment and Post-Therapy Questionnaire* (doctoral diss., Graduate School of Psychology, Fuller Theological Seminary, 1984). The post-therapy questionnaires were based on previous research reported in the following publications: C. R. Rogers and R. Dymond, *Psychotherapy and Personality Change* (Chicago: University of Chicago Press, 1954); H. H. Strupp, R. E. Fox, and K. Lessler, *Patients View Their Psychotherapy* (Baltimore: Johns Hopkins Press, 1969); H. H. Strupp, M. S. Wallach, and M. Wogan, "Psychotherapy Experience in Retrospect: Questionnaire Survey of Former Patients and Their Therapists," *Psychological Monographs* 78 (11, Whole no. 588).

[34]See A. A. Lazarus, *Behavior Therapy and Beyond* (New York: McGraw-Hill, 1971).

[35]The FSA Questionnaire is available from Family Service Association of America, 44 E. 23rd St., New York, NY 10010. See also D. F. Beck and M. A. Jones, *How to Conduct A Client Follow-Up Study* (New York: Family Service Association of America, 1980).

[36]See N. Fredman and R. Sherman, *Handbook of Measurements for Marriage and Family Therapy* (New York: Brunner/Mazel, 1987).

37See K. Corcoran and J. Fischer, *Measures for Clinical Practice: A Sourcebook* (New York: The Free Press, 1987).

38Ibid.

39Gary R. Collins, "Lay Counseling: Some Lingering Questions for Professionals," *Journal of Psychology and Christianity* 6, no. 2 (1987): 7–9, p. 7.

40See R. B. Basham, "Scientific and Practical Advantages of Comparative Design in Psychotherapy Outcome Research," *Journal of Consulting and Clinical Psychology* 54 (1986): 88–94.

41Alan E. Kazdin, "Methodology of Psychotherapy Outcome Research: Recent Developments and Remaining Limitations," in J. H. Harvey and M. M. Parks, eds., *Psychotherapy Research and Behavior Change (The Master Lecture Series*, vol. 1), (Washington, D.C.: American Psychological Association, 1982), 155–93, p. 166.

42See S. D. Imber, L. M. Glanz, I. Elkin, S. M. Sotsky, J. L. Boyer, and W. R. Leber, "Ethical Issues in Psychotherapy Research: Problems in a Collaborative Clinical Trials Study," *Journal of Consulting and Clinical Psychology* 41 (1986): 137–46.

43See L. S. Greenberg, "Change Process Research," *Journal of Consulting and Clinical Psychology* 54 (1986): 4–9; L. S. Greenberg and W. Pinsof, eds., *The Psychotherapeutic Process: A Research Handbook* (New York: Guilford, 1986); and L. Rice and L. S. Greenberg, eds., *Patterns of Change: Intensive Analysis of Psychotherapeutic Process* (New York: Guilford, 1984).

44See A. E. Kazdin and G. T. Wilson, "Criteria for Evaluating Psychotherapy," *Archives of General Psychiatry* 35 (1978): 407–16.

45These three organizations can be contacted at the following addresses:

Christian Association for Psychological Studies International
P.O. Box 628,
Blue Jay, CA 92317
(Tel. 714-337-5117, Dr. Robert R. King)

California Peer Counseling Association
3605 El Camino Real, Box 5
Santa Clara, CA 95051

The National Peer Helpers Association
2370 Market Street, Room 120
San Francisco, CA 94114
Tel. 415-626-1942

46J. Durlak, "Comparative Effectiveness of Paraprofessional and Professional Helpers," *Psychological Bulletin* 86 (1979): 80–92, p. 90.

10

The Local Church and Lay Counseling

In the previous nine chapters of this book I have described in some detail various aspects of a biblical approach to lay counseling, including the selection, training, supervision, and evaluation of lay Christian counselors, as well as building or establishing a ministry of lay counseling. In this chapter I will first describe briefly the major findings from a survey of fifteen church-based lay counseling ministries conducted by the Center for Church Renewal in Plano, Texas.[1] Second, I will provide examples of actual lay counseling ministries in various local churches, several of which have been described in a recent book on Christian peer counseling written by Joan Sturkie and Gordon Bear.[2] I will describe in more detail the lay counseling services I set up and directed at Peoples Church of Montreal and North Park Community Chapel in Canada. Finally, I will go beyond the local church by mentioning lay counseling ministries in other contexts like parachurch organizations (for example, Youth For Christ, Young Life, and the Navigators), prison ministries, retirement and nursing homes, Christian mental health centers or programs, and missions.

Lay Counseling Survey Findings

The Center for Church Renewal in Plano, Texas, conducted a survey in 1986 of fifteen evangelical church-based lay counseling ministries. The following churches, ranging in size from 450 to 9,000 members and representing a variety of denominational affiliations, geographical locations, and lay counseling models and philosophies, participated in the survey: Bear Valley Baptist Church, Bible Town Community Church, College Hill Presbyterian, Crystal Cathedral, Faith Presbyterian Church, First Baptist of Houston, First Presbyterian of Richardson, Glenkirk Presbyterian Church, Grace Community Church, La Canada Presbyterian Church, Living Faith Center, National Presbyterian Church, Northway Christian Church, Northwest Community Church, and Northwest Hills Baptist Church. Five of these churches described themselves as urban, ten of them as suburban, and none as rural. Fourteen churches described themselves as "large" and one of them as "small."

With regard to weekly attendance on Sunday mornings, there were five churches with under 1000, seven churches with between 1000 and 2000, one church with between 2000 and 3000, one church with between 4000 and 5000, and one church of 9000.

The following are the denominational affiliations of the fifteen churches: Assembly of God (1), Bible (1), Christian Church (1), Conservative Baptist (2), Evangelical Presbyterian (1), Independent (1), Missionary Church (1), Presbyterian Church USA (5), Reformed Church of America (1), and Southern Baptist (2). One church belonged to both the Conservative and Southern Baptist denominations.

I will now summarize the major findings from the survey under the three main headings provided: (1) lay counselor training, (2) lay counseling, and (3) evaluation.

Lay Counselor Training

A. Length of time programs have existed

The average age of the lay counseling ministries (including the provision of lay counselor training) in these churches was 6.1 years, with a range from 2 to 18 years.

B. Size

1. Number of people who have completed training. A total of 981 people have been trained as lay counselors by these fifteen churches, with an average of 65 trained people per church, and a range from 1 to 200. The actual number of trained lay counselors produced per year ranged from 3 to 38.

2. Number of people currently in training. A total of 82 people were still in training (in 4 of the 15 churches), with an average of 6 per church.

3. Number of teachers and trainers. The average number of trainers was 8, with a range of 2 to 50 (although not all 50 trainers are used in every session, in this particular church).

C. Description of the training process

1. Classes. The average number of classes used to train lay counselors was 36, with a range from 6 to 135. Most of the classes met weekly for one-to-two-hour sessions. In addition to weekly training sessions, some churches also used weekend retreats, an all-day Saturday seminar, attendance at outside seminars (one day to one week in length), home meetings, and required attendance at a seminary course.

2. Content. Out of the 13 churches which responded to this question, 4 of them noted that they were heavily influenced by Crabb's lay counselor training approach, although they described their training as eclectic in content. Two other churches indicated that their training course content was heavily influenced by the Stephen Series. One church depended completely on Egan's *Skilled Helper,* and another on Collins' *People Helper Pack.*

The most frequently covered topics (with frequencies of more than one) in the content of the training course provided were the following (with frequencies given in parentheses): counseling skills (12), training for specific issues (9), crisis counseling (8), marital counseling (8), use of the Bible in counseling (8), theology of man or human nature (7), theology of change (7), how or when to refer (5), relationship of psychology and religion (4), and self-understanding in lay counseling (2). Other topics mentioned only once included authority of Scripture, adult personality inventory, assertion training, assessment/diagnosis, categories of problems, Christian thinking, communication process, confidentiality, depression, feelings, issues of counseling, legal issues, organization, philosophy of counseling, prayer, psychopathology, relating to others, sin, telephone care, and thinking through your faith.

3. Who teaches? Eleven churches used staff pastors; ten used trained lay counselors; six used professional counselors from outside; one used a staff counselor; and another used chaplains from outside as trainers or teachers in their training programs.

4. Use of observation. Only two churches utilize observation of lay counselors in their training process.

5. Use of co-counseling. Seven churches offer some kind of co-counseling, especially in the contexts of premarital counseling and family counseling.

6. Personal discipleship. Eight churches described their training as including some component of personal discipleship.

7. Use of videos/films. Eleven churches use videos or films in their training programs, ranging from Christian ones on counseling to secular films on various topics.

8. Seminars. Fourteen churches included the use of seminars in their training programs (e.g., Larry Crabb's week-long seminars on biblical counseling, and other local, secular, topical seminars).

D. Length of lay counselor training process

The average length or duration of the lay counselor training process or program was about eight months. Eight churches had training programs that lasted six months or less. Four other churches finish their training process in a year or less. Two more churches take two years to complete their training, and one church had an indefinite length.

E. Selection process for lay counselors

1. Is participation in the lay counseling program open to all volunteers, or are those who do lay counseling chosen? None of the churches had completely open lay counseling programs. Eight churches have open participation in the training part of their programs, but the lay counseling is done only by specially selected lay counselors. The other seven churches limit both their training as well as the lay counseling ministry to specially selected or chosen lay counselors.

2. If the lay counselors are chosen, what criteria are involved? A wide variety of criteria was mentioned for selecting lay counselors. The counselor's character was listed most often, especially traits like teachability, flexibility, strength, and empathy. Second and third on the list were spiritual maturity and commitment to the lay counseling program respectively. Other criteria mentioned included demonstrated informal counseling ability, qualifying personal life experience, and successfully passing a screening interview (required by four churches).

F. Organizational structure

Fourteen churches had a paid staff person who oversees the lay counseling ministry (but not all of them actually direct the lay counseling programs per se), and one church used a lay volunteer to oversee the ministry.

Eight churches had one paid staff member direct all the lay counselors in the church, whereas in six others a supervising lay counselor actually directed the other lay counselors, but he or she in turn reported to a paid staff member of the church.

Lay Counseling

A. Number of active lay counselors

The average number of lay counselors functioning per church was 16, with a range from 7 to 40.

B. Time

1. Number of hours of lay counseling per week. The average number of lay counseling hours per week was 22, with a range from 4 to 50. The majority of the churches surveyed spent a little less than the average of 22.

2. Number of hours of staff counseling per week. The average number of hours per week spent by the staff of the churches surveyed in counseling was 34, with a range from 9 to 120. However, the majority of churches spent somewhat less than the average (i.e., about 20–30 hours per week).

C. Types of counseling situations in which the lay counselors minister

The following are the most frequently mentioned types of counseling situations seen by lay counselors (with frequencies of more than once), with the actual frequencies given in parentheses: parenting problems (12), depression (11), marital disputes (11), grief (10), premarital (10), drugs/alcohol abuse (8), self-image (7), anxiety (7), anger (6), child abuse (5), guilt (5), suicide (4), teen pregnancy (4), extramarital affairs (4), vocational (3), relationships (3), adjustment difficulties (3), adolescents (2), shut-ins (2), support counseling (2), family (2), and death (2).

The counseling situations, therefore, ranged from relatively light, calling activity to more serious situations such as suicide, substance abuse, and marital problems. There may therefore be very few limits in actual practice as to the ways lay counselors are being used.

D. Sources of referrals to the lay counselors

Most of the referrals to the lay counselors came from within the local church body, with church staff, the director of the lay counseling ministry, and church members doing most of the referring.

Other Christian organizations outside the church were the next most frequent referral sources. Non-Christian organizations like the police were also mentioned as referral sources. Other referral sources included the lay counselors themselves, recommendations by family members or former clients, recommendations by support groups in the church, or counselees coming forward after a church service for counseling.

E. Supervision

Fourteen churches responded to questions about the kind of supervision lay counselors receive, and whether it was formal or informal. Six churches described their supervision as informal, whereas eight others described their supervision as formal.

Different forms or structures of supervision were used. For example, four churches held follow-up sessions with church staff for the lay counselors, and three churches noted that staff actually observed the lay counselors at work. One church required written reports from the lay counselors. Other kinds of supervision, each mentioned once, included large group supervision meetings led by church staff, a layered accountability structure among the lay counselors themselves, and meeting with a professional psychologist.

F. Use

1. Are the members of the church using the lay counselors comfortably? Thirteen churches responded "yes," but two other churches indicated that their members were uncomfortable with using their lay counselors.

2. Is there reeducation needed for the church members to be more comfortable? Eleven churches responded "yes."

G. Financial

1. Are there any fees involved? None of the churches surveyed charged for their lay counseling services, with one exception being a $40 charge for premarital counseling conducted by lay counselors.

2. Are there any (requested) donations involved? Only three churches requested donations for their lay counseling services, but no specific amounts of donations were prescribed.

H. Extrachurch activity

What percentage of lay counseling is to nonchurch members? An average of 36 percent of the lay counseling services provided was to nonchurch members, with a range of 0 to 75 percent. The results indicated that the lay counseling ministries surveyed either did one-half or more of their lay counseling outside of the church membership, or did little counseling at all outside of the church membership.

I. Coordination with other ministries

1. What are some ways in which the lay counselor's efforts are able to dovetail with the pastoral staff? The following were some of the answers given: do pastoral care, pinpoint special needs, report visitation needs, lighten pastor's workload, serve as informal leadership core, serve as source of leadership, have women who take "female" counseling from male pastors, take overflow counseling, long-term counseling, or premarital counseling, take/screen walk-ins, take referral cases, take light cases, take prayer requests, do follow-up, provide support groups, and encourage church involvement.

2. *What are some ways in which the lay counselor's efforts are able to dovetail with the professional counseling community?* The following were some of the answers given: take referrals, take those too poor for professionals, give referrals, refer to physicians, pick up spiritual aspects of cases not dealt with by secular counselors, provide support and follow-up. One church, however, does not refer outside the church at all, while another describes itself as resistant to the secular counseling community.

J. Philosophy

What theorists most directly influence your counseling model and ministry? Most of the churches described their lay counseling approaches as philosophically eclectic. Ten of them mentioned Reality Therapy as influential in shaping their philosophy of counseling; seven of them mentioned Larry Crabb; three of them, Norman Wright; and Jay Adams, Egan, Collins, Haugk (Stephen Series Ministry), Rogers, and Satir were each mentioned twice.

Evaluation

A. Effect on church staff

The effects on the church staff of having a lay counseling ministry were varied and included the following: lightening the staff workload in general, lightening the pastoral workload but increasing the overall staff workload in the form of phone calls and secretarial workload, initially increasing the staff workload but eventually decreasing it, affecting the staff workload minimally, and overall edifying and sensitizing the church staff.

B. Effect on the church

Overall, the effect of a lay counseling ministry on the local church seemed to be positive. The range of responses included: prevented problems requiring counseling by education, responded more quickly to needs in the church or responded to previously unmet needs, edified the church body, enhanced the church's overall ministry, made the church a more sensitive and caring one with more listening and financial helping of hurting members, helped the church become more well-rounded, fulfilled mandate to help the weak, facilitated numerical growth of the church, benefited the family structure, marriages, and communication in general among people in the church, provided a real service to the poor and to those fearful of professional counseling, and impacted the church in a diverse but minimal way.

C. Lessons learned

1. What lessons have you learned that should be repeated in the future, i.e., what has worked especially well? The varied responses included: keep the training program free of charge; continue to use two-stage plan of lay counselor training—first level open to everyone, second level only open to some; require a high commitment on the part of the lay counselors; focus on the character and compassion of the lay counselor as more important than just training; work in teams; seek out quality leadership and strong administrative support; form support groups, and use the "excellent" ministry materials and valuable leadership workshops offered by the Stephen Ministry.

2. What lessons have you learned regarding things that should be avoided in the future? The different answers to this question included the following things to *avoid:* opening the lay counselor training program to everyone; overloading the lay counselors with too much specialized information or too heavy academics; following too much a "medical model" of counseling (rather than a "network model"); using a drop-in procedure; using the term *counseling* (which may threaten or frighten off some people); using a paid director to direct referrals (rather than a volunteer), which is a very time-consuming task; having unrealistic expectations for an overly large or quick response to the lay counseling ministry; having lay counselors who think too highly of themselves; letting people counsel or lead support groups without adequate preparation or training; using special training classes (rather than Sunday school classes) because of the greater possibility of legal liability; and advertising that the lay counseling is free, because it may lead to an overwhelming flood of referrals or clients.

3. What would you do differently if you were starting over?
Some of the various responses included: be more careful to
choose faithful people to be lay counselors; use a one-way
mirror in the training process; use videotape in training the lay
counselors; use more experiential training; include more
integration of the Bible; limit the training program in the second
half to only those who are qualified (many of the churches
surveyed were already doing this); pay more attention to
training the lay counselors; pay the director of the lay
counseling ministry; increase the degree of lay help in a
particular lay counseling ministry; and give greater
consideration to how to handle potential legal problems.

4. What do the lay counselors see as benefits of the program?
Among the benefits mentioned were the following: lay
counselors felt helped as they helped others; they felt they were
performing a genuine and fulfilling ministry; they experienced
personal growth in many areas, like development of personal
communication skills, growth in their marriages, personal
revival, discovery of their gifts, and an important step toward a
career. Some lay counselors also found the development of
positive relationships a significant experience for them, and
many benefited from a positive support group experience with
other lay counselors. The lay counseling ministry also enabled
several people to find their place or niche in the church by
functioning as lay counselors (and thereby closed the church's
"back door," so to speak).

5. Legal considerations.   The possibility of being sued for
something a lay counselor has done or said was a fairly common
concern among the churches surveyed. Some were considering
malpractice insurance, but it is too expensive or prohibitive for
most churches. A number of ways to decrease the risk of being
sued were mentioned, including the following: prayer; not
charging for the lay counseling services provided; requiring
clients to waive the lay counseling ministry's liability;
emphasizing *biblical* counseling; not using terms like *counselor*
and *counseling;* counseling only church members; providing
malpractice insurance for at least the director of the lay
counseling ministry, and, if possible, for all the lay counselors;
and having an emergency "malpractice suit" fund (to cover

court costs until the malpractice suit is thrown out of court, because one church's attorney felt a malpractice law suit would not stick), which is cheaper than buying malpractice insurance. Churches involved in the Stephen Ministry did not feel malpractice insurance was necessary since their lay caring ministry is primarily pastoral in nature.

While the findings of the Lay Counseling Survey just summarized are interesting and helpful, they must *not* be generalized to all lay counseling ministries in local churches. The number of churches surveyed was relatively small (i.e., fifteen), and while some attempt was made to survey evangelical churches representing a variety of denominational affiliations, geographical locations, and lay counseling models and philosophies, the overwhelming majority of the churches were relatively large ones (fourteen of them) in their respective communities. The Survey results are, therefore, limited to a small sample of relatively large evangelical churches in different parts of the United States. They should not be generalized to other smaller evangelical churches, to other churches which may not be as evangelical, to parachurch organizations and other contexts of lay counseling ministry, and to other countries. There are also some limitations inherent in the use of the survey method of collecting information, including questions regarding how accurate or reliable the answers given may be, since many of them have to be based on memory or retrospective reports. Nevertheless, more surveys of many more churches, and better evaluation of lay Christian counselors as described in chapter 9, including more systematic program evaluation, are still needed. The survey conducted by the Center for Church Renewal is definitely a valuable one and a significant step in the right direction.

Examples of Lay Counseling Ministries in Local Churches

It is difficult to estimate how many local churches in the United States and Canada actually have lay counseling ministries. The Stephen Series[3] alone has been successfully used in thousands of congregations throughout the country, in more than fifty denominations, in all 50 states, in 7 Canadian provinces, and in 6 other countries.

A number of churches have also been involved in starting a

Lay Pastors Ministry which includes lay pastoral care and counseling. Dr. Melvin J. Steinbron is the founder of the Lay Pastors Ministry, which began in 1978 with a pilot group of five laypeople when he was Minister of Pastoral Care at College Hill Presbyterian Church in Cincinnati, Ohio. This ministry has now expanded to at least 36 of the United States, five Canadian provinces, and two foreign countries, fulfilling the biblical injunction to "tend the flock of God" (1 Peter 5:2). Out of this ministry has grown a *network* of churches which have equipped their laypeople to provide pastoral care. Dr. Steinbron coordinates this network, conducts training seminars for lay pastors, and also edits a quarterly publication called *Network News*. He can be reached at Hope Presbyterian Church, 7132 Portland Avenue, Minneapolis, Minnesota 55423 (Tel. 612-866-4055) on Tuesdays, Wednesdays, and Thursdays. An International Conference on Pastoral Care of the Congregation by Lay People was held March 23–25, 1990, at Frazer Memorial United Methodist Church in Montgomery, Alabama, sponsored by the International Lay Pastors Ministry Network. It can be safely assumed, therefore, that many local churches are involved in some form of lay caring or counseling ministry.

Several of the better known local churches with successful lay counseling ministries have been briefly described by Joan Sturkie and Gordon Bear in their interesting and helpful book *Christian Peer Counseling: Love in Action.*[4] I will now mention their nine examples of local church lay or peer counseling programs under the two major models of lay counseling ministry which I have earlier described: the *formal, organized* and *informal, organized* models. The following four churches have successful lay counseling ministries using the *formal, organized* model:

Lay Counseling Ministry of La Canada Presbyterian Church (Presbyterian Church, U.S.A.), 626 Foothill Blvd., La Canada, California 91101 (Tel. 818-790-6708);

Neighbors Who Care—Lay Counseling Ministry of The Neighborhood Church (Assemblies of God), 625 140th N.E., Bellevue, Washington 98005 (Tel. 206-747-3445);

Christian Counseling Ministry of The Elmbrook Church (Nondenominational), 777 S. Barker Rd., Waukesha, Wisconsin 53186 (Tel. 414-786-7051); and

The North Heights Lutheran Church Counseling Clinic

(Evangelical Lutheran Church in America), 2701 N. Rice St., Roseville, Minnesota 55113 (Tel. 612-484-2049).

The following five churches have successful lay counseling ministries using the *informal, organized model:*

Lay Shepherding Program of First Baptist Church (American Baptist), 228 N. Main St., Fall River, Massachusetts 02720 (Tel. 508-672-5381);

Enrichment Builders Lay Counseling Program, First Baptist Church (Southern Baptist), Box 1158, Jackson, Mississippi 39205 (Tel. 601-949-1949);

Peer Ministry of The Christ Memorial Lutheran Church (Missouri Synod Lutheran), 9712 Tesson Ferry Rd., Afton, Missouri 63123 (Tel. 314-631-0304);

Stephen Ministry Program of The Union United Methodist Church (The United Methodist Church), 7582 Woodrow St., P.O. Box 705, Irmo, South Carolina 29063 (Tel. 803-781-3013), and

The Shepherding Ministry of The First Congregational Church (United Church of Christ), 2 Main St., Hopkinton, Massachusetts 01748 (Tel. 508-435-9581).

Sturkie and Bear also mentioned the following church, parachurch, or paraprofessional organizations involved in lay counseling training and ministry:

The Lay Academy of The Episcopal Diocese of California, 1055 Taylor St., San Francisco, California 94108 (Tel. 415-673-2183);

New Directions Counseling Center (Parachurch and Paraprofessional Organization), 996 Oak Grove Rd., Concord, California 94518 (Tel. 415-798-7500);

Love Lines, Inc. (Parachurch and Paraprofessional Organization), 2701 S.E. Fourth St., Minneapolis, Minnesota 55414 (Tel. 612-379-1199); and

Match-Two (M-2) Prisoner Outreach (Paraprofessional Organization), Statewide Headquarters, 500 Main St., P.O. Box 447, San Quentin, California 94964 (Tel. 415-457-8701).

In addition to helpful, brief descriptions of these thirteen lay or peer counseling ministries, Sturkie and Bear provide eight true stories from peer counseling in the field of ministry, giving a taste of what actually happens in the context of lay or peer counseling.

In the final section of their book, Sturkie and Bear reprinted the following fifteen practical and helpful sample forms and program ideas from different lay or peer counseling ministries: (1) Personal Interview Data Form; (2) Program Announcement of a Lay Counseling Ministry; (3) Philosophy of Ministry section from the Manual of the Christian Counseling Ministry of a local church; (4) Trainee Application Form; (5) Donation Policy Declaration; (6) An Interest/Availability Statement; (7) Release of Liability Form; (8) Intake Information Form; (9) Job Description (Director); (10) Release of Permission Form; (11) A Prayer and Counseling Report Form; (12) Counselee Referral Form; (13) Job Description (Assistant Director); (14) Evaluation (by Supervisor) Form; and (15) Counselor Evaluation Form.

A number of other local churches which have lay counseling ministries (including a few of the churches that participated in the Lay Counseling Survey mentioned earlier) are listed in appendix C, with their addresses and telephone numbers where available.

I have listed a number of local churches with lay caring and counseling ministries in this chapter and in appendix C, so that anyone interested in further information regarding setting up a lay counseling ministry in his or her church/area may contact any of these churches (or parachurch/paraprofessional organizations). It should be noted that some local churches like First Presbyterian Church of Hollywood actually have both a professional and a lay counseling center.

One recent exciting development is the establishing of lay caring and counseling ministries in ethnic churches, including Chinese churches. For example, North York Chinese Baptist Church in Canada (675 Sheppard Ave., E., Willowdale, Ontario M2K 1B6, Canada, Tel. 416-223-3121) has completed a training program for lay counselors and has just started a lay counseling service. Another example is First Evangelical Church in Glendale, California (522 W. Broadway, Glendale, California 91204, Tel. 818-240-5633), a Chinese church with an English-speaking congregation that recently completed a Stephen Series training program and started a Stephen Ministry of lay caregiving. This is my home church, and I am therefore especially delighted to see a lay caring and counseling ministry being established. I should also point out that as a result of the teaching and training ministry of Dr. Peter Chiu—a licensed marriage, family, and child counselor in California who was Director of the Department of Counseling and assistant to the General Secretary of Chinese Christian Mission (CCM), which serves Chinese churches worldwide—several Chinese churches and parachurch organizations in Houston, Vancouver, Singapore, Indonesia, and Taiwan are developing lay counseling programs. In Kowloon, Hong Kong, the Breakthrough Counseling Centre provides counseling training for paraprofessional counselors, seminarians, and church laypeople. The work of Selwyn Hughes in England in training lay Christian counselors using a biblical model is also well-known.

In writing about psychological services in the black church several years ago, Dr. Rose Edgar also noted that many black churches in the Los Angeles area provide after-school tutoring and family counseling services. She pointed out that one black Baptist church in Pasadena has established a counseling center using lay counselors and offering free counseling services, and Second Baptist Church in Los Angeles has a pastor in charge of counseling services who is developing and supervising small sharing groups for providing group counseling and support.[5] It is not easy in ethnic churches like Asian (e.g., Chinese) and black churches to establish lay caring and counseling ministries (partly because of the high regard such churches have for their pastors), but it is exciting to see that this is being done successfully in a few of these churches. The need for lay Christian counseling services or ministries in Hispanic churches is also great.

I will now describe in more detail two lay counseling centers or services that I set up and directed in Canada, using the *formal, organized model,* the first at Peoples Church of Montreal,[6] and the second at North Park Community Chapel in London, Ontario.[7]

The lay counseling service at Peoples Church of Montreal was set up in October 1976 with full support and cooperation from the two pastors and church board. This is an evangelical church with an average Sunday morning worship attendance of between 250 and 300 people. It is located in downtown Montreal, just across from the campus of McGill University, and is affiliated with the Associated Gospel Churches.

As an undergraduate student majoring in psychology at McGill University, I was involved for a couple of years in a secular, student-run peer counseling group called Interaction McGill. I was therefore exposed to peer or lay counseling training and services in a secular, community outreach context at a major Canadian university, just prior to organizing the lay counseling service at Peoples Church. I had also been involved for several years in leadership in Youth For Christ (Y.F.C.) ministries as a volunteer, both in Singapore (which is my country of origin and where I grew up and completed my high school/junior college education) and in Montreal, and therefore I had some experience in training volunteer and full-time Y.F.C. staff in youth ministry skills, including basic counseling skills.

With this background, and ongoing reading of the latest developments in biblical, Christian counseling (e.g., books by Adams, Crabb, Collins, etc.), I sensed the Lord leading me to set up a lay counseling service at Peoples Church to help lighten the load of pastoral care and counseling for the two pastors (who were already heavily involved in such ministry), and to facilitate the further development of the church body as a caring and therapeutic community.

After obtaining the full support of the pastors and church board, I also received, from the pastors, recommendations of certain church members or adherents as prospective lay counselors for the service to be established. Those recommended were generally warm and spiritually committed Christians who had a desire to be involved in a ministry of people helping or lay counseling. Several of them were already performing informal people-helping roles in the church, and a few were serving in different positions of church leadership. We also announced in the church that people interested in being involved in a lay counseling ministry should contact me or the pastors.

Prospective lay counselors were then approached and interviewed briefly, and those deemed appropriate who had the time to commit themselves to such a ministry were selected as lay counselors, with an original group of nine persons.

The initial training for these lay counselors involved a weekend seminar that covered the integrated, biblically based model of effective Christian counseling presented in some detail in chapter 3 of this book, as well as basic counseling skills and methods. We conducted role plays, with feedback and discussion, sometimes using audiovisual equipment (e.g., videotape), so that basic counseling skills like attentive listening, observing nonverbal cues, handling silence, wise questioning, and appropriate responding, could be taught and learned in a practical way.

The initial, basic training was therefore somewhat brief, but subsequent monthly staff meetings, lasting three to four hours each time, included further training sessions on a number of different topics pertaining to lay counseling (e.g., dealing with depression, recognizing signs and symptoms of severe disorders, terminating counseling, and making proper referrals). It took a few months before all the lay counselors were seeing counselees or clients. We also set up a small library for the lay counselors consisting of useful books, articles, and tapes on effective counseling and related topics, mainly from an evangelical, biblical perspective.

Supervision of lay counselors involved mainly case discussions either at staff meetings in a group, or individually between the lay counselor and myself as director of the service (with permission obtained from counselees or clients). Supervision and training through co-counseling was implemented later.

I also conducted special training seminars periodically for others, both clergy and laity, who were interested in learning more effective ways of helping people.

The counseling service had five basic functions, four of which were already mentioned in chapter 5 of this book (as a part of the brochure used at North Park Community Chapel, whose lay counseling service I set up later, patterning it after the one at Peoples Church of Montreal but with a few significant changes which I will describe). The fifth one was a telephone service for those who may want to call in and talk over the phone during the hours when the service was available. As a nonprofessional, volunteer ministry, the service did not charge any fees or ask for any donations, and it was publicized mainly at Peoples Church, although it did become known to other pastors and churches in the area. The service was open on two weekday evenings each week, from 7:00 to 10:00 p.m. Several lay counselors were available on each of the evenings. Some had appointments made in advance, but usually at least one lay counselor was free to answer the telephone or talk with those who just dropped in without an appointment.

Over the four years I directed it (1976–1980), the lay counselors who served in this ministry included two university students, a library assistant, a nurse, an engineer, an office worker, two schoolteachers, a medical intern, and one of the pastors. I was a graduate student and a candidate in the Ph.D. program in Clinical Psychology at McGill University, and I served as director of the service on a voluntary, unpaid basis. A Christian psychiatrist in Montreal served as a consultant and as a professional to whom appropriate referrals could be made. We also compiled a list of appropriate Christian professionals for use when other referrals were needed.

Many of the lay counselors informally commented over the years on how they had benefited from their training, supervision sessions, and counseling experience. Many counselees or clients also expressed appreciation for the help given them through the lay counselors and the service. Most of the earlier clients were referrals from the pastors, but referrals from other pastors and self-referrals became more common over the years.

Most of the clients were Christians, although several non-Christians also used the service. No files were kept on clients since the service was a nonprofessional, volunteer ministry, but names of clients were recorded to keep some basic statistics. Over a hundred clients had used the service in four years, with the average number of counseling sessions per client being about eight. The range was one to seventy sessions, but the majority of clients were seen for relatively short-term counseling. A few clients were seen for long-term supportive help.

The lay counseling service at Peoples Church continued to function for a while after I left Montreal for a job as a psychologist at University Hospital in London, Ontario. I also taught part-time in the Departments of Psychology, Psychiatry, and Oral Medicine at the University of Western Ontario in London. The majority of trained lay counselors at Peoples Church also moved out of Montreal in the early 1980s, so that the lay counseling service at Peoples Church had to be closed down. It has therefore stopped functioning on a formal, organized basis for several years now, although one or two of the remaining lay counselors still help informally in lay pastoral care and counseling when the need arises.

While in London, Ontario I set up another lay counseling service similar to the one at Peoples Church, at North Park Community Chapel, which is a nondenominational, evangelical local church with about one thousand members and adherents. I made a number of significant changes, however, based on my earlier experience at Peoples Church.

First, before starting the service, I conducted a longer and more comprehensive training program that lasted six months. The lay counselors were selected after being recommended by the pastors and interviewed by me and the senior pastor, using selection criteria described earlier in this book. Further details of the training program have been given in chapter 7 of this book.

Second, we did not provide a telephone or drop-in service, so all counseling sessions were by appointment only. This was done for convenience as well as for safety or security reasons, since a few thefts occurred at Peoples Church when the church side door was left open for people to drop in. At North Park Community Chapel church doors were left locked until the appropriate appointment time, or until a client rang the door bell.

Third, we continued to hold monthly staff meetings lasting four hours or so for further training and supervision (including role plays), but I also arranged individual supervision sessions between the lay counselors and myself when necessary, and this was done on a more frequent and regular basis than at Peoples Church.

Fourth, we did some basic evaluation of the effectiveness of the lay counselor training program using the self-report measure I developed (described in the previous chapter). Results were favorable, but no comparison group was used. However, we did not conduct a systematic evaluation of the effectiveness of the lay counseling provided.

Fifth, we held periodic retreats with the lay counselors for further training and support. Sixth, we scheduled some counseling appointments during the day, since a few of the counselors were homemakers and could meet with those who preferred day appointments to evening ones. Lay counseling was still available two evenings a week.

While no formal outcome or program evaluation has been done, many clients have expressed deep appreciation for the help they have received; the lay counselors have commented on how much they have learned and grown through their training and counseling experiences; and the pastors have appreciated the service because it has helped to lighten their own counseling load and given opportunities to gifted laypeople in the church to use their spiritual gifts and minister to others. I found being involved in such a ministry to be challenging but also deeply rewarding and fulfilling, especially as I have seen the Lord touch many broken lives with his healing and grace.

I directed the lay counseling service at North Park Community Chapel from 1981 until August 1983, when I moved to Toronto to become director of counseling and teach at Ontario Bible College, and subsequently, in July 1985, to Fuller Theological Seminary in Pasadena, California, where I am now teaching on the faculty of the Graduate School of Psychology. As I have recommended in this book, more direct observation of lay counselors and use of co-counseling, more systematic and comprehensive evaluation of the effectiveness of training programs as well as the lay counseling provided by trained lay counselors, and more frequent supervision sessions (biweekly or weekly) could and should be implemented in a lay counseling service like the one at North Park Community Chapel. I am glad to note that the lay counseling service at the Chapel continues to function under the leadership of a new director, and hopefully it will incorporate some of these recommendations, as I hope will many other local church lay counseling services, especially those using a formal, organized model.

Presently I am involved with several of my doctoral students in Clinical Psychology at Fuller Theological Seminary in the evaluation of the effectiveness of lay Christian counselor training programs and lay Christian counseling, particularly in the local church context. I have also consulted with several pastors both in the United States and Canada, as well as Singapore, who have subsequently used the ideas and guidelines presented in this book to establish lay counselor training programs and lay counseling ministries in their local churches.

More formally, each year I teach a four-unit elective theology course entitled "Training Lay Counselors in the Church," which has had good enrollments of students from all three Fuller Schools of Theology, World Mission, and Psychology, and hence from different parts of the world. I have also taught that course for Fuller's Extended Education program in Phoenix, Arizona.

I anticipate that more Bible colleges and seminaries or Christian colleges and universities will offer courses on Lay or

Peer Counseling. For example, Ontario Bible College in Toronto, Canada, continues to offer training courses on lay counseling, and I understand that Liberty University in Lynchburg, Virginia, has just begun a course of study on lay counseling, available by correspondence.

Lay Counseling Ministries Beyond the Local Church

In this section, I would like to point out that lay counseling ministries also occur outside the context of the local church, and provide some examples of such ministries.

Parachurch organizations like Youth For Christ (especially the Youth Guidance Division ministering to troubled youth), Young Life, the Navigators, and Campus Crusade for Christ also have counselor training programs either of their own or using available published materials, to train their staff members and volunteers, many of whom are not mental health professionals, in counseling skills. For example, Youth For Christ has published a manual for volunteer or associate staff called "The Whole Person Survival Kit," which can be used to train volunteers involved in either the Campus Life Division, which reaches out to young people in high schools, or the Youth Guidance Division, specializing in ministry to troubled youth. The manual or kit contains a section on "The Whole Person Counseling" (Section 4) with the following four chapters: Counseling Is a Life Well-lived; Counseling Is Providing a Relationship; Counseling Is Exploring for Solutions; and Counseling Is Having Appointments.[8]

Lay counselor training and lay counseling therefore are a crucial part of the ministry of many parachurch organizations.

Prison ministries is another area of outreach that often involves lay counseling. An example of a paraprofessional organization that specially trains and uses lay volunteer counselors to reach out to prisoners is Match-Two or M-2 Prisoner Outreach, mentioned earlier in this chapter. Although it is a secular organization, many Christians from various churches and denominations have been involved in the M-2 program since it was started in 1971. Its goals are to recruit and train adult volunteers from the community to provide caring relationships for prisoners or inmates in the California system who are interested in being matched with such volunteer lay helpers.

The volunteers agree to visit their assigned inmates at least once a month and also to write letters in between visits. Apparently, the M-2 program has been successful. Sturkie and Bear noted that the California Department of Corrections conducted a study in 1987 which showed that M-2 parolees who had twelve or more visits from an M-2 volunteer had an 81 percent better parole success than those parolees who had not participated in the M-2 program.[9]

Another area of expanding lay counseling ministry beyond the local church is in the *context of retirement and nursing homes.* For example, Dr. Paul Welter has developed a significant program for the training of retirement center and nursing home staff and residents in helping or counseling skills. This lay counseling program was funded by the Board of National Ministries of the American Baptist Churches for a seven-year period involving seven of their retirement centers/nursing homes, with a total of 450 staff members and 114 residents trained in helping or counseling skills. Also, a group of trainers was prepared in three of the centers. Most of the completed evaluations of the program were positive, but no control groups were used. Welter also provides a number of helpful implications or guidelines for lay counselor training in long-term care settings.[10]

Lay counselors or volunteers are also often used in *Christian mental health centers or programs.* For example, at The Psychological Center of the Graduate School of Psychology at Fuller, volunteer helpers or lay counselors are trained and used in a number of outreach programs and services,[11] including the Crime Resistance Involvement Council (C.R.I.C.) and Gero-Net. C.R.I.C. provides assistance to elderly victims of crime, and provides its volunteers who work directly with such victims training in areas such as sympathy skills and crisis intervention strategies.[12] Gero-Net, a component of the Community Assistance Program for Seniors (CAPS), is a volunteer-based program which offers friendly visitation and some case management services to low-income elderly who are at risk for institutionalization due to multiple physical and mental health problems. One other example of a program in The Psychological Center that trains and uses "lay counselors" is Project IV Family Outreach, which is really a cooperative outreach program with other community agencies, designed to serve children and families, primarily from disadvantaged minorities, who do not otherwise receive help from traditionally structured services. Parents and teachers are the main lay resources trained to implement treatments in the home and at school.

Another example of how lay counselors are trained and used in a Christian mental health agency or organization is New Directions Counseling Center, which is a church-related paraprofessional center in the San Francisco Bay Area. It was founded in 1974 to provide low-cost paraprofessional or trained lay counseling services to persons in lower-middle and lower income groups.[13]

One final area of lay counseling ministry beyond the local church is in the *context of missions.* Missionaries need training in interpersonal relationships, cultural adjustment, and coping with stress, as Johnson and Penner have pointed out.[14] However, they also need training in lay caring and counseling skills, not only to provide mutual support and help for themselves on the mission field, but also to help or counsel cross-culturally with those they are reaching out and ministering to, usually in Third World countries and places where there is only limited or even no access to professional counseling services. Much more work needs to be done in this area, in developing lay counselor training programs with special cross-cultural counseling skills included, and in developing lay caring and counseling ministries and services on the mission field.[15]

NOTES

[1]See "Lay Counseling Survey," available from Floyd Elliott, Director of Counseling and Family Renewal, Center for Church Renewal, 200 Chisholm Place, Suite 228, Plano, TX 75075. I would like to express my appreciation to Pastor Floyd Elliott for permission to summarize the findings of the survey.

[2]J. Sturkie and G. Bear, *Christian Peer Counseling: Love in Action* (Waco, Tex.: Word, 1989).

[3]For further information about the Stephen Series, contact: Stephen Ministries, 1325 Boland, St. Louis, MO 63117 (Tel. 314-645-5511).

[4]See Sturkie and Bear, *Christian Peer Counseling,* 136–63.

[5]R. Edgar, "Psychological Services in the Black Church," *CAPS Bulletin* 7, no. 4 (1981): 22–24.

[6]See S. Y. Tan, "Lay Counseling: The Local Church," *CAPS Bulletin* 7, no. 1 (1981): 15–20.

[7]See S. Y. Tan, "Training Lay Christian Counselors: A Basic Program and Some Preliminary Data," *Journal of Psychology and Christianity* 6, no. 2 (1987): 57–61.

[8]See Bruce B. Barton, ed., *The Whole Person Survival Kit for Volunteer Leadership* (Wheaton, Ill.: Youth For Christ International, 1976).

[9]See Sturkie and Bear, *Christian Peer Counseling*, 161-63.

[10]See P. Welter, "Training Retirement Center and Nursing Home Staff and Residents in Helping and Counseling Skills," *Journal of Psychology and Christianity* 6, no. 2 (1987): 45–56.

[11]See P. Clement, "The Psychological Center of Fuller Theological Seminary," *CAPS Bulletin* 7, no. 4 (1981): 27–30.

[12]See C. Zabriskie, "The Older Volunteer Role; A Model Program in Crime Prevention," *CAPS Bulletin* 7, no. 4 (1981): 19–22.

[13]See Richard and Flakoll, "Christian Counseling Centers: Two Effective Models," *CAPS Bulletin* 7, no. 4 (1981): 12–15.

[14]See C. B. Johnson and D. R. Penner, "The Current Status of the Provision of Psychological Services in Missionary Agencies in North America," *CAPS Bulletin* 7, no. 4 (1981): 25–27.

[15]For some preliminary work in this area, see C. A. Schaefer, L. Dodds, and S. Y. Tan, "Changes in Attitudes Toward Peer Counseling and Personal Orientation Measured During Growth Facilitator Training for Cross-Cultural Ministry," unpublished manuscript, 1988.

11

Potential Pitfalls
in Lay Counseling

I have emphasized in this book that lay caring and counseling ministries are biblically based and significant ministries for the building up of the body of Christ and for reaching out to people who are hurting or who have particular needs. Such ministries, however, do have potential pitfalls and hazards. Lay counselors need to be aware of these dangers and risks to minimize or avoid them. Then they can conduct their ministries of lay caring and counseling effectively and in a highly ethical and legal manner that honors and glorifies the Lord.

Legal and ethical issues in pastoral as well as lay Christian counseling have been "hot" topics in recent years, especially since the clergy malpractice suit against Grace Community Church in Sun Valley, California, was filed in March 1980 by the parents of twenty-four-year-old Kenneth Nally, who committed suicide by shooting himself on April 1, 1979. The Nallys claimed that the pastors who provided pastoral counseling to their son before his suicide were negligent, and therefore they sued them, the senior pastor, and the church for clergy malpractice. This case has received wide publicity and national attention because it is the first one on clergy malpractice that has been considered by any U.S. high court. It went right up to the California Supreme Court, which in November 1988 ruled against the Nallys on a five to two vote, and then on to the U.S. Supreme Court, which in April 1989 refused to review the California Supreme Court decision, thereby letting it stand. Essentially this means that pastors and church workers have no legal duty to refer troubled parishioners or church members to licensed psychiatrists.[1]

A ten-year legal battle over clergy malpractice has therefore ended with many pastors and lay counselors feeling relieved and vindicated in their pastoral and lay counseling ministries. However, the ethical and legal issues raised by the Nally case require further discussion and clarification. It is conceivable that another case with more substantial merit could succeed in the courts. In this chapter, therefore, I will cover legal and ethical considerations in the context of lay Christian counseling, but before doing so, I will first discuss other potential problems or pitfalls that lay counselors can fall into.

Potential Problems for the Lay Counselor

Dr. Gary Collins has written a particularly helpful chapter on the counselor and counseling in his textbook *Christian Counseling*, which covers comprehensively the major hazards or potential problems a Christian counselor may encounter, most of which also apply to a lay Christian counselor.[2] I will briefly summarize the main points he raises, but his chapter should be consulted for further details. Collins describes eight major areas of potential problems: the counselor's *motivation*, the counselor's *effectiveness*, the counselor's *role*, the counselor's *vulnerability*, the counselor's *sexuality*, the counselor's *ethics*, the counselor's *burnout*, and the counselor's *counselors*.

1. The Counselor's Motivation

Why does a person want to counsel in the first place? Some reasons are legitimate, others less so. Collins lists five possible needs that some counselors may inappropriately try to meet through their counseling ministry: the need for relationships (or intimacy and closeness with people); the need for control (of other people's lives); the need to rescue; the need for information (i.e., curiosity); and the need for personal healing.

2. The Counselor's Effectiveness

Some people are more gifted for a counseling ministry than others, and an honest evaluation of one's counseling effectiveness or lack of effectiveness is necessary. Some counselors may then realize that they are not particularly gifted or good at counseling, but can still help or minister to people through avenues other than counseling, like evangelism, social action, or teaching.

3. The Counselor's Role

Often counselors face role confusion. Based on Dr. Maurice Wagner's suggestions,[3] Collins describes the following nine potential examples of counselor role confusion: visiting instead of counseling; being hasty instead of deliberate; being disrespectful instead of sympathetic; being judgmental instead of unbiased; being directive instead of interpretive; being emotionally overinvolved instead of remaining objective; being impatient instead of realistic; being artificial instead of authentic; and being defensive instead of empathic.

4. The Counselor's Vulnerability

Counselors may experience power struggles, exploitation, and failure in the process of counseling or helping others. Three common ways that the counselor's vulnerability can be increased include *manipulation* of the counselor by the client, *countertransference* on the part of the counselor when his or her own needs and feelings interfere with the counseling relationship, and *resistance* on the part of the client. Such potential problems are best dealt with in consultation with a supervisor or colleague.

5. The Counselor's Sexuality

Sexual attraction to clients is real, and therefore there is the danger of falling into sexual contact and sin. While sexual feelings toward clients are common, Collins suggests the need to exercise self-control through the following means: spiritual protection (especially prayer, meditation on the Scriptures, and dependence on the Holy Spirit); awareness of danger signals (e.g., the counselor spending much time thinking about the client and admiring his or her qualities between sessions, beginning to have sexual fantasies about the client, etc.); setting of limits (e.g., regarding length of counseling sessions and telephone contacts); examination of attitudes (by remembering social consequences and implications as well as theological or biblical truth relating to sexual immorality); and support-group protection.

6. The Counselor's Ethics

Ethical problems include issues of confidentiality, and dealing with difficult decisions, and conflicts in values.[4] I will deal with this area in more depth later in this chapter in the section on legal and ethical issues.

7. The Counselor's Burnout

The counselor can be so involved in the ministry of counseling that he or she experiences "burnout." Collins points out that one writer has defined burnout as involving "a progressive loss of idealism, energy, and purpose" for people in the helping professions as a result of their work.[5] Collins suggests several steps to prevent burnout, including: having regular periods of prayer and meditation on the Scriptures for spiritual strength; receiving support from a few others; engaging in constant evaluation of the underlying drive to achieve; taking time off; seeking to improve ministry skills including counseling, conflict management, and assertiveness skills; and encouraging other Christians to be involved in lay caring and burden bearing.

8. The Counselor's Counselors

Every counselor needs to have a counselor or colleague to consult at times. The danger is that such a valid need may go unmet, or be neglected. Collins emphasizes first of all the counselor's need to depend on the Holy Spirit and on the Lord Jesus, who is himself the wonderful Counselor. He also points out the need for every counselor to have one or two colleagues to consult, share Scripture, and pray with regularly. Counselors need mutual support, because all counseling, including lay counseling, is draining work, even though it can also be fulfilling. At times counselors may need more formal counseling for their own needs and problems, in which case they should seek professional counseling or therapy, if necessary.

These eight problem areas should be borne in mind by lay counselors as well as those who train and supervise them, so that such problems can be minimized or avoided.

Dr. Michael Cavanagh, a clinical psychologist and professor at the University of San Francisco, has delineated several destructive myths about helping others that many ministers and church workers tend to hold, which lay counselors should also be careful to avoid. They include: love, good intentions, and common sense are all you need (the truth is that what is needed in counseling often is a love that is confronting and challenging and that sets limits, along with some counseling knowledge and skills); people define their problems accurately (not necessarily true!); most people just need advice and encouragement (some may need much more than this); people who seek help really want help (again, not necessarily; some may have other and possibly ulterior motives for seeking help); people are reliable eyewitnesses (sometimes they may be but often they are not); you should encourage people to ventilate their feelings (not always because sometimes ventilation per se may be unhelpful); and all religious problems have religious solutions (problems are often multifaceted and complex, with multiple causes and possible multiple solutions).

In addition to such myths about helping, Dr. Cavanagh also describes the following pitfalls that ministers and counselors often encounter in their attempts to help people: becoming a manager (or director of others' lives); becoming an agent (whom others can exploit); assuming a role other than that of minister or counselor; adhering to one theory; overestimating one's power; yielding to outside pressure; supporting behavior that should not be supported; and dealing with someone already in counseling with another counselor (open communication with the other counselor is then essential).[6]

Both Dr. Collins and Dr. Cavanagh have described and delineated a number of potential problems and pitfalls that not only pastors and counselors but also lay counselors can fall into. Hence lay counselors should be made aware of such dangers.

The rest of this chapter will focus on legal and ethical issues relevant to lay Christian counselors and their ministry.

Legal and Ethical Issues Relevant to Lay Counseling

Dr. Thomas Needham, who is now the Associate Dean heading the Division of Marriage and Family Therapy in the Graduate School of Psychology at Fuller Theological Seminary, wrote a helpful chapter in the book *Clergy Malpractice* on helping when the risks are great.[7] He has provided good answers to three key questions: What are potentially high-risk situations? Why are the risks increasing? and How can we care carefully? I will briefly summarize his main points for the potential benefit of lay counselors.

Dr. Needham listed *twenty potentially high-risk situations,* including direct violations of legal or ethical codes (e.g., sex with a counselee, or breach of confidentiality), reflections of poor judgment in counseling situations, examples of going beyond acceptable practices or standards in mental health or pastoral counseling, and situations which increase the risk of harming or embarrassing the counselee. The twenty high-risk situations are:[8]

1. Administration, interpretation, and storing of personality and psychological tests.
2. Belief in simple spiritual solutions for complex emotional and psychological problems.
3. Belief that all problems are spiritual or physical, with a denial of emotional and psychological dimensions.
4. Belief that pastoral and lay counselors need only biblical training to solve such severe problems as neuroses, psychoses, and suicidal intentions.
5. Belief that sincerity and good intentions are the major ingredients in pastoral and lay counseling.
6. Belief that pastors (and I would add lay counselors) should be all things to all people.
7. Counseling psychotic and suicidal individuals.
8. Counseling a mentally incompetent patient.
9. Advising against medical or psychological treatment.
10. Counseling regarding psychiatric medications.
11. Denial of the existence or severity of a psychological or psychosomatic disorder.
12. Improper care of records.
13. Inadequately trained lay and pastoral counselors.
14. Failure to give credence to violent intentions or statements.
15. Misdiagnosing psychotics as demon-possessed.
16. Misrepresenting one's title, position, degree, or abilities (i.e., psychologist, psychotherapy).
17. Poorly supervised lay counselors.
18. Recommending divorce.
19. Sexual relations with a counselee.

20. Violations of confidentiality (by ministerial or secretarial staff).

Not all of these high-risk situations are *unethical* in the sense of breaking ethical codes of mental health or pastoral counselors, or *illegal* in the sense of breaking the law, although many of them are. However, it would be wise for pastors and lay counselors to avoid these high-risk situations as far as possible, especially those which are obviously unethical or illegal. It should be noted that in some states, even the title "counselor" should be used with caution or qualification or even eliminated, depending on the licensing laws of a state governing the use of such titles. Some lay counseling ministries have therefore used alternative titles such as "lay caregiver," "lay helper," or "lay minister" in place of "lay counselor" and terms like "lay caregiving," "lay helping," "lay pastoring," or "lay shepherding" instead of "lay counseling."

As to possible reasons for the increasing risks of litigation or being sued in the context of pastoral and lay counseling, Dr. Needham mentions the following: (1) a litigious atmosphere; (2) increased demands for pastoral counseling; (3) new lay ministries; (4) a lag or gap between intention (which may be good and sincere) and ability (to carry out good and sincere intentions); (5) inadequate attitudes toward problems and problem-solving; (6) inadequate training; and (7) inadequate follow-up preaching after a suicide or other crisis situation.

Finally, Dr. Needham provides the following helpful suggestions for minimizing the risks of litigation in answering the question of "How can we care carefully?":

(1) Develop a formal counseling policy (which should include determining target needs, assessing resources, determining organizational channels and accountability, establishing selection procedures and training and supervision standards, formulating operational guidelines including policy on the issue of fees or contributions, checking insurance coverage, and developing a feedback loop);

(2) develop adequate selection, training, and supervision;

(3) avoid misleading claims;

(4) make a thorough evaluation of the problem (by taking a history, using tests where appropriate, determining chronicity and severity of the problem as well as whether it is psychotic, suicidal or psychosomatic, and evaluating the counselee's resources);

(5) learn to benefit from testing (where it is appropriate, and where adequately trained and qualified persons are available to conduct and interpret the tests used);

(6) determine your level of intervention (e.g., Dr. Needham points out that level four intervention involving the uncovering of repressed emotions causes the highest risk and should be conducted only by a *skilled* counselor);

(7) make use of consultation and referrals;

(8) take advantage of continuing education;

(9) guard records and information (i.e., maintain confidentiality); and

(10) provide follow-up care.

Dr. Needham aptly concludes: "The Nally lawsuit . . . has left an indelible concern over the future of pastoral and lay counseling in the local church. I believe we should expand rather than reduce our helping efforts, and this requires that we understand why the risks are increasing. Following the ten suggested guidelines should help churches have an active, effective, and careful, caring ministry."[9]

Dr. Walter Becker has written a concise article dealing specifically with the major legal and ethical considerations relevant to the lay or paraprofessional counselor in the church.[10] He emphasizes that trust is the essence of the therapeutic or counseling relationship, and therefore the risk of litigation or being sued by clients increases when trust is decreased or destroyed and clients feel harmed or wronged. There are three main areas in which trust in the counseling relationship should be developed: the *confidentiality* of the relationship, the *competence* of the counselor, and the client's freedom of *choice*.

In the first area of *confidentiality,* Dr. Becker recommends that the lay or paraprofessional counselor in the church should follow the ethical and legal standards of the professional counselor in order to maintain the requirements of the state as well as to hold to the highest standards of ethical conduct. Many states now require that professional counselors report incidents of child or elder abuse, or situations involving potential harm to self or violence to others. Dr. Becker, therefore, suggests that lay counselors in the church should follow such requirements to be on the safe side. Many lay counseling centers in churches in Southern California are already doing this by informing potential clients of such limits to confidentiality and requiring them to sign an informed consent form before beginning lay counseling. Directors of lay Christian counseling centers or even more informal lay counseling ministries need to familiarize themselves with the specific laws of the state in which they are working concerning mandatory reporting and limits to confidentiality in the professional counseling relationship, and then decide whether to follow them for the lay counselors. Even if lay counselors are exempted from following such laws for professional counselors, it may still be wiser for lay counselors to follow them.

Dr. Becker also noted that there are limits to confidentiality when counseling with minors, because their parents or legal guardians are responsible for the welfare of minors and therefore some sharing of information and cooperation with the parents or legal guardians is necessary. He further stresses the need to maintain confidentiality in a group counseling context, and to carefully store clients' records and guard their security and confidentiality, for example, by keeping them with a licensed professional supervisor.

One other significant issue raised by Dr. Becker in the area of confidentiality has to do with *church discipline*. He states the following guideline:

> Holding a dual relationship of lay counselor and church member active in disciplining a fellow member severely compromises the trust necessary in the counseling relationship. Paraprofessional counselors should not be agents of church discipline. The church counselor needs to be sensitive to the rules of discipline within his or her own denomination, as well as the importance of confession and repentance. Confession to appropriate church leaders should be encouraged so that healing within the church body can occur, but betraying the confidentiality of the therapeutic relationship for the sake of church discipline should be avoided.[11]

While this recommendation may be accepted by many, I am aware that some pastors and church leaders may not be able to follow it—for example, those who use a counseling approach like Adams' nouthetic counseling, in which scriptural direction, including church discipline where necessary and appropriate, is a crucial part of the counseling offered. In this case, I would suggest that the potential counselee or client be informed of all the limitations to confidentiality, including matters regarding church discipline, before starting lay counseling. The whole topic of church discipline, however, still requires much sensitivity and reflection, and I would recommend Dr. Samuel Southard's chapter "Church Discipline: Handle with Care," in the book *Clergy Malpractice,* for further reading.[12]

In the second area of *competency,* Dr. Becker emphasizes that the key here is to carefully and adequately select, train, and supervise lay or paraprofessional counselors so that they know and work within the limits of their training and helping ability (including learning how to refer to and work with mental health professionals).

In the third and final area of *choice,* Dr. Becker points out that freedom of client choice or informed consent means that the counselor should provide sufficient information about his or her qualifications, training, and values, as well as the process, goals, and possible consequences of counseling so that the client can make educated choices. The counselor's views and values should be clearly shared in order for the client to have the ultimate freedom to choose whether to continue with that counselor or to seek help from another counselor.

Dr. Becker briefly describes the following eight high-risk situations that lay counselors should avoid in order to minimize possible litigation or malpractice suits: charging fees or asking for "donations"; using psychological tests without proper training or supervision; having simplistic beliefs that can lead to superficial treatment, misdiagnosis, and harm; counseling those with severe problems requiring professional intervention; giving advice against medical or psychological treatment; ignoring statements of intent to harm or signs of violent behavior; counseling with a relative or employee; and developing a romantic or sexual relationship with the client.

Dr. Becker also provides several helpful suggestions for practice by lay counselors that can help build trust by maintaining confidentiality, facilitating confidence in the lay counselor, and ensuring freedom of choice for the client. Many of his suggestions have already been mentioned earlier in my discussion of Dr. Needham's recommendations, and I will therefore not repeat them here. However, one important suggestion that Dr. Becker makes is for lay counselors to follow the ethical standards and guidelines of professional counseling organizations like the American Association of Counseling and Development, the American Psychological Association, and the American Association of Marriage and Family Therapy. I would like to point out here that, in my opinion, the application of ethical standards and guidelines of professional counseling and therapy to lay counselors is *not* such an easy or clear-cut task. I believe that some modification of professional ethical guidelines is needed for lay counselors, especially those who are involved more in peer or friendship counseling, or in lay pastoral care or caregiving, which is broader than therapeutic counseling and where the informal models of lay counseling are more relevant. For example, the ethical guideline found in many professional ethical codes advising against dual relationships which could impair professional judgment or increase the risk of exploitation (for example, counseling with an employee, student, supervisee, close friend, or relative) has often been interpreted as an argument against counseling with *any* friend or even acquaintance. Such an interpretation, of course, cannot be applied to the area of lay counseling involving peer or friendship counseling.

Dr. Worthington has emphasized that supervisors of lay counselors should stress what friends and laypeople do well in counseling, for example, providing excellent emotional support and empathy for people in crisis, giving sound advice prefaced by careful empathic listening and understanding, and providing daily, multisituational support.[13] Such lay or peer counseling often involves counseling with acquaintances or friends, and this is appropriate in the context of nonprofessional lay counseling. However, it is still imperative for the lay counselor involved in such peer or friendship counseling to avoid counseling in situations where his or her objective judgment and helping capacity may be compromised or impaired (for example, counseling with very close friends, relatives, or employees).

The outcome of the Nally lawsuit has made it clearer that pastors, church workers, and lay counselors who are not licensed mental health professionals, are not *legally* accountable to meet the ethical codes and community standards for practice of mental health professionals. However, pastors and lay counselors should still be aware of the high-risk situations reviewed in this chapter and take steps to avoid them.

There are a few other issues I would like to deal with before ending this chapter. First is the issue of *malpractice insurance* for lay Christian counselors, especially those serving in a local church context. Malpractice insurance for lay counselors can be very expensive or not easily available today. Some church lay counseling centers have therefore decided not to purchase malpractice insurance but to have an emergency fund instead, to be used for obtaining legal advice or services in case they are sued for malpractice. Others have chosen to function without any malpractice insurance or emergency fund, but they follow the ethical guidelines and community standards for the practice of professional counseling in order to minimize the risk of litigation. Of course, there are still other centers which have continued to purchase malpractice insurance despite the great expense. Each lay counseling center or ministry will have to decide among the different options possible regarding obtaining or not obtaining malpractice insurance.

Second is the issue of what *legal standards* to follow for lay counselors functioning under the direction and supervision of a licensed mental health professional (e.g., licensed counselor, psychologist, social worker, psychiatrist, etc.). A number of directors of church lay counseling centers in Southern California have consulted attorneys on this matter and been told that lay counselors under the supervision and direction of a licensed mental health professional should follow the mandatory reporting laws and limitations to confidentiality that are relevant to that professional's practice. In the case of a director or supervisor who is both an ordained minister as well as a licensed mental health professional, the mandatory reporting laws pertaining to the licensed mental health professional's practice apparently still take precedence. It is important, therefore, for churches with licensed mental health professionals directing or supervising their lay counselors to require such lay counselors to adhere to the mandatory reporting laws and limitations to confidentiality that apply to the professionals involved. In the case of a pastor or lay leader who is *not* a licensed mental health professional directing or supervising lay counselors, such lay counselors are not bound by professional legal requirements, but it is safer to follow them as far as possible.

I have included in appendix D of this book the *Ethical Standards for Christian Counselors* as proposed in 1986 by Dr. James R. Beck, who teaches counseling at Denver Seminary, and Mr. R. Kent Mathews.[14] I have also included in appendix E the proposed *Code of Ethics for the Christian Association for*

Psychological Studies (CAPS) written in 1986 by Dr. Robert R. King, Jr., who is now the Executive Secretary of CAPS.[15] These proposed ethical codes contain biblical, Christian perspectives and foundations which are important to note.

It should be pointed out that attorneys like Mr. Dennis Kasper from Los Angeles have begun to conduct liability workshops for churches and religious or ministry organizations. They also consult with pastors and directors of church lay counseling centers on legal and ethical issues pertaining to lay counseling ministries. I highly recommend that pastors, church leaders, and directors of lay counseling centers and ministries avail them-selves of such workshops and consultations where possible. A listing of the dates and places for the liability workshops conducted by Mr. Dennis Kasper (mainly in California and Arizona) can be obtained by writing to the Institute for Continuing Education, Fuller Theological Seminary, Pasadena, CA 91182.

Third is the issue of ethical and legal considerations applied to the *supervision* of lay counselors. Space does not permit me to go into a detailed discussion of such considerations, but there is a good chapter on ethical and other issues in Cal Stoltenberg and Ursula Delworth's book, *Supervising Counselors and Therapists: A Developmental Approach.*[16] Essentially, they discuss ethical considerations in terms of competency of the supervisor (who should have received some training in supervi-sion skills, at the very least, some self-training through reading, consulting, and perhaps attendance at some relevant in-service training), dual relationships, respect for supervisees, and the supervisee's ethics (including respect for the supervisor). Re-garding legal considerations, Stoltenberg and Delworth note that the supervisory role carries with it a heavy responsibility. Potential areas of malpractice against the supervisor include situations in which the trainee or supervisee is incapable of providing proper counseling or therapy (even with the supervi-sor's help), or a counselee consenting to receiving counseling without knowing that the counseling will be offered by a trainee. They also discuss the significance of gender and ethnicity issues in the supervision of counselors. Lay counselors should, of course, obtain permission or written consent from their counselees to share information with their supervisors, and possibly other lay counselors in situations involving group supervision. Such information about counselees should be kept confidential by the supervisor or supervisory group involved. Counselees should be told clearly who the supervisor will be, how often supervision will be provided, and who else will be involved in the supervision, including other lay counselors.

Finally, I would like to mention the six major types of lawsuits that are typically filed against psychologists and counselors, as described by Dr. Archibald Hart, Dean of the Graduate School of Psychology at Fuller Theological Seminary, in his excellent book, *Counseling the Depressed:*[17] (1) *Breach of contract*, involving a failure on the counselor's part to keep a promise of providing "cure" or effective results. Counselors must, therefore, be careful not to promise "cures." (2) *Physical assault* or physical injury suffered by the client as a result of therapy or counseling. (3) *Sexual assault*, involving unauthorized or unreasonable touching, including having sex with a client. The largest number of lawsuits against psychologists today fall into this category. (4) *Abandonment*, involving failure to continue providing counseling when it is still needed or when counseling has not been properly terminated with clear documentation. (5) *Suicide* of a client may result in a lawsuit against the counselor for "failure to protect" or failure to follow the "usual degree of care." and (6) *Negligent infliction of emotional distress* (*not* just *intentional* infliction of emotional distress).

Let me conclude with this statement from Dr. Hart: "The overriding principle ... is that the counselor must *first* safeguard the well-being of the client. If you follow this principle, there's not much you can do to get yourself in trouble!"[18]

NOTES

[1]See D. G. Savage, "Court Ruling That Freed Clergy From Liability for Advice to Stand," *Los Angeles Times*, April 4, 1989, pt. 1, pp. 3, 26.

[2]See G. R. Collins, *Christian Counseling: A Comprehensive Guide* (Dallas: Word, 1988), 24–37.

[3]See M. E. Wagner, "Hazards to Effective Pastoral Counseling," pt. 1, *Journal of Psychology and Theology* 1 (July 1973): 35–41; and pt. 2, 1 (October 1973): 40–47.

[4]For a good book on the counselor's ethics written from a secular perspective, see G. Corey, M. S. Corey, and P. Callahan, *Issues and Ethics in the Helping Professions*, 3d ed. (Monterey, Calif.: Brooks/Cole, 1988).

[5]See J. Edelwich with A. Brodsky, *Burnout: Stages of Disillusionment in the Helping Professions* (New York: Human Sciences Press, 1980), 14. For some good and helpful material on dealing with burnout from a Christian perspective, see: R. T. Brock, "Avoiding Burnout Through Spiritual Renewal," in M. G. Gilbert and R. T. Brock, eds., *The Holy Spirit and Counseling: Theology and Theory* (Peabody, Mass.: Hendrickson, 1985), 88–102; A. D. Hart, ed., "Special Issue on Burnout," *Theology, News and Notes* (March 1984); and C. Perry, *Why Christians Burn Out* (Nashville: Nelson, 1982).

[6]See M. E. Cavanagh, "Destructive Myths About Helping Others," *International Christian Digest* 1, no. 6 (1987): 22–23. See also M. E. Cavanagh, *The Effective Minister: Psychological and Social Considerations* (San Francisco: Harper & Row, 1986).

[7]See T. L. Needham, "Helping When the Risks Are Great," in H. Newton Malony, T. L. Needham, and S. Southard, *Clergy Malpractice* (Philadelphia: Westminster, 1986), 88–109.

[8]Ibid., 89–90.

[9]Ibid., 109.

[10]See W. W. Becker, "The Paraprofessional Counselor in the Church: Legal and Ethical Considerations," *Journal of Psychology and Christianity* 6, no. 2 (1987): 78–82.

[11]Ibid., 79.

[12]See S. Southard, "Church Discipline: Handle with Care," in Malony, Needham, and Southard, *Clergy Malpractice*, 74–87. See also J. White and K. Blue, *Healing the Wounded: The Costly Love of Church Discipline* (Downers Grove, Ill.: InterVarsity Press, 1985).

[13]See E. L. Worthington, Jr., "Issues in Supervision of Lay Christian Counselors," *Journal of Psychology and Christianity* 6, no. 2 (1987): 70–77.

[14]See J. R. Beck and R. K. Mathews, "A Code of Ethics for Christian Counselors," *Journal of Psychology and Christianity* 5, no. 3 (1986): 78–84.

[15]See R. R. King, Jr., "Developing a Proposed Code of Ethics for the Christian Association for Psychological Studies," *Journal of Psychology and Christianity* 5, no. 3 (1986): 85–90.

[16]See C. D. Stoltenberg and U. Delworth, *Supervising Counselors and Therapists: A Developmental Approach* (San Francisco: Jossey-Bass, 1987), 168–80. See also W. R. Harrar, L. VandeCreek, and S. Knapp, "Ethical and Legal Aspects of Clinical Supervision," *Professional Psychology* 21 (1990): 37–41.

[17]See A. D. Hart, *Counseling the Depressed* (Waco, Tex.: Word, 1987), 244–45.

[18]Ibid., 250.

12

Conclusions About
Lay Counseling

In this concluding chapter, I would like to summarize a few of the major points I have made so far and mention briefly several other points relevant to lay Christian counseling.

A decade ago, Dr. Rodger Bufford wrote an interesting article on issues and trends in Christian counseling in the *CAPS Bulletin*, which was then the official publication of the Christian Association for Psychological Studies. He covered the topics of the concept of integration (of psychology and Christian faith), Christian approaches to counseling, lay counseling, insularity (of some leaders in the field of Christian counseling), demonology and psychopathology, graduate programs, publications, and ethics. With regard to lay counseling, Dr. Bufford said, "The decade of the eighties promises further development in this area."[1] This prediction has indeed come true, since lay Christian counseling has definitely developed further and matured much in this past decade. I would predict even greater development during the nineties, especially in regard to evaluation research investigating the effectiveness of lay Christian counseling and training programs; more refined, biblically based models of lay caring and counseling ministries; more adequate selection, training, and supervision of lay counselors; deeper appreciation of and greater sensitivity to ethical and legal issues; and heightened awareness of potential pitfalls and dangers inherent in any helping endeavor. I believe that many more churches or congregations, parachurch organizations, and mission boards will become involved in a more systematic and organized (but possibly still "informal") ministry of lay caring and counseling because it is biblically based and commanded by our loving Lord. While lay Christian counseling will probably continue to grow, it is crucial for leaders in this ministry *not* to elevate it above other significant ministries in the kingdom of God.

I would particularly like to strongly recommend that more biblical or biblically based models and approaches to lay Christian counseling be further developed and refined in the future. A key element in such models or approaches based on biblical truth should be the significance of the ministry of the Holy Spirit, including appropriate spiritual gifts and spiritual power in effective lay Christian caring and counseling ministries. I pointed out in an earlier chapter on the selection of lay counselors that spiritual gifts relevant to lay Christian counseling or a helping ministry may include exhortation, wisdom, knowledge, discerning of spirits, mercy, and healing. (Other relevant spiritual gifts may also include prophecy, teaching, faith, miracles, tongues, and intercession.) In this regard, it is interesting to note that Dr. Jerome Frank, Professor Emeritus of Psychiatry at Johns Hopkins School of Medicine and an authority in the practice, teaching, and study of psychotherapy, made the following statements several years ago:

> . . . Some therapists seem to obtain extraordinary results while the patients of a few do no better, or even fare worse, than if they had received no treatment at all. It would be highly desirable to weed out these "tone-deaf" therapists early in training, thereby preventing harm to patients and sparing the therapists from misery; but unfortunately, adequate screening methods for this purpose do not yet exist.
>
> My own hunch, which I mention with some trepidation, is that the most gifted therapists may have telepathic, clairvoyant, or other parapsychological abilities. . . . They may, in addition, possess something . . . that can only be termed "healing power." Any researcher who attempts to study such phenomena risks his reputation as a reliable scientist, so their pursuit can be recommended only to the most intrepid. The rewards, however, might be great.[2]

In a somewhat similar vein, Dr. Isaac Marks, a well-known British psychiatrist with special expertise in behavior therapy, after reviewing a documented case of transsexualism (transsexuals are those who have a gender identity opposite to their anatomical sex) showing a dramatic and complete cure through only two sessions of faith healing (versus generally poor results of behavior therapy with such cases), made the following conclusion just over a decade ago:

> The speed and durability of these faith healing cures leaves behavioral and other forms of psychotherapy far behind in terms of cost-effectiveness. The problem is repeatability.... When it works, faith healing has a power far surpassing existing psychotherapy technology. The order of magnitude of this difference is like that between nuclear and more conventional explosives. But we have not yet harnessed nuclear power satisfactorily, and our understanding of faith and religious processes is far more primitive than our knowledge of subatomic particles. Given a prepared mind, however, some paths into this labyrinth might be laid down. The important point is for hard-nosed experimenters to be alive to these possibilities, while retaining their methological [sic] rigor.[3]

I would therefore recommend that further research be conducted on the role of spiritual gifts like healing, exhortation, wisdom, knowledge, mercy, and discerning of spirits, and the ministry and power of the Holy Spirit, in effective Christian counseling, whether lay or professional. Christian mental health professionals and researchers should be bold enough to provide leadership in this endeavor, which I believe can reap great rewards as Dr. Frank has suggested, including much blessing and healing of broken lives. I am not suggesting here that counseling knowledge and skills are unnecessary for effective helping. However, as both Dr. Frank and Dr. Marks in a secular context have been honest enough to point out, there are other important, if not even more crucial, factors which may account for effective and efficient counseling or psychotherapy. They include "healing power," and in a Christian or biblical context, the presence and power of the Holy Spirit and spiritual gifts are crucial for effective ministry, including lay caring and counseling. Evaluation studies should be conducted to determine whether specially selected lay Christian counselors with such spiritual gifts as I have mentioned do better than other lay Christian counselors who may not have such gifts. Comparative outcome studies are also needed to determine whether a Christian counseling approach (whether lay or professional) that explicitly uses appropriate spiritual gifts and relies on the presence and power of the Holy Spirit is more effective than another Christian counseling approach that does not do this explicitly. Such evaluation research should, of course, be conducted with integrity and methodological rigor, as Dr. Marks has emphasized.

While spiritual gifts and the healing power of the Holy Spirit need more attention and research, it is still important for lay Christian counselors as well as pastors to learn to care and counsel in a systematic and skilled way, in order to be effective and truly helpful. Adequate training and supervision in Christian counseling skills are therefore still needed. As Dr. Wayne Oates pointed out over three decades ago, those involved in pastoral ministry cannot avoid counseling with people who are hurting. He stated that the "choice is not between counseling or not counseling, but between counseling in a disciplined and skilled way and counseling in an undisciplined and unskilled way."[4] I believe that this is true not only for pastors but for all of us who are committed to ministering to others and to serving the Lord in his kingdom. I have written this book to help provide the biblical perspectives and counseling resources needed for learning how to counsel in a disciplined and skilled way, so that Christians can be equipped for an effective helping ministry, especially those who may have appropriate spiritual gifts for such a ministry.

Let me end this concluding chapter as well as this book with the following words from an earlier paper I had written:

> The tremendous development of the field of lay Christian counseling in recent years is encouraging, and can result in much help and blessing in ministry to many troubled people to the glory of God, provided such counseling is done in a biblical, Christ-centered way, within appropriate ethical and legal limits, and with the best of selection, training, supervision, and evaluation possible of lay Christian counselors.[5]

NOTES

[1]See R. K. Bufford, "Christian Counseling: Issues and Trends," *CAPS Bulletin*, 6, no. 4 (1980): 1–4, p. 2.

[2]See J. D. Frank, "Therapeutic Components Shared by All Psychotherapies," in J. H. Harvey and M. M. Parks, eds., *Psychotherapy Research and Behavior Change (The Master Lecture Series*, vol. 1) (Washington, D.C.: American Psychological Association, 1982), 5–37, p. 31.

[3]See I. Marks, "Behavioral Psychotherapy of Adult Neurosis," in S. L. Garfield and A. E. Bergin, eds., *Handbook of Psychotherapy and Behavior Change: An Empirical Analysis,* 2d ed. (New York: Wiley, 1978), 493–547, p. 530.

[4]See W. Oates, *An Introduction to Pastoral Counseling* (Nashville: Broadman, 1959), vi.

[5]See S. Y. Tan, "Lay Christian Counseling: Present Status and Future Directions," invited paper presented at the International Congress on Christian Counseling, Lay Counseling Track, November 1988, in Atlanta, Georgia. Also see S. Y. Tan, "Lay Christian Counseling: The Next Decade," *Journal of Psychology and Christianity* 9, no. 3 (1990): 59–65.

Appendix A

Postcounseling Questionnaire—
Client Form

Your Name: _____

The following ratings give you a chance to give us an honest appraisal of your counseling experience. What we are interested in are your perceptions of the results of your counseling. Please be frank in your assessment, as this is the only way we can improve our services. Thank you, once again, for your cooperation.

The first 3 items should be rated on the following 6-point scale:

1	2	3	4	5	6
extremely poor	poor	adequate	good	very good	superb

_____ 1. How would you rate the overall success of your counseling?

_____ 2. How would you rate your overall satisfaction with the results of your counseling?

_____ 3. How would you rate the overall amount of improvement that has occurred as a result of your counseling?

Please answer the following questions by marking *one* option for each question. (Circle the answer which best applies.)

4. To what extent have your complaints or symptoms that brought you to counseling changed as a result of the counseling provided?
   (1) Completely disappeared
   (2) Very greatly improved
   (3) Considerably improved
   (4) Somewhat improved
   (5) Not at all
   (6) Got worse

5. How much do you feel you have changed as a result of the counseling provided?
   (1) A great deal
   (2) A fair amount
   (3) Somewhat
   (4) Very little
   (5) Not at all

6. How strongly would you recommend counseling with your counselor to a close friend with emotional problems?
   (1) Strongly recommend it
   (2) Mildly recommend it
   (3) Recommend it, but with

reservations
(4) Not recommend it
(5) Advise against it

7. On the whole, how do you feel you are getting along now?

(1) Extremely well
(2) Very well
(3) Fairly well
(4) Neither well nor poorly
(5) Fairly poorly
(6) Very poorly
(7) Extremely poorly

8. How well do you feel you are dealing with any unresolved or new problems now?

(1) Very adequately
(2) Fairly adequately
(3) Neither adequately nor inadequately
(4) Somewhat inadequately
(5) Very inadequately

9. How much in need of further counseling do you feel now?

(1) No need at all
(2) Slight need
(3) Could use more
(4) Considerable need
(5) Very great need

10. How helpful do you feel your counselor was to you?

(1) Completely helpful
(2) Very helpful
(3) Pretty helpful
(4) Somewhat helpful
(5) Slightly helpful
(6) Not at all helpful

11. How competent do you feel your counselor was?

(1) Completely competent
(2) Very competent
(3) Pretty competent
(4) Somewhat competent
(5) Slightly competent
(6) Not at all competent

12. How sincere do you feel your counselor was?

(1) Completely sincere
(2) Very sincere
(3) Pretty sincere
(4) Somewhat sincere
(5) Slightly sincere
(6) Not at all sincere

13. How likable do you feel your counselor was?

(1) Completely likable
(2) Very likable
(3) Pretty likable
(4) Somewhat likable
(5) Slightly likable
(6) Not at all likable

14. How interested do you feel your counselor was?

(1) Completely interested
(2) Very interested
(3) Pretty interested
(4) Somewhat interested
(5) Slightly interested
(6) Not at all interested

Your counselor: _____ Date: _____

Appendix B

Your name: _____

Client's name: _____

In filling out the following items, please feel free to use the full range of possible answers. If the outcome of the counseling has been excellent, indicate so. In the same manner, a poor or mediocre counseling outcome should also be rated as such. The first three items should be rated on the following six-point scale:

1	2	3	4	5	6
extremely poor	poor	adequate	good	very good	superb

_____ 1. How would you rate the overall success of the counseling provided?

_____ 2. How would you rate the client's overall satisfaction with the results of his/her counseling?

_____ 3. How would you rate the overall amount of improvement that the client has experienced as a result of the counseling provided?

Please answer the following questions by marking *one* option for each question. (Circle the answer which best applies.)

4. To what extent have the client's complaints or symptoms which brought him/her to counseling changed as a result of the counseling provided?
   (1) Completely disappeared
   (2) Very greatly improved
   (3) Considerably improved
   (4) Somewhat improved
   (5) Not at all
   (6) Got worse

5. How much do you feel the client has changed as a result of the counseling provided?
   (1) A great deal
   (2) A fair amount
   (3) Somewhat
   (4) Very little
   (5) Not at all

6. On the whole, how do you feel the client is getting along now?

(1) Extremely well
(2) Very well
(3) Fairly well
(4) Neither well nor poorly
(5) Fairly poorly
(6) Very poorly
(7) Extremely poorly

7. How well do you feel the client is dealing with any unresolved or new problems now?

(1) Very adequately
(2) Fairly adequately
(3) Neither adequately nor inadequately
(4) Somewhat inadequately
(5) Very inadequately

8. How much in need of further counseling do you feel the client is?

(1) No need at all
(2) Slight need
(3) Could use more
(4) Considerable need
(5) Very great need

Finally, please give two ratings for each of the following items. The first (Beginning) is for your sense of where the client stood at the beginning of counseling. The second (End) is for his/her standing at termination.

9. The degree of personal integration or psychological health of the client:

1   2   3   4   5   6   7   8   9
Highly disorganized   Optimally
or   integrated
defensively organized

Beginning _____   End _____

10. The life adjustment or social/vocational functioning of the client:

1   2   3   4   5   6   7   8   9
low   high

Beginning _____   End _____

Appendix C

Some Local Churches with Lay Counseling Ministries

Arcadia Presbyterian Church
Counseling Center
121 Alice
Arcadia, CA 91006
(Tel. 818-445-7470)

Bel Air Presbyterian Church
Counseling Center
16221 Mulholland Drive
Los Angeles, CA 90049
(Tel. 213-788-4200)

Centerline, Mt. Paran Church
of God
2055 Mt. Paran Rd. N.W.
Atlanta, GA 30327

Christian Counseling Service,
Inc.
Crystal Cathedral
12141 Lewis St.
Garden Grove, CA 92640
(Tel. 714-750-7077)

Counseling Resource Center
First Presbyterian Church
1820 15th St.
Boulder, CO 80302
(Tel. 303-442-3523)

Creative Counseling Center
First Presbyterian Church
of Hollywood
1763 N. Gower
Hollywood, CA 90028
(Tel. 213-465-6020)

Cross Bearers
Overlake Christian Church
9051 132nd Ave. N.E.
Kirkland, WA 98033
(Tel. 206-827-0303)

Family Counseling Center
First Assembly of God
Rockford, IL 61111

First Evangelical Free Church
2223 N. Mulford Rd.
Rockford, IL 61107

First Evangelical Free Church
of Fullerton
2801 N. Brea Blvd.
Fullerton, CA 92635
(Tel. 714-529-5544)

Glenkirk Presbyterian Church
1740 E. Palopinto Ave.
Glendora, CA 91740
(Tel. 818-914-4833)

Grace Community Church
13248 Roscoe Blvd.
Sun Valley, CA 91352
(Tel. 818-782-5920)

Lay Ministry Program
Walnut Creek Presbyterian
Church
P.O. Box 5606
Walnut Creek, CA 94956
(Tel. 415-935-1574)

237

New Life Counseling
Happy Church
455 S. Platte River Drive
Denver, CO 80223
(Tel. 303-777-4913)

North Park Community Chapel
1470 Glenora Drive
London, ON
N5X 1V2, Canada
(Tel. 519-438-6101)

Peer Counseling Ministry
Bear Valley Baptist Church
2600 S. Sheridan
Denver, CO 80227
(Tel. 303-935-3597)

Rolling Hills Covenant Church
2222 Palos Verdes Drive
North
Rolling Hills Estates, CA
90274
(Tel. 213-479-9406)

Sierra Madre Congregational
Church
170 W. Sierra Madre Blvd.
Sierra Madre, CA 91024
(Tel. 818-355-3566)

Stephen Ministry
Tabernacle Presbyterian
Church
418 E. 34th St.
Indianapolis, IN 46205-3795
(Tel. 317-923-5458)

Teleios Counseling Center
College Hill Presbyterian
Church
5742 Hamilton Ave.
Cincinnati, OH 45224
(Tel. 512-541-2222)

Appendix D

Ethical Standards for Christian Counselors*

Section A: Valuational Framework

Conflicting loyalties can exist among counselor, client, society, Scripture, and the profession. Such conflicts can be resolved only by response to a framework of values as found within the pages of Scripture.

Epistemology. God has revealed truth to humankind through His word, the inspired scriptures which are our sole objective referent. This revelation is exhaustive concerning salvific issues, not exhaustive regarding professional issues, yet is adequate for guiding our choices both here and in the future when facing ethical dilemmas.

Ontology. Every human being is created in the image of God; therefore, each person has real value to God the Creator. Humans experience freedom to make choices; they are not machines controlled by the whims of an impersonal universe. Humans can choose how they will influence the environment. Yet the human person is deficient because of sin, and can only meet created potential when rightly related to God through His Son, Jesus Christ.

The above valuational framework is used by the Christian counselor as a guideline for professional policies, aims, and objectives, for assessing the current status of one's relationship to society, and for assisting clients to become aware of their value orientation.

Section B: Relationship to Clients

Confrontation. The Christian counselor must always view the client as one who was created by God, is loved by God, is accountable to God, and who is given the right to make choices by God. The counselor must be sensitive to society's impact on the client in terms of values, motives, aims, and emotions. The counselor must respect any theological differences which the client may bring to the counseling setting and avoid any imposition of values which are not clearly mandated by Scripture. The counselor should assist the client in clarifying implicit assumptions, in developing a proper relationship with God, and a biblically motivated autonomy, consistency, and sense of responsibility. The counselor should challenge the client's inner contradictions, negative interpersonal relationships and aimless living; this confrontation will lead the client to search for the truth of God.

Confidentiality. Confidential information disclosed by the client should be revealed only for compelling professional reasons such as to protect the client or

*Reprinted with permission, from J. R. Beck and R. K. Mathews, "A Code of Ethics for Christian Counselors," *Journal of Psychology and Christianity* 5, no. 3 (1986): 78–84, pp. 82–83.

community from imminent danger, to comply with the order of a court, to comply with local law, or to comply with the written consent and wishes of the client. The limits of confidentiality shall be made clear to the client at the beginning of the counseling relationship.

Dual relationships. In situations where a counselor has other relationships with a client of an administrative, supervisory or social nature which might impair the counselor's objectivity, the counseling relationship should be terminated through referral to another counselor.

Competence. When a counselor is not qualified to be of assistance to the client, it is necessary to avoid entering into a counseling relationship with that person or to terminate the relationship through referral to a more qualified professional. The counselor will also terminate the relationship by arranging for other treatment when it is reasonably clear that the client is not receiving benefit from the current counseling relationship.

Section C: Relationship to the Community

Qualifications. Christian counselors must accurately represent their professional qualifications. They should continue their professional development through various means of continuing education, and must strive to maintain the highest level of Christian professional services.

Fees. In establishing fees, Christian counselors must consider the financial ability of the client as well as the community's standards.

Other professionals. Interprofessional relationships should be pursued by the counselor for the purpose of referral and mutual support. Clients who are in therapy with another professional should not be solicited nor serviced without prior consent of the original therapist.

Church. Christian counselors should have a vital and committed association with a local church, always seeking for an integration of theological and psychological concepts in order to understand more fully the dynamics of Christian living. The Christian counselor needs to be committed to service in the body of Christ, and to modeling servant leadership.

Publications. All statements shall be accurate and all publications will conform to the best of standard scholarship.

Standards. Christian counselors will exemplify the highest standards of professional competence and ethical behavior in the interests of the Christian community since any violations of these principles can be damaging to clients and to the testimony of the cause of Christ.

The general welfare. Because of the Christian counselor's commitment to God's program for this world, the counselor is called to work for the prevention and elimination of war, injustice and exploitation. Christian counselors must strive to provide their services for all persons and to expand the choices and opportunities available for all. The Christian counselor must function as an informed and active member of the electorate, working toward public policies which promote improved social conditions and which promote social justice.

Section D: Unethical Conduct

Counselors who have subscribed to this code but who appear to have violated its provisions should be held accountable by fellow peers. All allegations should be investigated within the guidelines of Matthew 18. If any charges are proven, efforts shall be made to inform the appropriate community that the counselor in question has been asked to remove his or her signature from this code of ethical standards. The counselor's peers shall make provision for future restoration when at all possible.

Appendix E

Christian Association for Psychological Studies
Proposed Code of Ethics*

APPLICABILITY OF THE CODE

This Code of Ethics (hereinafter referred to as the "Code") is applicable to all current, dues-paid Members and Associate Members of the Christian Association for Psychological Studies (CAPS). While CAPS is not a licensing or accrediting agency, it does desire that members who provide mental health, pastoral, or other personal services do so with the highest possible level of Christian and service or ministry ethics, whether professional, layperson, or student. Further, even though CAPS is not a licensing or accrediting agency, it does have the authority to set and monitor qualifications for membership in good standing. Thus, the Board of Directors urges each member to consider carefully and prayerfully the Code and to adopt it personally.

BIBLICAL FOUNDATION

Note: Each of the biblical blocks of the foundation that follows has one or more references. The references are not exhaustive, nor are they meant to be convenient "proof-texting." Rather, the Scriptures cited are meant to be representative of the many biblical references that build the foundation of this Code. The complete foundation is the total message of the Gospel of Jesus Christ. Also, it is recognized that each believer in Christ has the capacity—even the privilege and duty—to explore the depths of God's Word and discover personal guidance for daily living. This Code could not hope to explore all the richness of the Bible as it relates to ethical conduct.

Biblical "Building Blocks" of the Foundation

Conflicts, difficulties, power struggles, trials, and tribulations are normal and to be expected, whether one is a Christian or not (John 16:33; Psalm 37:7; Romans 2:9).

We are to grow and mature through the conflicts, problems, trials and tribulations, and discipline that we experience (James 1:2–4; 1 Thessalonians 5:18).

We are to support and encourage each other (John 15:17; Ephesians 4:32; John 13:35).

We are to admonish and, if necessary, discipline each other, especially those

*Reprinted with permission, from R. R. King, Jr., "Developing a Proposed Code of Ethics for the Christian Association for Psychological Studies," *Journal of Psychology and Christianity* 5, no. 3 (1986): 85–90, pp. 86–90.

Christians in positions of leadership and trust. However, such discipline is to be constructive rather than judgmental, done in love, and with caution about our own shortcomings (Matthew 18:15–17; 1 Corinthians 5:11–13; Galatians 6:1).

We are to demonstrate the lordship of Christ in our lives by servantlike leadership, a sense of community, and a life style that reflects the will of God (Matthew 20:25–28; John 12:26; 1 Peter 4:8–11; Colossians 3:12–17).

We are to reach out to others in love and concern (Matthew 25:31–40; Hebrews 13:16; 2 Corinthians 1:3–7).

BASIC CRITERIA AND PRINCIPLES OF THE CODE

1. The code includes a broad range of morality, yet it is specific enough in certain areas to offer guidance for ethical conduct in a variety of situations. It is intended to be universal without being platitudinous. On the other hand, it aims to be functional without being legalistic.

2. The Code calls for commitment to a distinctively Christian code of ethical behavior in our helping professions. Yet it recognizes that ethical behavior is certainly not the hallmark only of Christians, thus there is no implication of judging persons of different faiths or value systems.

3. The Code is not a credo or doctrinal statement of CAPS. Article II of the CAPS Constitution and By-Laws contains the basis for our association:

> The basis of this organization is belief in: God, the Father, who creates and sustains us; Jesus Christ, the Son, who redeems and rules us; and the Holy Spirit, who guides us personally and professionally, through God's inspired Word, the Bible, our infallible guide of faith and conduct, and through the communion of Christians.

4. The Code is not a position paper on major social issues. While CAPS has genuine interest in social issues, it has traditionally encouraged members to become involved personally, as led by God, rather than as prescribed by CAPS. Also, CAPS has traditionally encouraged the free exchange of ideas among members, rather than defining "truth" or a partisan viewpoint for its members.

5. All humans are created in the image of God. We are holistic in our being and thus most descriptions of our parts, such as mind, body, soul, spirit, personality or whatever, are primarily to make it easier to discuss and evaluate our nature. Much of being created in the image of God is still a mystery to us. However, it does mean that we and those persons we serve have basic dignity and worth, along with basic human rights and essential human responsibilities. Also, we are to glorify God in worship, service, and stewardship.

6. The family is the basic unit of our culture; it merits honor, encouragement, and protection. In addition, "family" to the Christian includes our "neighbor" (Luke 10:29–37). Thus, our "circle of love" embraces God, neighbor, and self (Luke 10:27). Not only that, we are to love our enemies (Matthew 5:43). Also, our influence, our activities in the helping professions, are to be "salt and light" in this world (Matthew 5:13, 14).

7. Scientific and humanistic activities in the helping professions are good, even excellent, but not good enough. While love without professional standards can become mere sentimentality, scientific observations and professional standards without love and godly ethics can become mere clinical experiments. Thus, the Christian is called to maximize helping others by integrating the distinctives of Christian commitment—including prayer—with professional education, training and, if appropriate, licensing.

8. The world as we know it is a temporal place of human existence with the

ever-present contrasts or polarities such as good and evil, order and disorder, joy and sorrow, generosity and selfishness, love and apathy, abundance and scarcity. Further, we do not necessarily know the reasons for any particular situation, event, or relationship.

9. Exploiting or manipulating another person for our own or yet another's pleasure or aggrandizement is unethical and sinful.

10. Pretending to have expertise beyond our abilities or practicing beyond the scope of our licensure is unethical, very likely illegal, and does not value the person who needs help, nor does it glorify God.

11. Attempting to do for others what they are able and responsible to do for themselves, especially those persons who are seeking counsel, tends to create dependency and is thus unethical.

12. Some persons—such as children, for example—are more dependent than others and thus merit a greater degree of protection from persons who would thoughtlessly or selfishly take advantage of or manipulate them.

13. Each of us, whether helper or the person being helped, is a fallible human being who has limits that are universal in the human nature yet unique in magnitude and proportion within each individual.

14. The helping professions are both art and science, with much to be learned. Also, each of us who serves, whether as professional or layperson, needs to be competent enough in what we do and of sufficient personal stability and integrity that what we do promotes healing rather than disorder and harm.

ARTICLES OF THE CODE OF ETHICS

Note: In an effort to avoid awkward and lengthy descriptions of persons we serve, the somewhat neutral word "client" is used. According to the perspective of members, words such as "peer," "parishioner," "communicant," "patient," "helpee," "counselee," or even "prisoner" may be used.

Also, the word "service" or "serving" is used frequently in the Code to describe what we do. Again, according to the perspective of members, words such as "helping ministries," "helping professions," "counseling," "ministering," or "pastoring," for example, may be substituted. Admittedly, no word is neutral, since language shapes (and reflects) our reality. Thus, the word "service" or its derivatives is meant to reflect Christ's statement that He came to serve, rather than to be served.

1. Personal Commitment as a Christian

1.1 I agree with the basis of CAPS, as quoted earlier in this Code, stated in the Constitution and By-Laws.

1.2 I commit my service, whether as professional or layperson, to God as a special calling.

1.3 I pledge to integrate all that I do in service with Christian values, principles, and guidelines.

1.4 I commit myself to Christ as Lord as well as Savior. Thus, direction and wisdom from God will be sought, while accepting responsibility for my own actions and statements.

1.5 I view my body as the temple of the Holy Spirit and will treat it lovingly and respectfully. Balance in my priorities will be prayerfully sought.

2. Loving Concern for Clients

2.1 Clients will be accepted regardless of race, religion, gender, income, education, ethnic background, value system, etc., unless such a factor would interfere appreciably with my ability to be of service.

2.2 I value human life, the sanctity of personhood, personal freedom and responsibility, and the privilege of free choice in matters of belief and action.

2.3 I will avoid exploiting or manipulating any client to satisfy my own needs.

2.4 I will abstain from undue invasion of privacy.

2.5 I will take appropriate actions to help, even protect, those persons who are relatively dependent on other persons for their survival and well being.

2.6 Sexual intimacy with any client will be scrupulously avoided.

3. Confidentiality

3.1 I will demonstrate utmost respect for the confidentiality of the client and other persons in the helping relationship.

3.2 The limits of confidentiality, such as those based on civil laws, regulations, and judicial precedent, will be explained to the client.

3.3 I will carefully protect the identity of clients and their problems. Thus, I will avoid divulging information about clients, whether privately or publicly, unless I have informed consent of the client, given by express, written permission, and the release of such information would be appropriate to the situation.

3.4 All records of counseling will be handled in a way that protects the clients and the nature of their problems from disclosure.

4. Competency in Services Provided

4.1 I pledge to be well-trained and competent in providing services.

4.2 I will refrain from implying that I have qualifications, experiences, and capabilities which are in fact lacking.

4.3 I will comply with applicable state and local laws and regulations regarding the helping professions.

4.4 I will avoid using any legal exemptions from counseling competency afforded in certain states to churches and other nonprofit organizations as a means of providing services that are beyond my training and expertise.

4.5 I will diligently pursue additional education, experience, professional consultation, and spiritual growth in order to improve my effectiveness in serving persons in need.

5. My Human Limitations

5.1 I will do my best to be aware of my human limitations and biases, and openly admit that I do not have scientific objectivity or spiritual maturity, insofar as my subjective viewpoint will permit.

5.2 I will avoid fostering any misconception a client could have that I am omnipotent, or that I have all the answers.

5.3 I will refer clients whom I am not capable of counseling, whether by lack of available time or expertise, or even because of subjective, personal reasons. The referral will be done compassionately, clearly, and completely, insofar as feasible.

5.4 I will resist efforts of any clients or colleagues to place demands for services on me that exceed my qualifications and/or the time available to minister, or that would impose unduly on my relationships with my own family.

6. Advertising and Promotional Activities

6.1 I will advertise or promote my services by Christian and professional standards, rather than commercial standards.

6.2 Personal aggrandizement will be omitted from advertising and promotional activities.

7. Research

7.1 Any research conducted will be done openly and will not jeopardize the welfare of any persons who are research, i.e., test, subjects. Further, clients will not be used as publicly identifiable test subjects.

8. Unethical Conduct, Confrontation, and Malpractice

8.1 If I have sufficient reason to believe a Christian colleague in CAPS has been practicing or ministering in a way that is probably damaging to the client or the helping ministries, I will confront that person. The principles and procedures specified in Matthew 18:15–17 will be followed in confronting the person who appears to be behaving unethically. In addition, the more stringent actions against pastors specified in 1 Timothy 5:19–20 will be considered, if relevant.

8.2 In addition to the confrontation procedures based on Scriptural guidance, civil law will be followed if relevant or applicable.

8.3 If the CAPS Board becomes aware that a member has been accused of unethical conduct, the Ethics Committee (either standing or ad hoc) will investigate the situation and recommend ethical discipline, including expulsion from membership, if appropriate.

8.3.1 If a person has been expelled from membership for unethical conduct, the Ethics Committee will maintain loving and concerned liaison with the person and others involved, as appropriate, and will attempt to bring about actions for repentance, forgiveness, and restoration to the membership.

8.4 The Ethics Committee will also provide consultation to CAPS as an organization and/or to individual members who may be confronting ethical dilemmas and want some guidance.

8.4.1 Since ethical concerns may be complex and/or have legal implications, the consultation provided will be primarily in helping think through a situation, without assuming responsibility for the case.

8.5 The value of malpractice insurance will be carefully considered, especially if a lawsuit—whether justified or not—would possibly drain financial resources of the ministry organization with which I am associated, or of my family.

9. General Prudential Rule

9.1 Recognizing that no code of ethics is complete, I will make day-to-day decisions based on the criteria and principles stated at the beginning of this Code. Even more important, I will do my best to serve and to live in a way that is congruent with the stated basic principles of this Code and with my faith as a Christian.

REVISIONS TO THE CODE

Any suggestions for improving the Code would be welcome and should be addressed to any current Board member, whether CAPS or regional, or to the Regional Director for your CAPS region.

Approval of any suggested revision would require a two-thirds majority vote of the CAPS Board.

Appendix F

Progress Notes

Meeting # ___

Counselee(s) _____ Date _____

Counselor(s) _____

Main Focus: (content) _____
_____
_____

Dynamics: (process) _____
_____
_____

Direction: _____
_____
_____

Meeting # ___

Date _____

Main Focus: (content) _____
_____
_____

Dynamics: (process) _____
_____
_____

Direction: _____
_____
_____

Informed Consent Form

LA CANADA PRESBYTERIAN CHURCH
LAY COUNSELING MINISTRY

The Lay Counselor is a person trained to listen and care for others. Lay Counselors are paraprofessionals (in other words, we are not licensed, paid professional therapists). As Lay Counselors we are trained in the skills of listening, clarifying, and goal setting. Our training and our counseling is supervised by licensed mental health professionals. We offer a response to your personal or family needs based on the Christian understanding of giving ourselves to our neighbors.

Lay Counseling Agreement Form

As a Counselee, I understand the following:
1. The contact I have with the Lay Counselor(s) is paraprofessional in nature.
2. In some cases, I may be seen by co-counselors.
3. All counseling is confidential. This confidentiality includes the Lay Counselor's supervisor(s) (see back side, "Duty to Warn" for exceptions).
4. I will meet with my counselor for 10 sessions, usually for one 50 minute session per week in the church counseling offices.
5. At the end of 10 sessions, a reassessment of the counseling situation will be made by both the Lay Counselor and myself. At that time, a new decision will be made concerning the best course of action for me. This may include: referral to a professional therapist, continuation of my counseling with the Lay Counselor, or termination of the counseling sessions.
6. Out of courtesy to my counselor, I will give at least 24 hours prior notice before cancelling an appointment.

I have reviewed the above conditions with my counselor(s) and agree to abide by them.

Counselee printed name	Date

Counselee signature	If under 18, Parent or Guardian

Counselor(s)	Date

I would be willing to allow my counseling sessions to be taped for professional supervisory purposes only.

Counselee signature	Date

DUTY TO WARN

The La Canada Presbyterian Church Lay Counselors abide by California law which requires incidences of "reasonably suspected child abuse" to be reported to California authorities (California Law—Penal Code Article 2.5, Paragraph 11166).

CONFIDENTIALITY AND PRIVILEGED COMMUNICATION REMAIN RIGHTS OF ALL COUNSELEES. HOWEVER, SOME COURTS HAVE HELD THAT IF AN INDIVIDUAL INTENDS TO TAKE HARMFUL, DANGEROUS, OR CRIMINAL ACTION AGAINST ANOTHER HUMAN BEING, OR ONESELF, IT IS THE COUNSELOR'S DUTY TO WARN APPROPRIATE INDIVIDUALS OF SUCH INTENTIONS. COUNSELORS ARE MANDATED TO REPORT ANY INCIDENCES OF "REASONABLY SUSPECTED CHILD ABUSE" (PHYSICAL OR SEXUAL).

Prior to informing anyone who should be warned, the counselor(s) will make concerted effort first to share the intention to warn with the counselee.

I HAVE READ THE ABOVE AND UNDERSTAND THE COUNSELOR'S SOCIAL AND ETHICAL RESPONSIBILITY TO WARN WHEN HARMFUL, DANGEROUS, OR CRIMINAL ACTION IS STRONGLY INDICATED. I FURTHER UNDERSTAND THE COUNSELOR'S LEGAL RESPONSIBILITY TO NOTIFY THE PROPER AUTHORITIES IN CASES OF "REASONABLY SUSPECTED CHILD ABUSE."

_____

Counselee printed name

_____   _____

Counselee signature   Date

_____   _____

Counselor   Co-Counselor

Informed Consent Form

LAY COUNSELING APPLICATION FORM
(ROLLING HILLS COVENANT CHURCH)

The Lay Counseling Ministry of Rolling Hills Covenant Church is a nonfee, short-term (10 sessions), biblically based, peer support and encouragement ministry that is available to all members and regular attenders. The counselors provided are nonprofessionals who are trained in listening, clarifying, and assisting in goal setting. We offer assistance in integrating your background, personality, and circumstances into a biblical style of living.

Date _____

Name _____ Phone: (Day) _____

Address _____ (Eve) _____

City _____ State __ Zip _____ Age __

Marital status _____ Spouse's name _____

Children and ages: _____

_____

1. How did you hear about this ministry? _____

_____

2. For what are you seeking help? _____

_____

3. When did you first notice this concern? _____

_____

4. Have you ever had counseling before? If so, what for and where? _____

_____

5. What were the results of that counseling? _____

_____

Supervision

In order to provide the best care possible, all lay counselors in this ministry are under the indirect supervision of the Pastor of Congregational Care and a licensed mental health professional.

Confidentiality

The confidentiality that you share with your lay counselor will be carefully guarded. However, it is required by California law that all counselors have a duty to warn the appropriate individuals if the counselee intends to take harmful, dangerous, or criminal actions against themselves or someone around them. Counselors are also mandated to report any incidences of "reasonably suspected child abuse" (physical or sexual), elderly abuse, or suicide attempts to the Department of Social Services and/or the Police Department.

Waiver of Liability

The undersigned, having sought biblical counseling as such as adhered to by Rolling Hills Covenant Church, a nonprofit religious organization, hereby acknowledges their understanding of the following conditions and further releases from liability Rolling Hills Covenant Church, its pastors, agents, employees, and lay counselors, from any claim or litigation whatsoever arising from the undersigned's participation in the above-mentioned biblical counseling ministry. It is further understood:

(1) That all biblical counseling will be provided by lay counselors and not licensed therapists.

(2) That all lay counselors used in this ministry are trained by mental health professionals and the pastoral staff of this church.

(3) That all counseling provided in this ministry is provided in accordance with the biblical principles adhered to by Rolling Hills Covenant Church (including the teaching on the discipline of wayward members), and is not necessarily provided in adherence with any local or national psychological or psychiatric association.

(4) That no representation has been made, either expressly or implied, that biblical counseling, as conducted by the above-mentioned lay counselors, is accepted as customary psychological and/or psychiatric therapy within the definitional terms utilized by those professions.

(5) That the undersigned has read and understands the contents of the waiver, and consents to and requests said counseling.

_____ Date _____
Counselee

_____ Date: _____
Pastor of Congregational Care

Release of Information Form

**Lay Counseling Ministry
La Canada Presbyterian Church
626 Foothill Boulevard
La Canada, CA 91011**

_____ has my permission to release to
(Agency or Counselor)

_____ the confidential information on
(Receiving Agency or Counselor)

_____.
(Counselee's Name[s])

The released information will inform (Receiving Agency or Counselor)

_____ about the educational, medical, psycho-

logical,   and/or   counseling   services   which   (Counselee)

_____ received from (Agency or Counselor)

_____ and will be used by (Receiving Agency

or Counselor) _____ in order to assist in the

counseling for (Counselee) _____.

This authorization for release of confidential information is valid from the date

the form is signed until _____.

_____   _____
Date   Counselee/Parent/Guardian/Conservator

_____   _____
Date   Second Parent/Guardian/Conservator,
                                 if legally responsible for Counselee

Name Index

Adams, J., 28, 33–34, 38, 40–41, 43, 45, 69, 71, 74, 123, 125, 128, 138, 180, 195, 203, 220
Albee, G., 14
Allender, D., 117
Allport, G. W., 170
Anderson, R., 128
Arnold, W., 71
Augsburger, D., 48
Backus, W., 33, 37, 46, 71, 123, 125–26, 128–29, 143, 153–54
Baldwin, C. L., 71, 125–26, 128, 143
Baldwin, M., 124
Barlow, S., 65
Bassett, R. L., et al., 103
Bear, G., 71, 188, 199–200, 209
Beck, A., 33, 140, 153, 166
Beck, J. R., 223
Becker, W. W., 219–21
Bergin, A. E., 64, 159, 172, 173
Berman, J. S., 63
Beutler, L. E., 143
Blanchette, M. C., 137
Boan, D. M., 72, 167
Bobgan, D., 71
Bobgan, M., 71
Brammer, L. M., 124
Brannon, D., 144
Brock, R., 41
Brown, S. D., 137
Buchanan, D., 71
Buckler, R., 28
Bufford, R. K., 28, 227
Burish, T. G., 65
Burlingame, G., 65
Carey, M. P., 65
Carifio, M. S., 144
Carkhuff, R. R., 33, 40, 44, 62, 98, 124, 165–66, 171

Carlson, D., 46
Carter, J., 28–29, 45, 159
Cavanagh, M. E., 215–16
Cawley, R. H., 40
Cerling, G. L., 99–101
Chapian, M., 125, 128–29, 153–54
Chiu, P., 201
Christensen, E. R., 172
Collins, G. R., 14, 33, 37, 39–40, 43, 48–49, 70–72, 74, 102–3, 106, 116, 122, 125, 127–31, 145, 179, 190, 195, 203, 213–16
Compton, J., 137
Corcoran, J., 73
Cormier, L. S., 46, 120, 124, 126, 166
Cormier, W. H., 46, 120, 124, 126, 166
Cowen, E., 68
Crabb, L. J., Jr., 32–34, 37, 43–44, 46, 70–71, 110, 117, 122–23, 125–29, 151–52, 155, 180, 191, 195, 203
Crimmings, A. M., 137
Cuvelier, B., 73
DeJulio, S. S., 172
Delworth, U., 135, 137, 141, 143, 224
Dobson, K. S., 115
Dodds, L., 72, 168
Dooley, D., 98
Drakeford, J., 71
Durlak, J. A., 62–63, 183
Edgar, R., 202
Egan, G., 33, 44, 99, 124, 190, 195
Estadt, B. K., Jr., 137
Ekstein, R., 137
Ellis, A., 33, 140, 153

Ellison, C. W., 103, 104, 169
Evans, C. S., 36
Feld, S., 61
Felner, R. D., 64
Flakoll, D. A., 73
Fleck, R., 159
Fohl, M., 71
Foster, R., 35, 71, 146–47
Foster, T., 71
Frank, J. D., 63, 228–29
Freeman, E., 144
Freud, S., 141
Friesen, D., 129
Friesen, R., 129
Garfield, S. L., 66, 172
Gilbert, M., 41
Goldstein, A. P., 46
Gomes-Schwartz, B., 44
Gorsuch, R. L., 73, 165, 170
Grunlan, S., 29, 49, 71
Guest, P. D., 143
Gurin, G., 61
Hadley, S. W., 63
Hardy, E., 135, 141
Harris, J., 73
Hart, A. D., 225
Hart, G. M., 137
Hart, L. E., 97–98
Harvey, J. H., 172
Haugk, K. C., 71, 84, 120, 122–23, 125, 195
Hess, A. K., 139, 144
Hesselgrave, D., 48
Hogan, R. A., 141
Holloway, E. L., 141
Hughes, S., 71, 202
Hunt, W. H. ("Skip"), 124
Hurding, R., 40
Imber, S. D., et al., 181
Jernigan, R., 73, 165
Johnson, C. B., 210
Kanfer, F. H., 46
Kaslow, F. E., 137

253

Kasper, D., 224
Kazdin, A., 181
King, C., 71
King, G. D., 97–98
King, R. R., Jr., 224
Korchin, S. J., 67–68
Lambert, M. J., 64, 172, 173
Lambrides, D., 29, 49, 71
Larson, D., 127
Lazarus, A. A., 38–39, 46, 178
Lent, R. W., 137
Lim, I., 71
Lim, S., 71
Lindquist,S., 71
Lipsker, L. E., 146
Loganbill, C., 135, 141
Lorion, R. P., 64
Lukens, H., 119–20, 122, 147
Malony, H. N., 169
Manthei, R., 175, 177
Marks, I., 228–30
Maslow, A., 168
Matarazzo, J., 63
Mathews, R. K., 223
Mayer, J., 144
Meichenbaum, D., 33, 140
Miller, P., 71, 99
Minirth, F., 29
Minuchin, S., 124
Morris, P., 71
Mowrer, O. H., 69
Nally, K., 212
Needham, T. L., 216–19, 221
Nicholi, A., Jr., 17
Norton, N. C., 63
Oates, W., 230
Oden, T., 74
Oglesby, W., 49
Olson, K., 129

Osborn, E., 124
Osburn, C., 110, 124
Owens, T., 72, 167
Paloutzian, R., 104, 169
Parks, M. M., 172
Parloff, M. B., 172
Partridge, T. J., 87, 89
Patterson, G. B., 124
Peck, S., 17
Penner, C., 129
Penner, D. R., 210
Penner, J., 129
Peterson, E., 71
Poser, E. G., 62
Prater, J., 48, 125
Reissman, F., 67
Rekers, G. A., 129
Richard, R. C., 73
Robbins, A., 137
Rogers, C., 195
Rosenblatt, A., 144
Ross, J. M., 170
Russell, R. K., 137
Sala, H., 71
Sarff, P., 72–73
Satir, V., 124, 195
Schaefer, C. A., 72, 168
Schmidt, P. F., 103–4, 169
Schmitt, A., 71
Schmitt, D., 71
Seamands, D., 126, 128
Shapiro, D. A., 64, 173
Shaw, B. F., 115
Shostrom, E. L., 168
Smith, F., 169
Solomon, C., 71, 123
Somerville, R., 71
Southard, S., 128, 221
Sparks, L., 71
Spitzer, R., 172
Steinbron, M. J., 71, 199
Stevens, P., 24–26
Stoltenberg, C., 137, 141, 143, 224

Strupp, H. H., 63
Sturkie, J., 71, 188, 199–200, 209
Sue,D., 48
Sweeten, G., 111, 118, 122–23
Tan, S. Y., 36, 46–47, 72–73, 100, 102, 125–30, 145–47, 163–64, 165, 168, 202–7, 230
Thompson, A. P., 162
Tozer, A. W., 35, 146
Truax, C. B., 40, 62
Varenhorst, B., 71
Venable, G. D., 170
Veroff, J., 61
Wagner, C. P., 27, 103, 105, 169
Wagner, M. E., 214
Wallerstein, R., 137
Walters, R. P., 71, 74, 143, 178
Ward, W., 71
Waskow, J. E., 172
Wayman, D., 103, 105, 111
Welter, P. R., 71, 73, 124, 209
Wheat, E., 129
Wheat, G., 129
White, J., 130
Wichern, F. B., 103, 106, 169
Wiley, M. O'L., 136
Williams, J., 172
Worthington, E. L., 33, 71, 125–26, 129, 137, 140–43, 146–48, 222
Wright, H. N., 33, 46, 71, 129, 143, 195
Yagel, J. C., 177
Yohn, R., 116
Zilbergeld, B., 66

Subject Index

Basic principles, 41–50
Basic training program, 125–27
Basic view: of counseling, 39–41; of humanity, 34–39
Biblical basis, 23–31
Biblical model, 32–60
Call to ministry, 24–26
Center for Church Renewal, 188–98

Choice of models, 87
Conclusions about lay counseling, 227–31
Counseling: basic principles of, 41–50; basic view of, 39–41
Counselor, spirituality of, 146–47
Crabb model of training, 117–18
Ethical issues, 216–25
Evaluation: of effectiveness, 176–79; of outcome, 172–81; survey findings on, 195–98; of training programs, 161–72
Example(s): in churches, 198–208; of supervision, 149–55; of training programs, 122–31
Formal, organized model, 85
Guidelines for establishing center, 87–94
Haugk model of training, 120–22
Holy Spirit, 228–30
Humanity, basic view of, 34–39
Hypothetical example of supervision, 149–55
"Ideal" supervisor, 144–47
Implicit trust model, 138
Informal, organized model, 84
Informal, spontaneous model, 83
La Canada Presbyterian Church, 106–9
Legal issues, 216–25
Literature: Christian, 69–74; secular, 61–69
Local church: and lay counseling, 188–211; examples of ministries, 198–208
Lukens model of training, 119–20
Measures: of knowledge and skills, 162–67; for outcome evaluation, 173–76; of personal and spiritual growth, 167–71
Methods: for screening, 102–6
Minimum intervention model, 137
Ministries: beyond local church, 208–10; examples in churches, 198–208; need for, 17–22

Ministry: call to, 24–26; lay counseling as, 26–29; steps for building, 85–87
Model(s), 83–85, 137–38; biblical, 32–60; choice of, 87; for lay counseling ministry, 83–85; for supervision, 127–40; for training, 117–22
Modes, theoretical or developmental, 140–44
Need for ministries, 17–22
North Park Community Chapel, 205–7
One-year training program, 127–30
Part-time training, 127–30
Peoples Church of Montreal, 202–5
Pitfalls, potential, 212–26
Problems, potential, 213–16
Professional training model, 138
Research design, 171–72, 179–81
Screening: methods for, 102–6
Selection: criteria for, 97–102; methods for screening, 102–6; example, 106–9
Spiritual gifts, 228–30
Stephen Series, as model of training, 120–22
Supervision: conceptual modes of, 140–44; definition of, 135–36; one-on-one, 149–55; practice models of, 127–40; hypothetical example of, 149–55
Supervisor: "ideal," 144–47; other issues for, 147–49; spirituality of, 146–47
Survey findings: training, 189–92; lay counseling, 192–95; evaluation, 195–98
Sweeten model of training, 118–19
Theoretical or developmental modes, 140–44
Training, 189–92; models of, 117–22; phases of, 116–17; programs, 122–31
Vertical intervention model, 138

Siang-Yang Tan

Siang-Yang Tan is director of the Psy.D. (Doctor of Psychology) program and associate professor of psychology in the Graduate School of Psychology at Fuller Theological Seminary in Pasadena, California. He is a licensed psychologist with a Ph.D. in Clinical Psychology from McGill University. He has published articles on lay counseling and lay counselor training, intrapersonal integration and spirituality, cognitive-behavior therapy, epilepsy, pain, and psychopathology and culture in the Asian-American context. He is associate editor of the *Journal of Psychology and Christianity* and serves on the editorial boards of the *Journal of Consulting and Clinical Psychology, Journal of Psychology and Theology,* and *Journal of Pastoral Counseling.*

Dr. Tan has worked and taught at University Hospital and the University of Western Ontario, and Ontario Bible College in Canada, where he established and directed the Institute of Christian Counseling for training lay or paraprofessional Christian counselors. He has had extensive experience in the area of lay Christian counseling, especially in the local church context. He was director of the Lay Counseling Service at Peoples Church of Montreal (1976–80), and North Park Community Chapel in London, Ontario, Canada (1981–83). He was also pastor of the Malaysian-Singaporean Bible Church in Toronto and has served as Director of the Campus Life Division of Montreal Youth For Christ. He lives in Arcadia, California, with his wife, Angela, and two young children, Carolyn and Andrew. Dr. Tan also serves as Assistant Minister to the English Congregation at First Evangelical Church in Glendale, California. He is originally from Singapore.